History Begins

History Begins

A Global History of the Ancient World

Sheena Coupe and Barbara Scanlan

Longman
New York

History Begins

Longman, 10 Bank Street, White Plains, N.Y. 10606

Associated companies:
Longman Group Ltd., London
Longman Cheshire Pty., Melbourne
Longman Paul Pty., Auckland
Copp Clark Pitman, Toronto

Designed by R T J Klinkhamer

History Begins   ISBN 0-8013-1044-X
                  ISBN 0-8013-1040-7 (pbk)
Threads of Time   ISBN 0-8013-1045-8
                  ISBN 0-8013-1041-5 (pbk)

1 2 3 4 5 6 7 8 9 10-VH-9695949392

Contents

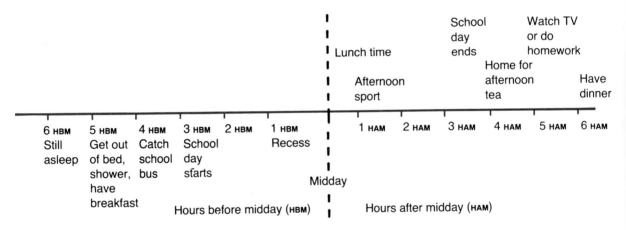

Fig. 1.1 A typical school day. What time does school begin, according to this time-line?

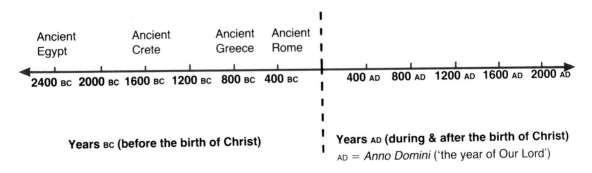

Fig. 1.2 A time-line showing years BC and years AD.

1

The world before history

TIME is when things happen. Things may happen right now (in the present), they may have happened yesterday (in the past) or they may happen tomorrow (in the future). To measure or record time we use a number of different devices. A clock measures time in hours, minutes and seconds. A stop-watch can measure time in parts, or fractions, of a second. A calendar records the time passing in days, months and years.

When we study history we use time-lines to show when things happened. In Fig. 1.1 the hours of a typical school day have been placed along a straight line, with midday as the mid-point. On this time-line anything that happens before midday happens in the *hours before midday* (HBM). Anything that happens after midday happens in the *hours after midday* (HAM).

Historians have a way of expressing the time when things happened on a time-line that uses the birth of Jesus Christ as the point from which time is measured. On this time-line (Fig. 1.2) anything that happened before this point happened in the years BC (*before* the birth of *Christ*).

Anything that happened after this point happened (or will happen!) in the years AD (from the Latin words *Anno Domini*, which mean 'in the year of our Lord'). The year 1987 is actually 1987 years after the birth of Christ, or 1987 AD.

Sometimes you might see a date expressed as, for example, 30 000 BP. This means that the event happened 30 000 years *before the present*. This way of writing dates is often used to record things that happened many thousands of years ago. Often things that happened thousands of years ago cannot be placed on a time-line precisely. In these cases, an approximate date is used. On Fig. 1.2, some of the ancient societies you will be studying in this book have been placed on a time-line, according to when they happened.

Some people, such as Jewish people and Moslems, have a different way of expressing the time when things happened, according to their religion. However, the system described above and used in this book is the one used throughout most of the world.

Time to understand

1 In our own lifetimes events have happened that could be represented on a time-line as a history of our lives. In Fig. 1.3 'Kate Jones's life' has been placed on a time-line in this way. Using this as a guide, draw the time-line of your own life. You need to mention all the important things that have happened in your life.

2 We live in the twentieth century AD. This means that we live in a period of time between 1900 and 2000 AD. A century is a period of time 100 years long. Fig. 1.4 shows us how to count centuries. From the birth of Christ to year 99 AD is the *first* century AD. From 100 AD to 199 AD is the *second* century AD, and so on. If we work backwards from the birth of Christ the same system applies. For example, the years 100–199 BC are the *second* century

Fig. 1.3 Kate Jones's life.

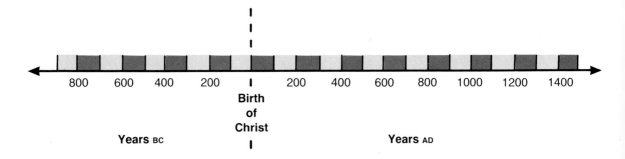

Fig. 1.4 A time-line of centuries.

2

BC. Sometimes, in history, if we do not know exactly when something happened, we say it happened in a particular century. Use Fig. 1.4 to answer the following questions.

    a   In which centuries did the following dates occur?

        i   44 AD
       ii   957 AD
     iii   99 BC
     iv   225 BC
      v   1206 AD
     vi   682 BC
    vii   781 AD
   viii   382 BC

    b   What centuries are the following periods of time?

        i   400 to 499 AD
       ii   399 to 300 BC
     iii   900 to 999 AD
     iv   299 to 200 BC
      v   1200 to 1299 AD

3 A period, or an era, is a length of time between two important events. The things that happened during that period of time may have been influenced by the first of the two events. An example from history is the period or era when a king ruled. Which would be the event that began the period — the date of the king's birth or the date he began to rule? What event would end the period?

Before history?

When we study history we are studying the story of the past. It may be the story of a particular country, a society of people or one individual person. It could be the history of music or the history of medicine or the history of anything whatsoever. This book covers the history of a number of different societies. All these societies existed thousands of years ago. Some of them existed *before* history!

How could anything exist *before* history? Easily! The word 'history' refers to the study of the past that has been recorded in some form of writing. Writing was first used about 5000 years ago. Anything that happened before writing was invented happened *before* history and is called *prehistoric*.

Learning about prehistory

Even though there are no written records about things that happened over 5000 years ago, we are still able to understand much about the way human beings lived and worked. This is because wherever people have lived they have left things behind. The study of these things, or remains, is called *archaeology*.

These remains include every possible aspect of human life: houses, cooking utensils, weapons, jewellery, toys, graves, even rubbish dumps. All these things provide clues as to how people lived before history, or in prehistoric times. These clues are pieced together, like a jigsaw puzzle, by *archaeologists*. Sometimes there are pieces missing and so the story of the past is unclear. You will learn more about the work of archaeologists later in this chapter.

Sometimes both the remains of a society and written records exist. This makes piecing together the story much simpler.

Places or sites where people once lived are often now deserted or even forgotten. Many of these sites are buried beneath layers of sand or soil. They have to be *excavated*, or dug up, by archaeologists before we can know anything about them. Sometimes archaeologists discover that over thousands of years one site may have been occupied several times. After the first settlement was deserted or destroyed, another was built on its ruins, and so on. Fig. 1.5 shows how this might have happened.

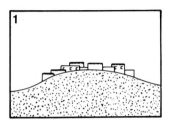
A mud-brick town is built on a small hill.

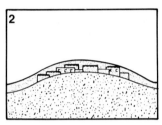
The town is destroyed by floods and covered by a layer of silt.

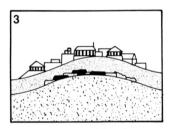
A new town of stone and timber is built on the higher hill.

The town is attacked and burned.

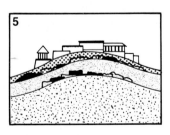
The ruins are destroyed and a new town is built many years later.

Fig. 1.5 Some archaeological sites have been occupied more than once.

Finding ancient sites

How does an archaeologist know where to dig to find an ancient site? There are several ways that a site may be detected. In countries such as Turkey, Iran and Iraq there are hundreds of small hills or mounds. Almost all of these are ancient places of settlement. They are called *tells*.

Aerial photography can sometimes show an archaeological site that cannot be seen at ground level. Take, for example, an ancient wall, the crumbled remains of which have been covered over the years by soil. The soil directly above the wall will be drier than the deeper soil around the wall. Therefore the grass growing above the buried wall will be sparser than the grass growing beside it. The difference shows up in an aerial photograph. The outline of the wall is often clearly visible.

Once an archaeologist has decided to excavate a site, permission must first be obtained from the government of the country where the site is. Then a team of workers start the *dig*, as an excavation is sometimes called.

If a site has been occupied more than once, each settlement will form a distinct layer as the dig progresses. The layers are

Fig. 1.6 An aerial photograph showing the outline of a large house built about 60 AD in Britain.

dug up in the reverse order to that in which they were laid down. The top layer will therefore be more recent than the bottom layer, as long as the site has not been disturbed over the years.

These layers are very important to archaeologists. They can help to date the site. In each layer (or *stratum*) objects, mostly broken pieces of pottery, are found. Sometimes these pieces of pottery are similar to those found in another excavation. The archaeologist can then say that both sites were occupied in roughly the same period of time. Perhaps the two sites had some contact with one another through trade. If the date of one site is known, the other site can be given a similar date.

Another method of dating is called the Carbon 14 method. This method uses scientific analysis of objects from the site. The amount of carbon present in organic materials decreases as the object breaks down. By measuring how much carbon is present, scientists can tell how old something is. However, most dates in archaeology are *approximate*. The further back in time something happened, the more approximate is its date.

Every item unearthed during a dig is carefully recorded and its precise position noted. Sometimes the items are passed on to specialists for examination. Once the dig is over and the finds have been examined, the archaeologist studies all the records and reports, to make a final report on the site.

Time to understand

1 An archaeologist often needs the help of other specialists to analyse the finds of a dig. Use a dictionary to find out what the following specialists do:

   a   zoologist
   b   numismatist
   c   palaeographer
   d   Egyptologist
   e   physicist
   f   botanist
   g   palaeontologist
   h   epigraphist

2 Pottery and pieces of broken pottery (called *potsherds*) are often the most common finds at digs. This is simply because pottery was the most common material in everyday use in many ancient societies. Today we use other materials. What materials are used today to make the following items which would have been made of pottery thousands of years ago?

   a   drinking vessel
   b   storage jar
   c   dinner plate
   d   writing material
   e   lamp base

Lake Mungo

In 1968 Jim Bowler, from the Australian National University, was studying land formations in western New South Wales when he made a very exciting discovery. He found the remains of an ancient campsite. A little further away he saw some bones sticking up out of the ground.

Carbon dating of some of the objects from the campsite showed that the camp had been occupied over 30 000 years ago. Archaeologists discovered that the bones were the skeleton of a young woman who had died about 26 000 years ago.

Fig. 1.7 A view of Lake Mungo, showing the lunettes or sand dunes.

Further research in the area over the next few years showed that the site, called Lake Mungo, had been a large freshwater lake some 30 000 years ago with several different groups of Aboriginal people living on its shores. They had fished in the lake, eaten the freshwater mussels found in its mud, roasted emu eggs over fires and hunted for small animals around the lake.

Lake Mungo is one of a number of lakes called the Willandra Lakes. These once covered about 1088 square kilometres. It is hard to imagine that the barren landscape of today was once much cooler and moister. The lakes dried up between 15 000 and 18 000 years ago, when the climate of Australia was changing in the last Ice Age.

The Ice Ages were long periods of time during which the ice of the Arctic and Antarctic circles extended much further than it does today. The advance of the ice caused the level of the sea to drop throughout the world. At times the ice melted and the sea level rose again. About 15 000 years ago the sheets of ice were probably at their furthest extent. Because the temperature became so much colder,

the atmosphere became drier. This was probably the reason why the lakes dried up.

When the ice melted, the sea level throughout the world rose and the temperature became warmer. The Willandra Lakes remained dry, probably because of the higher temperatures.

The bones of the young woman found in 1968 showed that she had been cremated. The skeleton had then been deliberately smashed before the remains were placed in a small pit. This is the earliest evidence of cremation in the world.

In 1974 another skeleton was discovered. Carbon dating showed that it was over 30 000 years old. Archaeologists said that it was a very rare find, because it was the *complete* skeleton of a rather tall man. His hands were clasped together and his body had been covered with a red-coloured ochre.

Fig. 1.8 The first complete skeleton found at Lake Mungo.

Ochre is a powder obtained from minerals mixed with clay. It is not found naturally at Lake Mungo. This tells us that the ochre was deliberately brought to the site, perhaps especially for the burial.

The two burials are evidence of careful thought and action taken by the people who lived on the shores of the lake. Some archaeologists think that the burials are evidence of some form of religion.

Most of the evidence is found along the *lunettes*, or sand dunes. At Lake Mungo these have become eroded into fantastic shapes. In the 1860s the dunes were named 'The Walls of China', because of their shapes.

The remains of animal skeletons have also been found in the lunettes. Among these are the bones of the extinct *Procoptodon*, a kangaroo that was over three metres tall. Did the Aboriginal people hunt giant procoptodons? Did procoptodons become extinct because of this?

There are many unanswered questions about prehistoric life in Australia. Evidence at Lake Mungo is still being discovered, as it is in many other sites. Very slowly, the pieces of the jigsaw puzzle are being put together. Some of them may never be found.

Fig. 1.9   An artist's impression of two procoptodons.

Prehistoric animals in Australia

The Aboriginal people first came to Australia at least 40 000 years BP, probably by crossing by boat from South-East Asia. When they arrived, animals that are now extinct were living in Australia. They may have become extinct because the changes in climate made it impossible for them to survive. (Remember how the Willandra Lakes dried up?) They may have been hunted to extinction by the Aboriginal people. Perhaps the burning of large areas of land drastically changed the environment. How do we know these animals existed? How do we know Aboriginal people hunted them?

At Tambar Springs in New South Wales, a skeleton of a large prehistoric animal called *Diprotodon australis*, dating from 35 000 BC, was found. Cut marks on the skeleton look like the work of a butcher, who was perhaps an Aborigine using stone tools.

Some of the animals living at that time were much bigger than their modern relatives. They are called the *megafauna*. When some of these animals died their bones gradually became *fossilised* or preserved in a layer of earth. Palaeontologists study these *fossils* to find out about life on earth long ago. When animal bones are found along with human remains they are used by archaeologists as pieces in the jigsaw puzzle of life in the past.

Time to understand

1   Dr Michael Archer, a palaeontologist from the University of New South Wales, has been in charge of excavations at Riversleigh in north-western Queensland. He has uncovered the fossils of many

7

animals that have never been known before. On the dig one morning:

Archer looked down at the rock he was standing on — and almost passed out with excitement; the rock was literally bristling with the teeth and jaws of mammals of every kind imaginable.

The events of the next five minutes remain a bit of a blur in all of our memories. The whole group, responding to the incoherent and decidedly unscientific shouts of its leader, descended on the area. Despite the carpet of prickly spinifex grass which almost covered the rocks, everyone was crawling around on hands and knees shouting out to each other all of the new delights they were finding. In that brief handful of moments, in a mere 10 square metres of area, we spotted well over 100 mammal specimens representing about 30 species that no one had ever seen before.

One of the fossils discovered at Riversleigh is a 'weird thing'. It was a small animal the size of a rabbit. It had only cutting cheek teeth. This means it would not have been able to grind its food before swallowing it. The animal has been nicknamed 'Thingodonta'.

What kind of food do you think it ate?

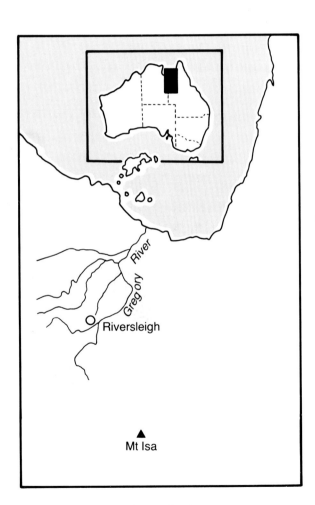

Fig. 1.10   The site of Riversleigh.

Fig. 1.11   This large rock at Riversleigh contains the fossilised jaw of an ancient animal. Can you see its teeth?

8

Before you answer, consider the following facts.

   a Some animals, such as snakes, swallow then digest their food whole.

   b Sharp teeth are able to puncture things such as eggs.

2 Ancient societies often used· mythological stories to explain natural events. Today we know the scientific explanations. Aborigines explained a flood after a drought in the following way.

Tiddalik, the largest frog ever known, awoke one morning with an unquenchable thirst. He started to drink, and he drank until there was no fresh water left in the world. The creatures everywhere were soon dying and the trees were shedding their leaves because of the lack of moisture . . .

The animals could not think of a way out of their terrible plight, until a wise old wombat suggested that if Tiddalik could be made to laugh, all the imprisoned water would flow out of his mouth.

So everyone gathered by the giant frog's resting-place. For a long time they tried to make him laugh, but in vain. The kookaburra told his funniest stories, so good that he could not help laughing at them himself . . . but the frog's face remained blank and indifferent.

Then, when the animals were in despair, the eel, Nabunum, driven from his favourite creek by the drought, slithered up to the unresponsive frog, and began to dance. He started with slow, graceful movements, but as the dance became faster he wriggled and twisted himself into the most grotesque and comical shapes, until suddenly Tiddalik's eyes lit up and he burst out laughing. And as he laughed, the water gushed from his mouth and flowed away to replenish the lakes, the swamps, and the rivers.

Below is an illustration of two animals found at Riversleigh. This is how an artist has imagined they looked. He first studied the skeletons carefully. Then he studied modern animals that have similar characteristics.

Fig. 1.12 The *Neoholos* (left) was about the size of a rhinoceros. It ate plants, which means it was herbivorous. The *Palorchestes azael* (right) was about the size of a bull. It probably used its huge claws to strip branches or bark from trees. It was herbivorous and became extinct approximately 20 000 BP.

Using the story of Tiddalik as a guide, write a story about one of these extinct animals.

Çatal Hüyük

In 1958 an archaeologist called James Mellaart decided to excavate a large mound lying in the middle of a plain in Turkey. The Turkish word for mound is *hüyük*. That particular mound was known to the locals as Çatal. The site became known as Çatal Hüyük (pronounced *Chat-arl Hoo-yook*).

When the team began to excavate in May 1961, Çatal Hüyük had lain undisturbed for approximately 8000 years. Mellaart and his team discovered much more than they expected. Çatal Hüyük was not a simple village; it was large and complex enough to be called a city.

The prehistoric city

What makes up a city? One of the most obvious 'parts' of a city are the buildings. These are used in many different ways. There are also open spaces such as parks, public squares, roads and rubbish dumps. Then there are the people who actually live in the city. Their daily work and lives

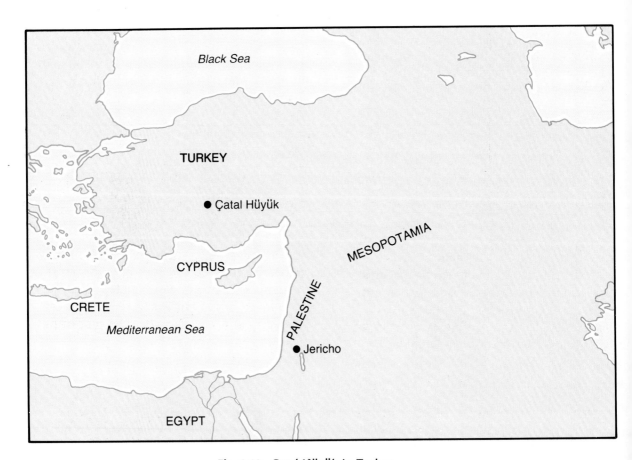

Fig. 1.13 Çatal Hüyük in Turkey.

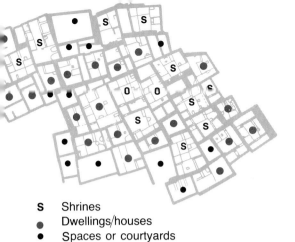

S Shrines
● Dwellings/houses
• Spaces or courtyards

Fig. 1.14 A groundplan of part of Çatal Hüyük.

keep the city going. They build the buildings and use the spaces.

Most of the buildings in the part of Çatal Hüyük that has been excavated were either houses or shrines. Look carefully at the groundplan of this area (Fig. 1.14). Most of the buildings and the spaces are the same size. This is because the spaces were often ruined houses which had not been rebuilt.

Look carefully at the plan in Fig. 1.14 again. What else is unusual about it? There are very few doorways and all the houses are built right up against one another. There are no streets, no laneways, no front or back gardens. Entrance to the buildings was through an opening in the roof. Communication between them was also by rooftop. This meant that the outside of the settlement would have looked like a solid wall. It made defending the settlement from attack much easier. (Remember that it was located on a plain.) It may also have been protection from the flooding of a nearby river.

Inside, the houses were all very similar. Cooking was over an open fire which was always at the south end of the room. The entrance also doubled as the smoke hole.

Sometimes there was also an oven. There were two raised platforms that were used for sitting, sleeping and working. Each house usually had a small storage room as well. The only other pieces of furniture were a ladder, perhaps a workbench and storage bins for grain. Walls and floors were plastered each year. This all indicates a fairly simple day-to-day life (See Fig. 1.16, over).

There is, however, another feature of the houses at Çatal Hüyük that is not obvious when you look at the plan. It tells us much more about the lives of the people who lived in the houses than the simple furnishings.

Burials and religion

All the burials at Çatal Hüyük were found beneath the raised platforms inside the houses. This was not as unhealthy as it may seem. Only the bones, held together roughly by the ligaments, were buried. Under some houses were several generations of one family. Perhaps the dead were still considered to be part of the family.

Gifts buried with the dead tell us that women and children wore jewellery such as necklaces, bracelets, anklets and pendants made of various stones, shells, clay and mother-of-pearl. Sometimes mirrors made of highly polished obsidian and even cosmetic sets had been buried. Weapons of stone and obsidian were sometimes buried with men.

Most of the burials under the platforms were those of women and children. Perhaps many of the men died while away from home, hunting or fighting.

The shrines, which were used for worship, were very similar to the houses. The main difference was that the shrines were decorated with wall paintings and sculpture. There were forty shrines in the small area of Çatal Huyuk that has been

11

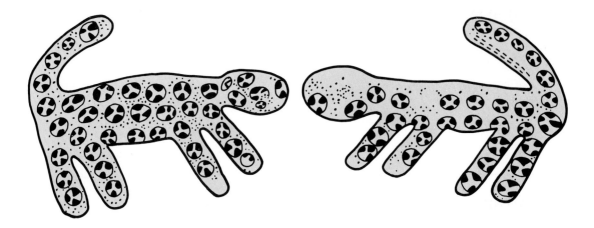

Fig. 1.15 A wall decoration showing a pair of leopards.

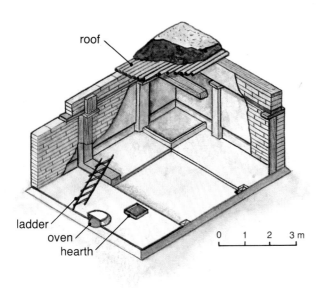

Fig. 1.16 Inside a house at Çatal Hüyük, showing the raised platforms, the hearth and the oven. Do you remember why there was a ladder in each house?

excavated. Mellaart concluded that religion was important. The main goddess worshipped was a 'mother goddess', sometimes depicted with a daughter and a young son.

From the evidence at Çatal Hüyük it appears that the people ate different kinds of grains, meat, peas, lentils, nuts, fruits and berries. This diet may sound unimportant but to Mellaart it was an exciting discovery. It showed that 8000 years ago the people of Çatal Hüyük were successful farmers. They grew a variety of crops and they herded sheep and cattle. They also hunted for game and gathered other foods. To archaeologists, that showed an important step in the history of world civilisation.

What we have learnt from the discoveries

Both Çatal Hüyük and Lake Mungo show us how prehistoric people developed ways of living that were suitable to their environment. At Lake Mungo the earliest settlers used the lakes as their main source of food. When the lakes dried up the Aboriginal people began to grind wild grass seeds into flour, on large sandstone grinding stones which have been found in the lunettes.

At Çatal Hüyük the people seem to have been farmers and traders. The large number of obsidian goods suggests that the people of Çatal Hüyük exchanged obsidian, which was available nearby, for other items such as stone and shells.

12

The beginning of recorded history makes the task of piecing the puzzle of the past together much easier. This does not mean that the picture is complete. In the following chapters you will be studying societies that have left behind many different kinds of evidence of their histories.

Time to understand

1 Many of the remains found at Çatal Hüyük were *manufactured* goods. This tells us quite a lot about the activities of the people who lived there.

What craftspeople would have produced the following goods?

a textiles
b baskets
c pottery
d copper beads
e leather bags
f wooden bowls

How would these people have obtained food?

2 What kind of workers would be needed to perform the following tasks?

a building houses (at least 2)
b decorating shrines

3 Use an encyclopaedia to find out what *obsidian* is. Then explain why it was used to make daggers, spearheads, arrowheads, sickle blades, scrapers and even mirrors found at Çatal Hüyük.

Fig. 1.17 Tollund Man, sacrificed to the gods in the Iron Age. His body was discovered in a bog in Denmark in 1950, 2000 years after he had been killed. (See over.)

13

A rare discovery

In 1952 the body of a teenage girl was found in a peat bog in Denmark. She had been led to the place, blindfolded, and drowned in half a metre of water. Like a man found nearby with his throat cut, and another found with a leather noose around his neck, the girl had been murdered as a sacrifice to the mother goddess. They had all died in the first century AD.

The most amazing thing about these people is that their bodies were found, almost perfectly preserved, in the peat of the bog almost two thousand years later.

By examining what was in one man's stomach, scientists were even able to tell what he had eaten for his last meal (a gruel made from barley, linseed and weeds).

The photograph in Fig. 1.17 shows the head of Tollund Man, with the leather rope by which he was killed still around his neck. His remains are the best preserved of all the human remains that have yet been discovered. Would you agree with the archaeologist who wrote that 'the head is still full of life and more beautiful than the best portraits by the world's greatest artists, since it is the man himself we see'?

2

Sumer: the land between the rivers

READ THE EXTRACT below. Can you understand how the boy felt? What do you think of his teacher? Why do you think the boy was so pleased with his idea of inviting his teacher to eat at his home?

The people in this story are so real that it could almost have been written today — except, of course, for a few different ideas about schools and the old-fashioned words of the teacher. In fact, this story was

I woke up late and knew I would be caned if I was late for school. So I asked my mother to make my lunch quickly and I got ready as fast as I could. Even so, I didn't get there in time and the monitor asked me why I was late. I bowed to my teacher but that day everything went wrong. I was caned for talking, standing up at the wrong time and trying to walk out the gate when I should have been in class. Then I was caned again because the teacher thought my writing was not good enough. That's when I thought of a plan. I asked my father to invite the teacher home. He was happy to come because his pay was not very good and he always liked a bit of attention. The teacher sat at the place of honour at our table and I acted as the waiter while he ate and drank with my father. We gave him some new clothes, a ring and other presents. The plan worked well. My teacher was so pleased with his treatment in our house that he turned and said to me:

'Young man, may you reach the pinnacle of the scribal art, may you achieve it completely. Of your brothers may you be their leader, of your friends may you be their chief, may you rank the highest of the schoolboys. You have carried out well the school's activities, you have become a man of learning.'

Fig. 2.1 Originally this extract would have been written on a clay tablet in cuneiform writing in the Sumerian language (See Fig. 2.16, p. 30).

Fig. 2.2 The flatlands of the Tigris–Euphrates valley today. It was in land like this that civilisation began in Sumer.

written down almost 4000 years ago! The boy lived in Sumer, which was then one of the world's most civilised places. The school he went to was among the first in the world; the writing he was in trouble for not doing properly was perhaps the first writing in the world; the city he lived in was one of the first ever built.

This chapter is about Sumer, this boy's home. In it we shall learn about the kind of life he led and why his people were so important in the history of human development.

Settling down

Imagine the world before human beings had ever built a town, or even a village. People wander (as they have for many thousands of years before) hunting animals, stopping in caves or perhaps throwing a few branches together to make a windbreak. They can talk but have not invented writing; they hunt but do not farm.

In the area we now call the Middle East, the hills and grasslands where the hunters roam overlook flat, muddy plains.

Perhaps the hunters come to the hilly edges of these valleys many times. Perhaps they find water and camp there for longer than usual. They watch the native grass growing, quickly and high, in the valleys below. They learn to pick the grass — barley we call it today — and use it for food. Then they learn to save some of the seed and plant it to produce another crop. They find that some animals will come to the camp and stay there if grass is left for them. These animals — cows, sheep and goats — can be tamed and used for clothes and food. Some are put into pens so that they will always be there when they are needed. The wandering hunters have become settled farmers.

It took thousands of years for this change to happen. In Chapter One you read about one of the first human settlements, Çatal Hüyük in Turkey. People lived there about 8000 years ago.

About 5000 years ago a group of farmers left their villages in the hills of the Middle East and moved to the flatlands below. We do not really know why. Perhaps they were attracted by the rich and fertile land in the valley. Perhaps they had fought with their neighbours. Perhaps they were pushed out by a stronger group of farmers. Can you think of any other possible explanations?

The land these people moved to was called Sumer. Here they established schools and cities; here they found a way of writing. They made other exciting discoveries, too, and invented many things that human beings still use.

Time to understand

Human beings have existed for more than 100 000 years — a thousand centuries. Let

16

us imagine that those 100 000 years are represented by the 24 hours of a day and night. Draw a line 24 centimetres long to stand for this period. Each centimetre stands for one hour, so you can mark the hours along the line. Midday will be at the 12-centimetre mark and midnight at the end of the line. Each centimetre represents about 4000 years. Midnight is the present.

Now make a mark at 9.30 pm along the line. How many years ago was that? Until that time, human beings were wandering hunters. At about 9.30 pm in our diagram a few humans in one part of the world started growing food as well as hunting for it. Make another mark at the point on the line that stands for 10.45 pm. This is when the first people settled in Sumer. The

inventions and changes that made Sumer so important all took place within the next half-hour on our scale.

Can you work out at what point along the line Jesus Christ was born? How do we describe the time before this? How do we describe the time after it?

The land between the rivers

Look carefully at the map in Fig. 2.3. Can you find the Tigris and Euphrates rivers? The land between them — a crescent-shaped arc from the Persian Gulf west to the Mediterranean Sea — was called

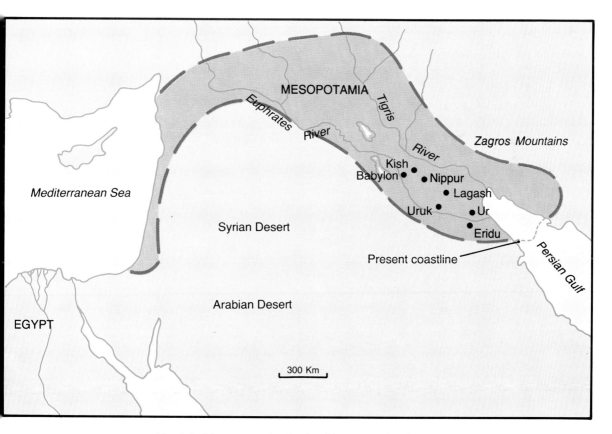

Fig. 2.3 Mesopotamia, the land between the rivers.

Mesopotamia, 'the land between the rivers'. The southern part of Mesopotamia was known as Sumer. Today it is the country called Iraq. Find Iraq in a modern atlas. What are its neighbouring countries today?

If you visited the site of Sumer you would find it hard to believe that it was one of the world's first settled places. For most of the year it is hot, dry and dusty. The soil is baked as hard as rock by the scorching sun, and crops wither and die. In winter the rains come and turn the plains into a muddy, slimy mess. There are very few trees and almost no stone for building.

Despite all these disadvantages, the flatlands of Sumer had one overwhelming advantage in the eyes of its new settlers. The Tigris and Euphrates rivers regularly flooded and their waters covered the plains around them. This had happened for thousands of years. The mud and silt brought down by these rivers had gradually built up to form natural islands and banks of rich, fertile land ideal for planting crops. It was this land that attracted the earliest settlers to Sumer. There was another advantage, too. Along the banks of the rivers were reedy marshes and swamps, the homes of fish and waterbirds that could easily be caught for food. In spring the reeds were thick enough to be cut down and used to feed goats and sheep.

Time to understand

1 You can see from the map in Fig. 2.3 that the shape of the Persian Gulf has changed since the area was first settled. Using the information in this section, can you explain why there is now much more land at the entrance to the gulf?

Why did people settle in this area?
2 Imagine you were among the earliest Sumerian settlers. Describe the first flood you experienced. What happened to your home and your possessions? What happened after the flood? What did you learn from the flood?

From village to city

The first Sumerians lived in family groups near the marshes and swamps by the river. They built their homes from the reeds around them. They used reeds, too, for making boats and rafts to travel through their marshy land. The seed they planted grew quickly in the rich soil. They soon learned to dig out canals to spread the river water further through the crops.

There was plenty of food and families grew bigger and spread further. Some moved away from the marshes into the plains between the rivers. It was drier here and houses could be made of sun-baked clay. Over a period of about a thousand years these villages became larger and more complex. By 3000 BC there were several large cities, which you can see in the map in Fig. 2.3. Ur was a harbour city with quays and wharfs made of mud bricks, at which trading boats tied up.

Each city was an independent kingdom and owned the land around its walls. These cities are sometimes called 'city-states' because of this. At first these cities were ruled by an assembly or council of adult free men. Later, when they began fighting each other, a king was elected to rule each city. These kings became important and powerful leaders and the position of king became hereditary — it passed from father

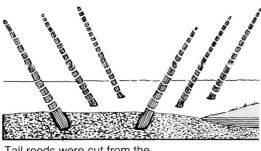

Tall reeds were cut from the riverbank, tied together in bundles and pushed into the earth.

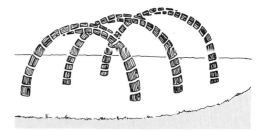

The tops of bundles opposite each other were bent together and fastened.

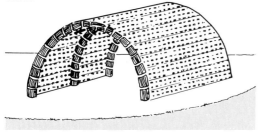

The arches were covered with mats made of reeds. A floor was made of reed mats.

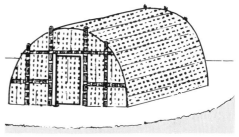

Reeds were used to make frames for the ends. They were covered with matting. A door was fixed to a pole.

Fig. 2.4 The earliest Sumerian homes.

to son in one family. The Sumerians came to believe that their city's king was a representative of the god of the city who owned the city and everything and everybody in it.

The temple

The temple was the highest and grandest building in each Sumerian city, for it was here that the people worshipped and paid homage to the god who owned and protected the city. The first temples were simple mud-brick buildings but as the cities grew, so their temples became larger and more elaborate. The temples were built on mounds inside walled enclosures. Terraces led from one level to the next, climbing upwards all the time because the Sumerians believed that the higher they

reached, the closer they were to their god. For this reason, the temple — the house of the god — was built on a mound, the mountain of the god. In the centre of the temple, on the highest level, was the *sanctuary* or most sacred place. Here the king spoke to the city god and learned the god's wishes. Here sacrifices were made to the god and food was left out for the god to eat. Sometimes the king or his priests would spend the night in the sanctuary, hoping that their god would visit them while they were asleep and give them wisdom.

By the end of the Sumerian period the temples had become so high that they have been given a special name — *ziggurat*, from an old word for 'pinnacle'. The terraces continued higher and higher, up to

19

Fig. 2.5 The ruins of the ziggurat of Ur.

88 metres into the air, each connected by a long staircase. The remains of more than 30 ziggurats, or temple-towers, have been found by archaeologists in Mesopotamia.

The death pit of Ur

It is 1927. A British archaeologist, Leonard Woolley, has been supervising an excavation, or dig, in the cemetery just outside the wall of the ancient Sumerian city of Ur for many months. He has found some large burial chambers, some covered with domes. The burial chambers had been robbed thousands of years earlier, and there is nothing of interest inside them.

Despite his disappointment, Woolley digs further. One day he finds five corpses lying in a shallow grave. By digging along a sloping ramp near the bodies he finds another group of corpses, men and women lying in neat rows as if they had been lined up. Further on are the remains of a

Fig. 2.6 A harp found in the 'death pit' at Ur. The bull's head is made of gold.

20

Fig. 2.7 A reconstruction of the 'death pit' at Ur. Servants prepare to be sacrificed near the tombs of two powerful Sumerians.

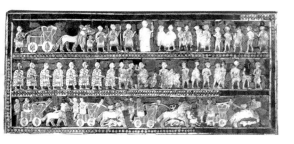 

Fig. 2.8 The Royal Standard of Ur consists of two wooden panels, each about 45 centimetres long. The pictures on the standard show peace and war — the two sides of life in Sumer. The figures were carved in shell and set in lapis lazuli, a kind of precious stone.

harp and the bones of the harpist, and then the bones of animals and what is left of a decorated chariot. As they move along the ramp Woolley and his team uncover an extraordinary collection of objects: wooden chests, tumblers of gold, silver and glass and tools of gold and copper.

Slowly and carefully they move along the ramp, sifting the earth and taking notes of what they find. They are about to make an exciting and frightening discovery. The ramp leads to an underground tomb and there they find the reason for all the bodies they have so far discovered. For there, in a great square pit, lie the bodies of two people who may have been the rulers of Ur. One is a woman called Shub-ad, on whose head is a magnificent headdress of gold and jewels. Near her lips is a gold cup and around her are the bodies of her attendants.

Beside her tomb is the grave of a man called A-bar-gi. On the ramp nearby lie the bodies of servants, women and soldiers, all well dressed, and the remains of two wagons and the oxen that had pulled them into the tomb.

Who were these people? The Sumerians kept lists of their kings but neither the name of the man nor the woman in the main tombs appears on them. Were they, perhaps, a priest and priestess who had been sacrificed to the gods? Were they the victims of a battle between two cities, prepared to die rather than to surrender to their enemies?

There is another mystery. There was no sign of any struggle either in the main tombs or along the ramp leading to them. All those who had died had done so quietly and peacefully. They had even arranged themselves in order, lying down in the place where they would eventually be found in 1927. Had they all drunk from a cup of poison? (Remember the gold cup near the body of Shub-ad.) Had they all *wanted* to die? Or were Shub-ad and A-bar-gi really king and queen and all the others sacrificial victims, forced to die with them and be buried forever in their tombs? How did they feel as they marched in procession, dressed in their best clothes, into the pit, with music playing, knowing that they were going to their deaths? Did they even realise that they *were* going to die? We may never know.

Time to understand

1 Leonard Woolley believed that the tombs he had discovered at Ur were those of a king and queen who had died and whose servants and attendants were killed with them so that they could serve them in the after-life. From what you have read above, do you think this is the most likely explanation? Are there any facts in the story that do not fit in with Woolley's explanation? Can you suggest another explanation? Do you think your explanation is more or less likely than that of Leonard Woolley? Why?

2 Like their mistress, Shub-ad's female servants wore elaborate headdresses. They had thick, heavy wigs decorated with artificial flowers and gold and silver ribbons. It seems that one of these ladies-in-waiting had not had time to put on her ribbon, for Woolley found it by her side in the pocket of her dress. She had slipped it there, still rolled up, rather than be late for her own funeral.

Imagine you were this young woman. Why were you late for the funeral procession? How did you feel as you hurriedly prepared for your death? Why did you bother decorating your hair? Why did you put the ribbon in your pocket?

Did you want to die as well dressed as the other ladies-in-waiting?

3 Make a list of the things we can learn from Leonard Woolley's discovery about Sumerian beliefs about death and the after-life.

City life

Sumerian cities, you will remember, were independent and often at war with their neighbours. For this reason they were surrounded by high walls built, like the other city buildings, of sun-dried clay. Inside the walls were narrow, winding streets along which were the mud-brick homes of the people. Most were simple buildings — just two or three rooms around an open courtyard in the centre. There were no garbage collections or sewerage systems, so the cities must have been uncomfortably smelly as all rubbish and waste were simply thrown into the streets.

A few streets were set apart for all the city's people to use. There were public squares where they could watch wrestling matches or listen to storytellers, or try their luck at gambling. There was the bazaar, shaded by awnings and lined with the stalls of shopkeepers. Here people could buy vegetables and fruit, meat and fish, pots and clothes. Traders brought in luxuries from other countries — precious metals and jewels, wooden objects, ivory, shells and pearls.

As we have seen, the temple was the most important building in a Sumerian city. The second-grandest building was the king's palace. In the biggest cities the palace stretched over many blocks and contained hundreds of rooms. Elaborate carving and wall paintings decorated some of these rooms. It was here that the king received his visitors and advisers, here that he feasted with other wealthy people and here that he listened to the problems of the people of his city. As well as being the representative of the city's god, the king was also concerned with the everyday life and problems of the citizens. He sent troops to fight against enemy invaders, discussed local matters with his officials and made judgments about quarrels and family problems.

As food became more plentiful, not all Sumerians had to work on the land to produce it. Many people lived and worked in the cities. There were carpenters and stonemasons, potters and teachers, metalworkers and priests, servants and merchants, soldiers and boatbuilders, clerks and toolmakers, jewellers and entertainers. All of them — and many more — had a place in Sumerian society.

At the very bottom of the social ladder, however, were the slaves, people who had a much less happy life. Some of them were prisoners of war, captured in one of the many battles between the Sumerian cities or between the Sumerians and enemy tribes from the surrounding regions. Others were forced to become slaves or to sell their children as slaves when they could not grow enough food or make enough money to feed themselves. Most Sumerian slaves were owned by the priests of the temple or the king in his palace.

Time to understand

Like other societies, past and present, the Sumerians were divided into a number of different groups or classes. Use the outline in Fig. 2.9 to make a diagram showing the main classes in Sumerian society.

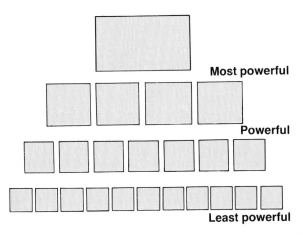

Most powerful

Powerful

Least powerful

Fig. 2.9 Make a diagram of Sumerian social classes.

1   Which person should go at the top of the diagram? Why was this person so powerful in Sumerian society?
2   Which group of people should go immediately below this first person? Why were they powerful?
3   Many kinds of people fit into the middle of the diagram. These were ordinary people who went about their daily lives as best they could. Add some of them to the middle part of your diagram.
4   Which group of people were at the bottom of Sumerian society? Why? Where did they come from? Add them to the bottom part of your diagram.

Taming the rivers

The Tigris and Euphrates rivers were both friend and foe to the Sumerians. The rivers brought down the rich silt in which their crops grew so quickly and so well. The rivers, too, sometimes flooded and destroyed whatever had been built around them. The success of Sumer depended upon the people's ability to tame these rivers, to use their waters without being ruined by them.

To do this, Sumerian farmers dug a network of canals and dykes to channel the water where they wanted it to flow and to stop it from washing away homes and crops. The irrigation system grew so large that many people were employed to work on it and keep it in order. Canals had to be dug and cleaned; dykes had to be built and repaired. This work had to be organised and supervised: it had to be *planned*. The need to plan the irrigation system probably helped the Sumerians to learn and practise the skills they needed in their city-based society.

In their irrigated fields, Sumerian farmers were able to grow much larger crops than they could have grown without irrigation. The number of Sumerians increased quickly but there was usually enough food for them all, including those who worked in the cities and had to buy food from the marketplace.

Time to understand

1   'Before Sumer, people *preyed* on nature; in Sumer, people were *partners* with nature.'
Can you explain what this statement means? Do you agree with it?
2   The diagram in Fig. 2.10 shows one of the ways that the Sumerians irrigated their land. Explain how this method would have worked.
3   A small clay tablet found in the Sumerian city of Nippur has helped us understand how Sumerian farmers worked. The tablet, only 76 millimetres wide and

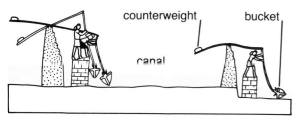

Fig. 2.10 Irrigating the fields. How did the system work?

Fig. 2.11 A Sumerian plough-seeder. How did it work?

114 millimetres long, contained instructions written by a father for his son to help him through the farming year — a kind of farming textbook. Here are some extracts from this ancient tablet:

> When you are about to cultivate your field, keep a close watch on the irrigation works so that the water does not rise too high in your field when you flood it. When you have emptied the field of water, make sure the wet ground stays even. Let no wandering oxen trample over it. Clear it with ten narrow axes. Tear out the stubble by hand and tie it in bundles. When you have ploughed straight furrows, then plough diagonal furrows. Keep an eye on the man who puts in the barley seed. Let him drop it in uniformly, two fingers deep. If the barley seed does not go in properly, change your ploughshare, 'the tongue of the plough'.

a   Why was the young farmer advised to flood his field with water? How do you think this would have been done? How would the water have been emptied out again?

b   What is a ploughshare? Why would it have been called 'the tongue of the plough' in this old document?

c   Fig. 2.11 shows a farming implement invented by the Sumerians. It is a combined plough and seeder. What do you think each of the men in the picture is doing? How did the plough-seeder work?

d   In another part of this tablet the young farmer was reminded that on the day when the seed broke through the ground he was to pray to Ninkilim, the goddess of field mice and vermin, to ask her help in keeping these pests away from the growing grain. What does this tell us about Sumerian beliefs?

e   From the evidence of this ancient 'textbook' and the illustrations in this section, what conclusions can you draw about Sumerian farming? Make a list of the five most important things you have learned about it.

Sumerian inventions

At its greatest — between about 4500 BC and 3000 BC — Sumer was a wealthy and powerful society. The irrigation schemes and farming methods meant that there was food for all, and people had time to stop and think, to experiment and plan. It was during this time that the Sumerians produced an amazing number of inventions and ideas, many of which we still use today. You can read about writing —

perhaps the greatest of these new ideas — in the next section of this chapter, and you have already learned about the Sumerians' new ideas about cities and farming. Here are some of their other inventions.

The wheel

Around 4000 BC a Sumerian built the first known wheeled vehicle. The wheels were made of solid wood. With wheels on axles, the Sumerians were able to build carts and chariots, drawn by oxen, mules and horses. The carts helped farmers and merchants with their work; the chariots were used in processions and in battle.

Fig. 2.12 This model, about 20 centimetres high, was found in the ruins of Sumer. It is one of the first known examples of the wheel.

Schools

You read about a Sumerian schoolboy at the beginning of this chapter. Schools were set up to teach wealthy boys how to be scribes, or writers. Scribes worked in the temple or palace or on large farms where they kept records of crops grown and sold. It was hard work learning to be a scribe. A boy had to go to school day after day for many years, with only six days off each month. The teaching was dull and students were caned for even the slightest mistake or bad behaviour. They had to learn the complicated way of Sumerian writing and to memorise hundreds of different signs.

Girls did not work as scribes, so they were not able to go to school. Education was only for the wealthy and most Sumerians were unable to read or write. In fact, some scribes earned their living by setting up a stall in the marketplace and acting as writers for those who could not write themselves.

Law

Some scribes studied law, and archaeologists have found thousands of clay tablets on which are recorded contracts, IOUs, wills, deeds of property, receipts and court decisions. From these we know that the Sumerians had a well-developed system of laws. A clay tablet dug up in 1950 records a murder trial in which three men were tried by the citizens' assembly at Nippur for murdering a temple official. It seems that after the murder they told the official's wife of their crime but she did not report it to the authorities. At the trial, some people argued that the wife should also be punished as an 'accessory' to the crime. However, the assembly decided that 'the punishment of those who actually killed should suffice'. The three men were executed and the woman was allowed to go free. When this tablet was translated, it was sent to an American lawyer who said that modern judges would agree with the decision made in that

Sumerian court almost four thousand years ago!

Medicine

A Sumerian doctor once decided to write down his prescriptions and remedies. They lay buried on a clay tablet at Nippur until it was excavated and deciphered — and that was not an easy task because the medical descriptions were very specialised, just as doctor's prescriptions are today.

From these dozen or so remedies we know that the Sumerians used herbal medicine and made mixtures from seeds, roots, gum and bark. They made ointments by grinding substances to powder and mixing them with certain oils. They understood chemistry and knew how to extract one substance from another.

Time to understand

1 The wheel has been called 'the greatest mechanical invention of all time'. Why? What do you think? Are there any other mechanical inventions that are more important than the wheel? Could they have been made without the wheel?
2 All the inventions and ideas listed below were developed or improved by the Sumerians, although some had been invented by other people. Try to imagine why each one was invented. What kind of person might have developed it? Why? Are these inventions still important to us today?

sailing boat	potter's wheel
numbers	paint
surveying instruments	cosmetics
leather	dyeing cloth
casting copper and bronze	engraving

Writing

The system of writing invented by the Sumerians is the earliest known writing in the history of the world. It was used in western Asia for about 2000 years — well after the Sumerians themselves had disappeared. Writing enabled people to record what they thought and felt, what they did and what they believed. Because they wrote down so many things about their world, we know quite a lot about the Sumerians today. We pass this knowledge on to others by writing — in a different language and using different symbols, but using the same basic ideas as those developed by the Sumerians so long ago.

Pictographs

The first written symbols were really pictures. These pictures were used as seals, or signatures. Sumerian scribes used them to mark goods and record information. Sometimes these pictographs, as they have been called, were made with a cylinder seal. You can see a drawing of one of these seals in Fig. 2.14 (over). The picture was carved into the surface of a cylinder of stone. When the stone was rolled over soft clay it left an impression of the picture. Then the clay was left to harden and the picture would be there as a permanent record. Other pictographs were made with a sharp reed, or stylus.

As Sumer grew and priests, kings, merchants and farmers produced more work for the scribes, the pictures became simpler. What had begun as a realistic picture of, say, a cow's head became more *stylised*. The lines on the clay tablet now suggested the shape of a cow's head instead of showing a full picture of a cow's head.

Fig. 2.13 This statue of a Sumerian scribe comes from the city of Lagash. On the back of the statue the story of the scribe's life has been engraved.

Fig. 2.14 A cylinder seal.

From pictograph to cuneiform

Pictographs were used on small clay pieces that were tied to bags of grain to record who had grown them and where they were being sold. They were like ancient labels. They were used, too, on larger tablets on which priests, merchants and farmers kept lists of goods of all kinds. Starting at the top right-hand corner of the clay tablet, the scribe would draw the pictographs in long columns. It was a long and messy task, partly because the pointed stylus produced fine, curved lines that had to be carefully drawn, and partly because the scribe's hand was always smudging his work as he moved from column to column.

The next change — an important one — took place about 3000 BC: The scribes turned the clay tablets sideways and wrote in horizontal rows, top to bottom, from left to right. This overcame the problem of smudging. At the same time they developed a new kind of stylus with a thicker, wedge-shaped tip. This could be pushed down into the clay to make sharp, clear lines but it was no good for drawing the finer lines of the earlier pictographs.

In time, the pictographs became simpler and more abstract. A few lines drawn with the wedge-shaped stylus came to stand for each word. You can see some examples of this change in Fig. 2.15. The first column shows the earliest pictograph, the third column shows the pictograph turned sideways and the fourth column shows how it had developed by about 1900 BC when it was written with a wedge-shaped stylus. The symbols later became more complicated but they still kept the basic patterns of the earlier writing.

You can see from the diagram that some ideas were represented by combining two other words. 'Mouth' and 'water', for example, were joined to make the verb 'to

Earliest pictograph 3000 BC	Meaning of pictograph	Pictograph turned sideways	Cuneiform sign 1900 BC	Meaning
	Head and body of a man			Man
	Head with mouth indicated	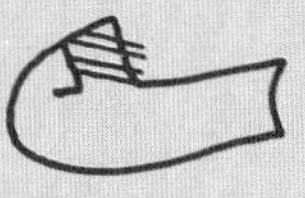		Mouth
	Bowl of food			Food, bread
	Mouth and food			To eat
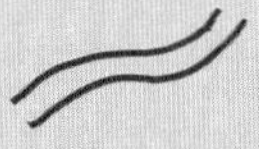	Stream of water			Water
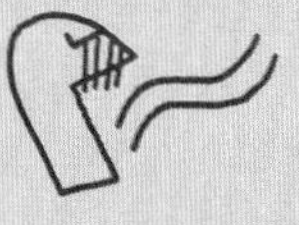	Mouth and water		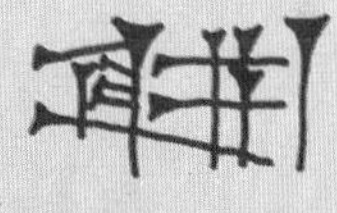	To drink
	Bird	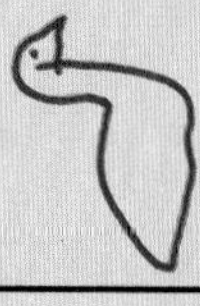		Bird
	Ear of barley			Barley

Fig. 2.15 The development of writing from pictograph to cuneiform.

drink'. Sometimes one symbol was used to represent an idea related to it. The symbol for 'mouth' was in this way sometimes used to mean 'speak'; the symbol for 'pot' also stood for 'food'.

The last stage in the development of Sumerian writing happened when the scribes started using the symbols to stand for sounds as well as ideas. If all the writers knew and accepted that certain symbols made certain sounds, they could combine the sounds together in many different ways, just as we do in English today. Imagine that a scribe knew the symbol for 'sea' and the symbol for 'sun'. He could then put them together to make a new word 'season', which *sounds* like a combination of the two words, although in fact it is not.

The kind of writing invented by the Sumerians has been called *cuneiform* writing. If you know that 'cuneiform' is the Latin word for 'wedge-shaped' you should understand why it has been given this name. By the end of the Sumerian period there were about 150 well-known cuneiform signs. Some of them were symbols for objects; others were symbols for sounds.

Time to understand

1 Try your hand at some cuneiform writing. You will need a stylus which you can make from a short stick. Sharpen it at the end with a penknife so that it has a thick wedge-shaped writing edge. To write on you will need a small piece of flat clay. Look back to find out the size of the tablet on which the farming instructions were written to get an approximate size. Practise on scraps first to learn how to use the stylus and then try to copy some real cuneiform signs onto the clay. You may be able to bake it hard in a school pottery kiln; otherwise dry it in the sun as the Sumerians did.

2 A *rebus* is a sentence or message written in pictures — rather like early Sumerian writing. Each picture can stand for a whole word or part of a word. In a rebus the word 'potatoes' would be written like this:

a   Can you work out why the rebus above means 'potatoes'?
b   Work in groups to make up your own rebus. Try them out on other people in the class.

3 Make up some pictographs for these names:

   Shusin (Sumerian ruler)
   Kabta (Sumerian god of bricks)

Fig. 2.16 Cuneiform writing on a clay tablet.

Im-dugud (Sumerian name)
Aratta (Sumerian town)
Ashnan (Sumerian goddess of grain)
Enki (Sumerian god of wisdom and
   water)
Nippur (Sumerian city)
Nanna (Sumerian moon god)

Divide each name into its parts or syllables and think of a picture to represent that syllable. By joining the pictures for each part you will make a pictograph or sign that stands for the whole word, just as the Sumerians did.

Deciphering the tablets

Throughout this chapter you have read several passages that were written by Sumerians in a different language, using a different kind of 'alphabet', many thousands of years ago. Have you wondered how we came to know what this writing means? It was as if the writing on the clay tablets used by the Sumerians was written in code. Until the code was broken, the information on the tablets was useless. The story of the breaking of the code will help you to understand a little more about how historians work.

Much later than the period we are studying — about 500 years before the birth of Christ — Darius, a Persian king, defeated his enemies and became the strongest ruler in the Middle East. To boast of his greatness he had a message engraved on the Rock of Behistun in what is now Iran. The rock rose over 500 metres above the plain and on it, about 100 metres up, was carved the message of Darius, 20 metres wide and 7 metres high. The wedge-shaped characters in which it was written baffled historians for many centuries.

The code was broken by an English soldier and scholar called Henry Rawlinson. He first saw the engravings in 1835 while he was working in Persia (now Iran). He worked out that the message was written in three different kinds of cuneiform and guessed that it was the same message three times over, written in the three main languages of the people Darius had conquered. Rawlinson knew that if he could decipher just one of the messages he would have a key to the other two.

It was a difficult and complicated task. His first problem was how to make a copy of the signs on the rock. Darius had made sure that his message was engraved in a place that was almost impossible to reach. Rawlinson used ropes and ladders, balancing precariously on narrow ledges as he carefully copied the signs. For one particularly difficult section he had to rely on a young local boy who edged his way up to the engravings and made impressions of the letters as Rawlinson called out to him from below.

One of the scripts looked much simpler than the others and Rawlinson guessed that it was Old Persian, the language spoken by Darius. Slowly and patiently he worked through it, using his knowledge of modern Persian and lots of guesswork. He found one set of symbols that occurred over and over again and worked out that they meant 'king'. Another frequent sign was a divider that broke up the words. Gradually Rawlinson broke the Old Persian code. It was many years before the other two kinds of cuneiform were deciphered, and scholars are still working on more exact translations of cuneiform signs. Everything that is discovered from Sumer and the surrounding lands adds to

Fig. 2.17 The Rock of Behistun. Beneath the engraving is inscribed the cuneiform message praising Darius the conqueror.

their understanding of cuneiform writing and the languages it represents.

The literature of Sumer

Much of what was written down by the Sumerians was practical, everyday information: lists and accounts, rules and records of one kind or another. However, the Sumerians also wrote down stories and poems, songs, prayers and hymns. From them we know that the Sumerians had gods and heroes, demons and villains whose adventures were told and retold many times.

One clay tablet records a story about how two brothers brought barley to Sumer. Others tell of the gods and their adventures — the sun god who lit the earth with rays from his shoulders; the god of water whose shoulders were rivers; the goddess of love and war; and Mother Earth herself, who was the source of all life. From these stories we know that religion was very important to the Sumerians and we can begin to understand why they built such mighty temples to honour the gods who ruled their world.

One story begins with a message from the gods to Ut-Napishtim:

> Tear down this house, build a ship!
> Aboard the ship take thou the seed of all
>   living things . . .

Ut-Napishtim obeyed and built his ship, into which he took his wife and family and seeds and animals. The poem continues:

> Six days and six nights
> Blows the flood wind, as the south storm
>   sweeps the land
> When the seventh day arrives . . .
> The sea grew quiet, the tempest was still,
>   the flood ceased,
> I looked at the weather; stillness had set
>   in . . .
> And all of mankind had returned to clay.

You may recognise this as similar to the story of Noah in the Old Testament of the Christian Bible. People throughout Mesopotamia would have seen mighty floods many times in their lives. Perhaps their stories were told over and over until they merged together into the idea of one huge and disastrous flood that could only be survived by those who obeyed the gods.

Fig. 2.18 Gilgamesh, Sumerian super-hero.

Time to understand

1 The most famous of all the Sumerian heroes was Gilgamesh, part god and part king, who with a very strong man called Enkidu roamed the land in search of adventure. The story of Gilgamesh has been written in modern English for young people to read and enjoy. Find a copy in your school or public library and read for yourself this ancient legend.

2 As well as writing down their stories, the scribes of Sumer recorded their most popular *proverbs*, or sayings. Some of these are listed below. What do they tell us about life in Sumer? Could any of them be comments on our life in Australia today?

a You can have a lord, you can have a
      king,
   But the man to fear is the tax collector!
b You go and carry off the enemy's land;
   The enemy comes and carries off your
      land.
c Friendship lasts a day;
   Kinship lasts forever.
d Who possesses much silver may be
      happy;
   Who possesses much barley may be glad;
   But he who has nothing at all may sleep.
e Pay heed to the word of your mother as
      though it were the word of a god.

The fall of Sumer

Sumer, you will remember, was a land of
independent city-states. The different city-
states were often at war with each other,
trying to keep or increase their power.
Around 2300 BC all these cities were
conquered by a mighty leader called Sargon.

This conqueror stopped the squabbles
between the cities and gave Sumer a unity
it had never had before. Sumer became
part of his empire, which was made even
larger by his grandson, who called himself
'king of the four regions of the world'. But
Sumer was again conquered and there
were years of confusion as cities were
destroyed and battles fought by rival
groups. For a while the king of Ur, a ruler
named Ur-Nammu, managed to unite the
Sumerians again. But time was running out
for Sumer and in about 1720 BC the last
Sumerian king was defeated by
Hammurabi, king of Babylon in northern
Mesopotamia.

Sumer became part of the Babylonian
empire. The Sumerians were no longer a
separate people; their language was no
longer spoken. It seemed that they had
been forgotten. Only through the work of
archaeologists such as Leonard Woolley
and scholars such as Henry Rawlinson
have we been able to discover the secrets
of their civilisation and understand their
contribution to the history of our world.

Fig. 2.19 Sargon the Mighty of Sumer.

3

The Egyptians

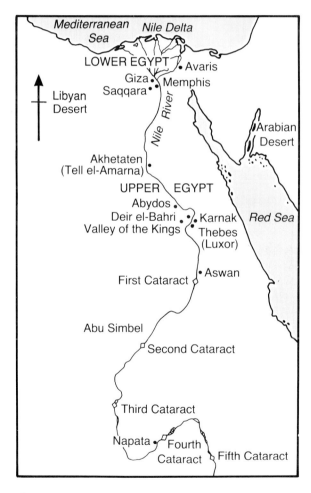

Fig. 3.1 Ancient Egypt.

I F YOU LOOK at Fig. 3.1 you will see that the Nile River flows right through the country of Egypt. It fans out into a number of small channels as it reaches the Mediterranean Sea. On each side of the river is a narrow strip of fertile land, known as the Nile valley. High limestone cliffs surround the valley. Beyond these cliffs lie two deserts. The eastern desert is called the Arabian Desert and the western one is called the Libyan Desert.

About two and a half thousand years ago, Herodotus, a Greek traveller in Egypt, wrote that the land of Egypt was the 'gift of the river'. What did he mean by this?

The Nile is formed by the joining of two other rivers further south at Khartoum. One, known as the White Nile, flows north from Lake Victoria in Uganda. The other, the Blue Nile, comes from Ethiopia.

Each year, heavy winter rains in Ethiopia flooded the Blue Nile. The floodwaters surged along the river until they burst the banks of the Nile River in Egypt. The Nile valley was then flooded. When the waters subsided the ancient Egyptians planted their crops in the layer of fertile, moist silt left behind.

Fig. 3.2 Crops growing on a flood plain.

Fig. 3.3 Desert stretches out across Egypt.

Fig. 3.4 A *shaduf*, used for irrigation.

Fig. 3.5 Flood plain and desert — contrasts of the Egyptian landscape.

Do you understand why Herodotus said that Egypt was the 'gift of the river'?

The rise and fall of the Nile's waters regulated the lives of the ancient Egyptians in many ways. By watching the annual flooding of the river, the Egyptians observed the cycle of the seasons.

They called the time when the valley was flooded the Inundation. As the earth reappeared the season was called the Seed, and finally came the Harvest. Each of these seasons was four months long. By observing the changing seasons the Egyptians developed a calendar similar to the calendar we use today.

In some years the Nile did not flood as highly as others. The Egyptians set up *nilometers* along the river to measure the height of the flood. They knew that if the floods were low, the crops would not be as good.

The fields that were furthest away from the river were watered by irrigation. Egyptian farmers used the *shaduf* to raise water from the river to canals flowing to the fields. There is a picture of a *shaduf* in Fig. 3.4. Can you explain how it worked?

The course of the Nile divided Egypt into two distinct areas. Look again at the map in Fig. 3.1. You can see that the Nile river has five *cataracts*. These are sections where large boulders in the river change the way the water flows. As the water

36

flows past these boulders it is churned up into rapids. The land between the First Cataract (near Aswan) and Giza, near modern Cairo, was called Upper Egypt.

From Giza the Nile branched out into several channels. This area was called Lower Egypt — even though it is at the top of the map! Sometimes it was called the Delta because its triangular shape resembled 'delta', the fourth letter of the Greek alphabet. You can see this letter in the diagram in Fig. 9.11 on p. 158.

The river was a fast, easy way of travelling from one part of Egypt to another. Egyptian towns were built near the river but out of reach of the floodwaters.

Time to understand

1   The following lines come from an Egyptian hymn in praise of the Nile.

> Hail to thee, O Nile, that issues from the earth and comes to keep Egypt alive! . . .
> He who makes barley and brings wheat into being, that he may make the temples festive.
> If he is sluggish . . . everybody is poor . . .
> The bringer of food, rich in provisions, creator of all good, lord of majesty, sweet of fragrance . . .
> He who brings grass into being for cattle . . .
> He who makes every beloved tree to grow . . .

  a   How were the Egyptians dependent on the yearly flooding of the Nile?

  b   Why did the Nile 'make the temples festive'?

  c   What do you think is meant by the line 'If he is sluggish . . . everybody is poor'?

2   As well as the Nile River, Egypt had good natural defences.

  a   How did the deserts on either side of Egypt help prevent invasion?

  b   How did the cataracts prevent attack?

  c   Which part of Egypt was the easiest to attack? Why?

3   Ancient Egyptians divided the year into three seasons.

  a   How many seasons are there in our calendar?

  b   How do we tell one season from another?

  c   How did Egyptians distinguish one season from another?

  d   Does this tell us anything about the climate in Egypt?

The Pharaoh

In many ways, the early history of Egypt is similar to that of Sumer. In Chapter Two you read how the land between the Tigris and Euphrates rivers attracted hunters and gatherers. These people gradually settled in the area and over thousands of years built farms, towns and cities there.

The earliest settlers in Egypt hunted and fished along the banks of the Nile. There are very few records of this prehistoric period of Egyptian history. However, we can guess that the people in the Nile valley lived in mud-brick houses and grew crops in the fertile silt left behind each year after the flood. By about 3400 BC, Upper and Lower Egypt were probably separate kingdoms. They may have been governed by separate rulers.

Recorded history began in Egypt in 3100 BC. At that time a ruler called Menes

became Pharaoh of both Upper and Lower Egypt. He is the first known Pharaoh. The Egyptian word *Pharaoh* has been translated into English as *god-king*. The Pharaoh was not just the king of Egypt; he was also looked up to as a god.

The Pharaoh was the most important person in ancient Egypt. People believed that he had the power to keep law and order not only in Egypt, but in the whole universe. The authority of the Pharaoh was *absolute* — he made the final decision about everything. A ruler as strong and powerful as this obviously could not make decisions about everything by himself. He usually chose a close relative to help him in the daily governing of Egypt. This person was called the *vizier*.

Today, kings and queens sometimes wear crowns as a symbol of their power. We associate the crown with the position of king or queen. The Pharaoh, too, had symbols of his power. When people saw these things they knew they referred to the Pharaoh.

In paintings the Pharaoh was often shown holding a flail, a short stick with a number of leather tails. The flail was a symbol of the Pharaoh's power to punish wrongdoers. Another symbol of the Pharaoh's power was the shepherd's crook, which showed his right to rule and look after his people.

Later, other symbols were used as well. The Pharaoh was always shown wearing a ceremonial wig and beard. On his forehead was a serpent's head and a vulture's head. The Egyptians believed that the Pharaoh ruled in the life after death. The serpent and the vulture may have symbolised his power in the 'next world'. You will read more about the belief of Egyptians in the 'next world' later in this chapter.

The Pharaoh passed the right to rule Egypt to his son. This formed a *dynasty* or

Fig. 3.6 The Pharaoh Chephren.

ruling family. Sometimes another family took on the position of Pharaoh if the old Pharaoh had no son to follow him. Sometimes another family took the throne by force.

Time to understand

1 Look carefully at Figs 3.8 and 3.9 (over). These show the two sides of an ancient Egyptian cosmetic palette. In Fig. 3.8 there are two animals whose long necks are intertwined, leaving a circular space in the middle. In this space, eye paint was either mixed or ground up. The two sides show scenes of a Pharaoh conquering his enemies.

   a   Which person is the Pharaoh in Fig. 3.8? How can you tell?

   b   Which person is the Pharaoh in Fig. 3.9? Do you think he has won or lost the battle? How can you tell?

   c   The two Pharaohs are wearing special headdresses. Fig. 3.8 shows the Pharaoh wearing the crown of Lower Egypt, while Fig. 3.9 shows the pharaoh wearing the crown of Upper Egypt. When Egypt was united under one Pharaoh a double crown combining the shapes of the two crowns was formed. What do you think this would look like? (You may prefer to draw it rather than describe it in words.) See

if you can find an illustration that shows a Pharaoh wearing a double crown.

   d   What is unusual about the position of all the figures on both sides of the palette? Is it possible to stand like one of the figures? Draw someone in this position.

   e   Some historians think that this palette tells the story of the joining of Upper and Lower Egypt. Can you find anything on the palette which could tell the story of one Pharaoh making himself king of all Egypt?

2 Fig. 3.6 shows a statue of the Pharaoh Chephren. Imagine you are an Egyptian farmer living about 2000 BC. You have never seen the Pharaoh in person, but you are given the privilege of viewing this statue. How would you describe Chephren's face and its expression? Would you believe he was a god?

A time-line of Egyptian history

The history of Egypt from the time of Menes down to the conquest of Egypt by Alexander the Great in 332 BC was divided into thirty-one *dynasties*, by a historian called Manetho. He wrote in approximately 270 BC. This long recorded

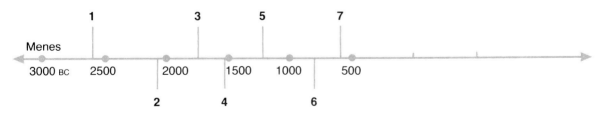

Fig. 3.7 A time-line of Egyptian history. The numbers on this time-line correspond to the numbered sections on p. 40.

39

Fig. 3.8 Egyptian cosmetic palette.

Fig. 3.9 The reverse side of the cosmetic palette shown in Fig. 3.8.

Fig. 3.10 The stepped pyramid at Djoser, built in the period of the Old Kingdom.

history has been divided into three main periods or *kingdoms* (see Fig. 3.7).

1 The *Old Kingdom* begins with the Third Dynasty. This period has also been called the Pyramid Age because of the number of pyramids built during this time.

2 Egypt was divided into small districts called *nomes*. Each of these was governed by a *nomarch* or local governor. Gradually the nomarchs became more powerful and finally threatened the Pharaoh himself. By about 2160 BC there was war in Egypt between one nomarch and another. They fought over who should rule Egypt.

3 Mentuhotep of Thebes was strong enough to unite Egypt under one ruler again. He became the first Pharaoh of the *Middle Kingdom*. The main difference between the Old Kingdom and the Middle Kingdom was that the Pharaoh was not as powerful as he had been in the Old Kingdom.

4 A strong group of people called the 'Hyksos' invaded the Delta about 1674 BC. They came from either Palestine or Syria. The Hyksos set themselves up as the rulers of Lower Egypt. One even took the title of Pharaoh.

Fig. 3.11 The Great Sphinx at Giza (see p. 69).

5 Ahmose of Thebes built up a strong army. He drove the Hyksos out of Egypt. He united the country again under one Pharaoh and became the first Pharaoh of the *New Kingdom.*

During this time Egypt began to strengthen its influence over neighbouring countries. The Egyptian empire was established. It included Nubia in the south and Palestine and Syria in the north-east. People believed that the Pharaoh was a warrior as well as a god. He had to be able to lead his army into battle, to keep the empire under Egypt's control. By the twentieth dynasty the empire no longer existed.

6 During the Twenty-first Dynasty Lower Egypt was ruled by Pharaohs while Upper Egypt was ruled by priests.

7 From the Twenty-second Dynasty to the Thirty-first the Pharaohs were often foreigners. This was because Egypt was invaded at different times by Libyans and Persians.

Fig. 3.12 Hieroglyphics from the temple at Karnak (see p. 47). (see p. 47)

Hieroglyphics

Like the Sumerians, the Egyptians developed a way of writing. They used a kind of picture writing called hieroglyphics to record important events. Another script, *hieratic*, was used for less important records and everyday accounts. After about 300 AD a new script was introduced and hieroglyphics were no longer used. People soon forgot how to read them.

In 1798 some French soldiers dug up a large stone tablet covered with three different kinds of writing. The stone has been called the Rosetta Stone after the town where it was discovered.

The Rosetta Stone contained the same message, or inscription, in three different scripts. One was in hieroglyphics, the second in Greek and the third in another Egyptian script called demotic. The stone was an important discovery because scholars could compare the hieroglyphics — which they did not know how to read — with the Greek script, which they understood. In 1822 a French scholar, Jean Francois Champollion, deciphered the hieroglyphics on the Rosetta Stone.

The Egyptians wrote on a kind of paper called papyrus. It was made from the reeds that grew on the banks of the Nile. Papyrus was probably invented around the same time as hieroglyphics, that is, around 3000 BC. The earliest piece of papyrus comes from a tomb of the First Dynasty at the beginning of Egyptian history.

Fig. 3.13 Part of a papyrus scroll written in hieratic script.

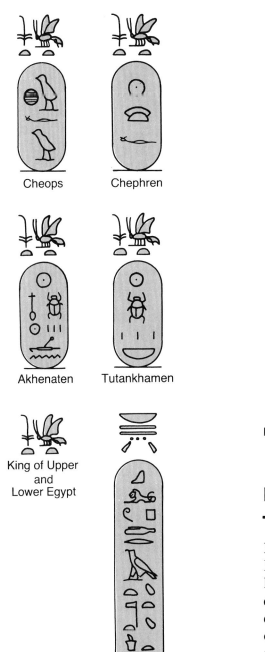

Cheops

Chephren

Akhenaten

Tutankhamen

King of Upper
and
Lower Egypt

Cleopatra VII

Fig. 3.14 The names, in cartouches, of some Egyptian Pharaohs.

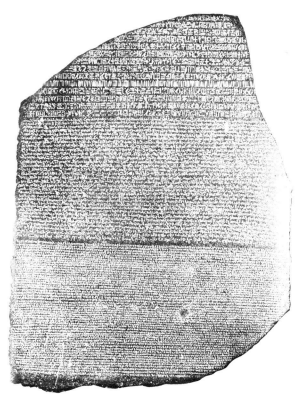

Fig. 3.15 The Rosetta Stone.

Life after death

Most of our knowledge of life in ancient Egypt comes from the many tombs that have been excavated. These tombs are decorated with hundreds of scenes from everyday life. Sometimes miniature models of houses, animals and even people, were also 'entombed'.

Why did the Egyptians spend so much time decorating and furnishing their tombs? Very simply, Egyptians believed that there was life after death. The tomb in which the dead person's body was put had to be equipped with everything the person needed for life in the next world. Because there was not much space in a

43

The Great Pyramid at Giza

Fig. 3.16 The Pharaoh Cheops was buried in the Great Pyramid. We know little about him as the treasures of the pyramid were stolen thousands of years ago. Only this small statuette of Cheops, about the size of a large chess piece, remains. ▷

Fig. 3.17 The pyramid entrance and below it an opening made by 9th century Arabs. ▽

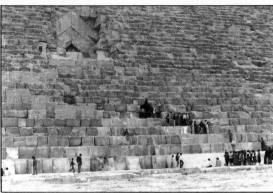

Fig. 3.18 The Great Pyramid. The pyramids have always fascinated visitors to Egypt. There are about eighty along the banks of the Nile. They were built between four and five thousand years ago and are the oldest stone buildings in the world. The most famous of them all is the Great Pyramid at Giza, measuring 230 metres long on each side and 146 metres high. It is part of a complex of pyramids dating from the Fourth Dynasty. Near to the Great Pyramid are the pyramids of Chephren and Menkure. ▽

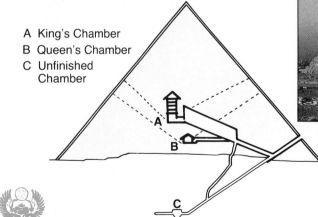

A King's Chamber
B Queen's Chamber
C Unfinished Chamber

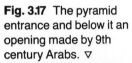

◁ **Fig. 3.19** The passageway leading to the King's Chamber was originally blocked with huge granite plugs, probably to protect the contents of the tomb. Robbers may have used the shaft connecting the ascending and descending passageways to remove the contents of the two burial chambers.

calculations. However, the mystery of the Great Pyramid may never be solved. The entrance to the Great Pyramid remained hidden for thousands of years. In 820 AD Al Mamun, an Arab ruler of Baghdad, forced his way into the pyramid. He and his fellow workers were ten courses of stone below the original entrance, but they found a descending passageway. After many weary hours of exploring the dark, mysterious tunnels, the Arabs found the burial chamber of Cheops. It contained nothing but a large, empty stone coffin. The limestone blocks used to build the pyramid were quarried nearby or across the Nile in the Mokattam hills. The granite blocks came from Aswan, hundreds of kilometres away, and were floated down the Nile on barges. The blocks may then have been hauled to the site by gangs of labourers. No one knows exactly how the blocks of stone were lifted into place.

. 3.20 Egyptologists, thematicians and entists have put ward many theories out how the yptians built the eat Pyramid and how vas used. The four es of the pyramid are gned with the four ints of the compass. cause of this some ople have said that e Great Pyramid was ed to make ographical and ronomical

Fig. 3.21 Monumental sculpture depicting Rameses II (1304–1237 BC) at Abu Simbel.

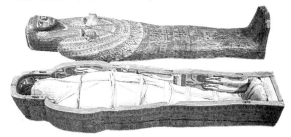

Fig. 3.22 A mummiform coffin.

Fig. 3.23 A naturally mummified body from prehistoric Egypt.

45

Fig. 3.24 The god Amun at Thebes blesses Hatshepsut, one of the few female Pharaohs in Egyptian history. Female Pharaohs were usually depicted as men.

Fig. 3.25 The chapel of Rameses II at Karnak.

tomb it was not possible to include everything from real life. The Egyptians solved this problem by building models and painting scenes from everyday life on the walls.

Egyptians also believed that a person's soul or 'ka' needed a body in the next life. For this reason they preserved the body of a person who died. This process was called *mummification*.

It took up to three months to prepare a mummy properly. When the mummy was ready the body was wrapped in fine linen bandages. It was then placed in a *mummiform* coffin as shown in Fig. 3.22.

What do you think the word 'mummiform' means?

At first only Pharaohs and nobles were mummified, but later other people were as well. The climate of Egypt is hot and dry. This helped to 'mummify' bodies.
Fig. 3.23 shows a burial from prehistoric Egypt. The body dried out naturally in the hot sand.

During the Old Kingdom Pharaohs were buried in pyramids when they died. Noblemen and women were buried in much simpler tombs called *mastabas*. Later in Egyptian history, anyone who could afford to, built a large tomb.

The family of the dead person held the funeral after the body had been mummified. All burials were on the west side of the Nile. The crossing of the river during the funeral from the east bank (where most people lived) to the western 'city of the dead', showed that the person had crossed from one life to the next.

Usually the building of a tomb began during a person's lifetime. To us, it may seem that the Egyptians were preoccupied with death. However, they believed that life in the next world was going to be much the same as life in this world. The scenes painted on tomb walls tell us that Egyptians enjoyed life in this world. Naturally they wanted to prepare for their next life.

Gods and goddesses

Osiris was the Egyptian god of the dead. He ruled in the next world just as a Pharaoh ruled in this world. He is often shown in tomb paintings.

The Egyptians worshipped many gods and goddesses. Each one was in charge of some aspect of life. They were usually shown with animal heads and human bodies. Each village or town worshipped its special god or goddess.

In the New Kingdom period the main god worshipped right throughout Egypt was Amun of Thebes. This was because the rulers at the beginning of the period came from Thebes.

At Karnak a huge temple was built for Amun. Each time a battle was won the Temple of Amun and its priests received a share of the booty. Huge farms and large herds of cattle were given to Amun. They provided a regular source of money for the temple. The priests of Amun became so wealthy and powerful that they were a challenge to the power of the Pharaoh himself.

One Pharaoh, Akhenaten, who ruled from 1363 to 1347 BC, tried to introduce a new religion. He wanted to abolish the worship of all gods except the Aten, the sun-god. He believed that nothing could exist without the sun. However, when Akhenaten died, so did the new religion.

Time to understand

Pharaohs and nobles wrote curses inside their tombs to protect them from robbers. There were also charms against the snakes that lived in the ground where mummies were buried. Two of these curses are written below. The first is from the tomb of Unis at Sakkarah. The second is from the tomb of the official Meni at Giza.

> Words to be spoken: 'Back with thee, hidden snake! Hide thyself! . . . Thou shalt not come to where King Unis is, lest he tell that name of thine against thee: Nemi, the son of Nemit . . . O Monster, lie down!

The eldest of the House of Meni says:

> The crocodile be against him in the water, the snake be against him on land . . . him who may do a thing to this tomb. I never did a thing to him. It is the god who will judge him!

1 Why would Unis fear snakes after he had died? What does this tell us about Egyptian beliefs?
2 Why was it important to try to protect tombs in ancient Egypt? Do you think the curses worked?

Life beside the Nile

Most of the people of ancient Egypt were peasants or labourers. Some of them can be seen in paintings on tomb walls, ploughing fields, raising water in a shaduf to irrigate fields and being beaten because they cannot afford to pay their taxes.

All these paintings are in the tombs of Pharaohs and nobles. Poor people could not afford to build tombs. We shall probably never know how peasants themselves thought because they never had the opportunity to record their ideas. They were *illiterate*, that is, they were unable to read and write.

The story told by the tomb paintings is that peasants worked very hard. When the Nile flooded they had to make sure that the irrigation channels were clear. As the water subsided they had to drain the marshy soil near the river. They then sowed seed into the fresh silt and used a plough to turn it into the ground. As the soil became drier their work became harder. The fields furthest from the river had to be watered by hand.

Peasants or labourers worked for wealthy nobles and landowners. They looked after the noble's fields of grain and his herds of cattle. They baked his bread, brewed his beer and even made his clothes. Peasant families lived in small villages close to their fields. Those who looked after cattle probably camped with them in the fields.

It was quite dark inside the peasants' small mud-brick houses. They were probably lit only by slits in the flat roof. On summer nights the whole family slept on the roof because it was unbearably hot inside the house.

The family room or living room was separate from the kitchen. Sometimes a small storeroom was added onto the kitchen. Furniture was made of rushes and wood. It probably consisted of no more than a couple of chairs or benches and perhaps a table or workbench. Clothes were stored in chests, and food — such as grain — was kept in pottery jars.

When a group of labourers, craftsmen, artisans, builders, sculptors and scribes were working on a pyramid or tomb they often lived in a special village nearby. The Valley of the Kings was the burial ground of about thirty Pharaohs. On the other side of the cliffs around the Valley of the Kings are the remains of a workers' village or tomb community.

The artisans and craftsmen who lived in this village were paid with their daily needs. These included wheat, barley, vegetables, fish and wood for fuel. Occasionally they were given bonuses of salt, wine, beer and even silver. They worked ten days before having a rest day. In addition to this they had time off for religious festivals. The pyramid workers were supplied with slaves to chop their wood, bring water to the village and grind their corn.

Whenever a large-scale project such as the building of a pyramid was about to start, hundreds of people were called up for duty. Most of these people were peasants, labourers and slaves.

Slaves were usually people who had been captured after battles in places like Nubia or Palestine. Sometimes they were bought in foreign slave markets. They were usually quite well treated because slave owners did not want to lose them. Some slaves belonged to the temples. They helped to look after the temple and the temple's land.

Criminals were much more harshly treated than slaves. For example, there are records of criminals having their noses cut off and then being forced to work in the gold mines of Nubia.

Egyptian women

Women in ancient Egypt are often shown in paintings as the silent companions of men. The wives of Pharaohs and nobles

Fig. 3.26 Nefertiti, wife of Akhenaten.

Fig. 3.27 A pair of boats.

Fig. 3.28 A weaving shop.

Fig. 3.29 The cattle inspection.

49

are often shown beside their husbands, sometimes affectionately arm-in-arm.

We know from tomb paintings and models that women ground cereals, made bread from wheat and beer from barley, wove cloth, cared for children and washed clothes in the river. Sometimes they are shown entertaining guests at a feast, playing musical instruments and dancing.

Only a few individual Egyptian women have been recorded in history. One of the first was Hatshepsut. Her stepson, Tutmosis III, was only five years old when his father died. She ruled Egypt instead of Tutmosis. She wore a ceremonial wig and a false beard like an ordinary Pharaoh so that people would accept her. When Tutmosis III was twenty-five he began to reign as Pharaoh and no more is recorded of Hatshepsut.

Nefertiti, the wife of Akhenaten, has been called one of the most beautiful women in the world. You can see a picture of her in Fig. 3.26. Akhenaten's third daughter, Akhesenamen, also earned a place in history as the wife of Tutankhamen. You will read much more about her unfortunate life later in this chapter.

Time to understand

In the 1920s an American archaeologist, H.E. Winlock, was working on a rock-cut tomb near Thebes. He thought that he would find nothing for all his efforts. Then one of his Arab workmen noticed a crack between the wall and the floor of the rock-cut corridor in which he was working. Winlock peered in with the aid of a torch:

> The beam of light shone into a little world of 4000 years ago and I was gazing down into the midst of a myriad of brightly painted little men going this way and that. A tall slender girl gazed across at me perfectly composed; a gang of little men with their sticks in their upraised hands drove spotted oxen, rowers tugged at their oars on a fleet of boats, while one ship seemed foundering in front of me in the air. And all of this busy coming and going was in uncanny silence, as though the distance back over the forty centuries I looked across was too great for even an echo to reach my ears.

Winlock had discovered a storeroom of models in the tomb of Meket-Re, a noble who died about 2000 BC. Meket-Re was equipped with numerous labourers, made to scale and of wood. These men and women were supposed to work for him in the next world. These models give us a vivid impression of everyday life in ancient Egypt.

1 Look at Fig. 3.29 on the previous page.
   a Describe what is happening to the cattle in Fig. 3.29.
   b Which carved figure in the model is Meket-Re?
   c How many scribes are recording this event?
   d Would you say this is a special event or a regular one? Why?
   e Do you think cattle would have been important in Egyptian society? If so, why?

3 Fig. 3.28 shows the interior of a weaving shop.
   a How many different activities can you name?
   b If Meket-Re had weavers working for him, how do you think less wealthy people obtained their clothes?
   c Do you think that the figures in this model are men or women? How can you tell?

5 a How would you describe the two boats in Fig. 3.27? What materials could have been used in their construction?

b Why do they have a trawl between them?

c Is Meket-Re in this scene? How can you tell?

Working beside the Nile

Peasants and labourers produced the food of Egypt, built temples for the gods and tombs for the Pharaohs. What did the rest of the population do for their living?

The civil service

You can imagine that the organisation and day-to-day running of Egypt was complicated. The Pharaoh was the head of the government. To help keep things running as smoothly as possible he employed many people to assist him. They made up the *civil service* or government of ancient Egypt. One official in the civil service was called Overseer of the Granary of Upper and Lower Egypt. He supervised the harvesting, recording and storage of wheat and barley. To be Fanbearer on the Right of the Pharaoh meant that you had won the Pharaoh's favour and become his personal friend.

There were hundreds of jobs in the Egyptian government. This was because Egyptian life was highly organised. For example, each year the Nile flooded. Each year grain was planted, harvested and collected as a form of tax. People were needed as tax collectors, assessors, recording scribes and so on.

Only men could become civil servants. Sometimes soldiers who had fought with the Pharaoh in battles were given important jobs in the government as a reward for bravery or loyalty. But the usual way to join the civil service was to enrol in a scribal school as a young boy. Subjects taught at a scribal school included reading, writing in different scripts such as hieroglyphics and hieratic, geography and mathematics. After studying these subjects, the young scribe could enter the civil service in a low-ranking position.

It was possible to work up from the position of a scribe to higher ranks. Many nobles have recorded in their tombs the number of different jobs they took in the civil service. Often the sons of civil servants followed in the footsteps of their fathers.

There was also the possibility of a foreign posting in some part of the empire. In Palestine and Syria native princes were allowed to govern their own towns with

Fig. 3.30 The Egyptian empire.

51

the 'help' of Egyptian civil servants. An Egyptian garrison of soldiers made sure that each town paid its tribute of goods to Egypt. The garrison also protected the town from attack.

Nubia was governed by a civil service like that in Egypt itself. The governor of Nubia was called the King's Son and Overseer of the Southern Countries. The title tells us that it was an important position and the official was close enough to the Pharaoh to be his son. The government of Nubia had to be well organised because Egypt obtained much of its wealth from the gold mines there.

The army

The empire and the gold trade routes had to be protected and guarded. Law and order had to be kept in Egypt. So the Egyptians organised an efficient army.

The army was a group of trained, professional soldiers. They fought in foreign wars or guarded towns in distant parts of the empire. In Egypt they marched in royal parades or worked on royal monuments, such as tombs, if more labourers were needed. When the Pharaoh wanted extra soldiers, fit and healthy young men were called up for service.

Men often worked their way up through the ranks to a high position in the army. The Pharaoh himself was the commander-in-chief. He planned and led campaigns.

There were other rewards if a soldier was successful. If he showed courage in battle he was given gold or a good job in the civil service. Each soldier received a share in the booty that had been captured after a successful campaign. Booty was usually slaves, cattle or treasure.

You probably remember that Egyptians thought of tombs as their houses for the next life. It was important to protect them.

Policemen called *medjays* guarded cemeteries. They also patrolled the deserts and kept law and order in Egypt.

Time to understand

Boys who were learning to be scribes were taught by qualified scribes. The boys had to copy out long exercises of advice and instructions on papyrus. Scribes were always in demand to record all kinds of information. The extracts below, from an apprentice scribe's papyrus, compare the benefits of being a scribe with other occupations.

> See for yourself with your own eye. The occupations lie before you.
> The washerman's day is going up, going down. All his limbs are weak, [from] whitening his neighbours' clothes every day, from washing their linen.
> The maker of pots is smeared with soil, like one whose relations have died. His hands, his feet are full of clay; he is like one who lives in the bog.
> The cobbler mingles with vats. His odour is penetrating. His hands are red with madder, like one who is smeared with blood. He looks behind him for the kite, like one whose flesh is exposed.
> The watchman prepares garlands and polishes vase-stands. He spends a night of toil just as one on whom the sun shines.
> The merchants travel downstream and upstream. They are as busy as can be, carrying goods from one town to another. They supply him who has wants. But the tax collectors carry off the gold, that most precious of metals.
> The ships' crews from every house [of commerce], they receive their loads. They depart from Egypt for Syria, and each man's god is with him. [But] not one of them says: 'We shall see Egypt again!' . . .
> Imagine this, you are dressed in fine

clothes; you own horses. Your boat is on the river; you are supplied with attendants. You stride about inspecting. A mansion is built in your town. You have a powerful office, given you by the pharaoh. Male and female slaves are about you . . . Put the writings in your heart, and you will be protected from all kinds of toil. You will become a worthy scribe.

1 How many of these occupations do you recognise? Are they still occupations today?

2 Why would the washerman be 'going up, going down'? Why would his limbs be weak?

3 What did the relations of someone who had died do in ancient Egypt? Does this make the potter's work seem attractive?

4 What is a 'cobbler'? Why would he use 'madder'? Do you think he would always be looking over his shoulder for a 'kite'? Why?

5 Where do you think watchmen were employed? How can you tell?

6 What were the disadvantages of being a merchant or a sailor?

7 What were the advantages of being a scribe? Do you think the writer is trying to encourage young boys to be scribes?

The discovery of Tutankhamen's tomb

In 1922 Howard Carter was digging in the Valley of the Kings in search of the tomb of Tutankhamen, a Pharaoh who had died in 1325 BC. Lord Carnarvon, a wealthy Englishman, was helping to pay for the excavation.

Carter had been trying to locate the tomb since 1917 and was almost ready to give up. He decided to dig under the remains of some huts which had been occupied by workmen thousands of years earlier. These workmen had probably built one of the tombs in the Valley of the Kings, where many Pharaohs had been buried.

One morning Carter arrived at the tomb to find an 'unusual silence'. The others working on the dig were waiting to give him the good news. They had found a step cut into solid rock. Perhaps it was the first step of an entrance to a tomb.

The digging continued for several days before Carter found the entrance to the

Fig. 3.31 Tutankhamen shown as a warrior in a chariot.

Fig. 3.32 The exterior of Tutankhamen's tomb.

Fig. 3.33 The first view of the antechamber.

Fig. 3.34 The sealed door faintly visible at the back of the antechamber.

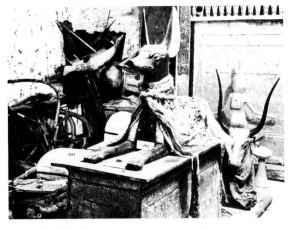

Fig. 3.35 Anubis, jackal god of embalming, guarding the entrance to the Innermost Treasury.

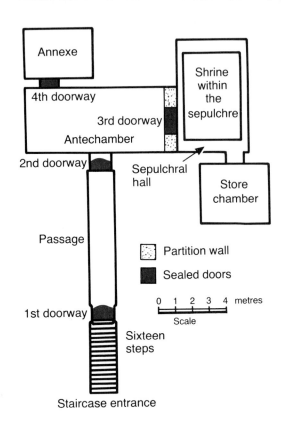

Fig. 3.36 Plan of the tomb.

Annexe

4th doorway

3rd doorway

Antechamber

Shrine within the sepulchre

2nd doorway

Sepulchral hall

Store chamber

Passage

Partition wall

Sealed doors

0 1 2 3 4 metres
Scale

1st doorway

Sixteen steps

Staircase entrance

Fig. 3.37 Howard Carter working on the third coffin in the tomb; this coffin was of solid gold.

54

tomb. It was at the end of a descending passageway cut into bedrock. It was sealed!

Unfortunately, Carter discovered that the seal had been broken before and then resealed. He was very disappointed. Perhaps the tomb had been robbed, like so many others in the Valley of the Kings.

Behind this entrance was another descending passageway filled with rubble. The rubble may have been placed there to prevent thieves entering the tomb.

At the end of the second passageway was a second doorway. It had also been sealed, broken into and later resealed. The workmen cut a hole in the door. Carter pushed an iron rod through the hole to see if there was anything behind the door. There was nothing but air. He then held a candle to the hole to see if any foul gases were coming from a tomb which had been sealed for thousands of years. Then came the moment for which Carter, Lord Carnarvon and the others on the dig had been waiting. Carter pushed the candle through the hole.

> At first I could see nothing . . . But presently, as my eyes grew accustomed to the light, details of the room within emerged slowly from the mist, strange animals, statues and gold — everywhere the glint of gold. For the moment — an eternity it must have seemed to the others standing by — I was struck dumb with amazement and when Lord Carnarvon, unable to stand the suspense any longer, inquired anxiously, 'Can you see anything?' it was all I could do to get out the words, 'Yes, wonderful things.' Then, widening the hole a little further, so that we could both see, we inserted an electric torch.

Time to understand

Fig. 3.33 shows the antechamber, or first room of the tomb. It is exactly as Carter saw it. Many of the objects had been overturned or were piled one on top of the other. Carter drew the conclusion that thousands of years earlier robbers had entered the tomb. They had been disturbed before they had gone very far. Then the tomb had been resealed and once again covered with rubble.

Fig. 3.34 shows a sealed doorway in one of the walls of the antechamber. Towards the bottom a large hole had been made but then resealed. There was no coffin in the antechamber.

Imagine you are one of the first to see the antechamber.
1 Give a description of some of the objects you see before you.
2 How were some of the objects used?
3 What could some of the boxes and other containers hold?
4 What could possibly be behind the sealed doorway?
5 Why would a hole have been cut in it and then resealed?
6 Who, do you think, resealed the doorways and filled the passageway with rubble?

Tutankhamen, the boy Pharaoh

Tutankhamen is the most famous of all Egyptian Pharaohs. This is not because he ruled the longest or was the most powerful. It is simply because his tomb is the only one to have survived almost untouched in the Valley of the Kings. The

Fig. 3.38 The gold mask which covered the mummy's head.

tomb was filled with a fantastic array of goods and treasure. Howard Carter and his team worked for six years emptying the tomb. Each piece had to be carefully photographed and recorded before it was removed.

Tutankhamen was probably only about nine years old when he became the Pharaoh. He was married to Ankhesenamen, the young daughter of the previous Pharaoh, Akhenaten.

Akhenaten had changed the religion of Egypt. He allowed only one god, the Aten or sun-god, to be worshipped. This had caused much trouble in Egypt. When Tutankhamen came to the throne, Ay, an important official in the government, advised the young Pharaoh to bring back the old religion. Tutankhamen did this when he was about thirteen. On a stone pillar Tutankhamen wrote:

> I found the temples fallen into ruin, with their holy places overthrown, and their courts overgrown with weeds. I reconstructed their sanctuaries, I endowed the temples, and made them gifts of all precious things. I cast statues of the gods in gold and electrum, decorated with lapis lazuli and all fine stones.

Tutankhamen died when he was about eighteen. He had no son to take the position of Pharaoh. So the young queen asked the king of the Hittites to send one of his sons to marry her. The Hittites lived to the north of Syria. Ankhesenamen promised that she would make the Hittite prince Pharaoh of Egypt.

The marriage was finally arranged. Unfortunately for Ankhesenamen the prince was murdered on his way to Egypt. The murderers may have been a group of Egyptian officials who did not want a foreigner to become Pharaoh.

Ay, the official who had advised Tutankhamen, became her co-ruler

instead. Four years later Ay died. There is no further record of Ankhesenamen either.

A strong army leader called Horemheb became the Pharaoh. He chipped Tutankhamen's name off many new buildings and pillars. Horemheb then had his own name engraved on them. Yet Horemheb did nothing to harm Tutankhamen's tomb. Apart from the attempt to rob it soon after it was first sealed, the tomb remained untouched for over 3000 years.

The mummy's curse!

Four months after witnessing the opening of Tutankhamen's tomb, Lord Carnarvon died. Newspapers immediately claimed that his death was the result of a curse protecting the tomb. In fact Lord Carnarvon died of pneumonia, which had developed from an infection caused by a mosquito bite.

Fig. 3.39 Howard Carter and Lord Carnarvon working on the tomb of Tutankhamen.

Mystery of King Tut's curse may rest in its culture

By MILAN RUZICKA,
of Associated Press

Burial mask of Tutankhamen.

PARIS, 30 July. — "I have succumbed to a curse," the British Egyptologist Hugh Evelyn-White wrote in his own blood in 1924 just before he hanged himself.

He was among the first to enter the tomb of the Pharaoh Tutankhamen when it was opened in November 1922, and one of two dozen explorers who were to die after going into the tomb. The Pharaoh's Curse theory was born.

Now a French physician says the curse was mostly a severe allergic reaction to mould.

Ms Caroline Stenger-Philippe has concluded that at least six of the deaths were directly linked to the penetration of the tomb. Evelyn-White's suicide and the mysterious demise of many others were not among them.

The tomb of Tutankhamen, dating to about 1350 BC, was found in the Valley of the Tombs near Luxor, Egypt.

In her doctoral thesis submitted recently to the Strasbourg University School of Medicine, the Frenchwoman concluded that "the directly linked deaths were due to the same illness from the same cause — allergic reaction to fungi, or mould, which grew in the airtight chambers of the tomb".

According to Ms Stenger-Philippe, the victims contracted allergic alveolitis, a severe inflammation of the tiny air chambers in the lungs, and died of pulmonary insufficiency.

She said the fruits and vegetables the Egyptians placed in the tomb to nourish the pharaoh through eternity, as well as all other organic substances, decayed over the centuries, creating mould and later organic dust.

"Much of the fungi did not survive the millenia, but the microscopic dust did and may have, in fact, increased its antigenic properties," she said.

Ms Stenger-Philippe said the dust could have remained in the tomb for up to two years after its opening, but then it dissipated and there were no more victims.

She told the Associated Press in an interview that the explorers came to look for gold and treasures and paid no attention to the pink, grey and green patches of fungi on the walls. That's what killed some of them.

She dismissed such theories as the presence of deadly rays, bacteria or dormant viruses as unsupported hypotheses.

"Many more would have died if there were radioactive materials or bacteria deliberately placed in the tomb," she said.

Dr Arthur Maier, one of France's pioneers in allergy studies, agreed. As head of pneumology at the Saverne Hospital in eastern France, he supervised Ms Stenger-Philippe's research and was among the physicians to review her findings. But he said the thesis offered no more than a very plausible scientific explanation.

Fig. 3.40 The *Age*, 31 July 1985

The legend of the mummy's curse was revived each time someone associated with the opening of the tomb died. Many people believed that the mummy's curse was true, and that the mysteries of ancient Egypt should not be disturbed.

The newspaper extract on the right is an example of the public's reaction to the news of Lord Carnarvon's death.

In July 1985, newspapers once again took interest in 'the mummy's curse'. The article above explains why. Which would you believe, the scientific explanation or the theory of 'the mummy's curse'? Write a paragraph, using your knowledge of the beliefs of the ancient Egyptians, to explain why.

Fig. 3.41

The Argus, Melbourne, Monday, 9 April 1923.

LORD CARNARVON'S DEATH

COLLECTORS IN PANIC.

Antiques Sent to Museum.

"Rising Tide of Superstition."

(Australian Press Association.)

LONDON, April 8.

The "Daily Express" states that a panic has been created among many superstitious owners of Egyptian antiques, as the outcome of the death of Lord Carnarvon. An avalanche of parcels containing mummies, shrivelled hands and feet, porcelain and wooden statues, and relics from ancient Egyptian tombs has descended on the British Museum. Some of these are regarded as valuable additions to the museum; others admittedly are ancient, but are not of much account.

An official of the British Museum said that he hoped people suffering from panic would forward valuable specimens. As a scientist, he rejected the superstition, but as a public servant he would not make any statement.

The British Museum had a similar experience before, when the story of the curse of the High Priestess of Amen-ra alarmed the superstitious. This arose from the story of a rich American, who purchased the actual mummy of the High Priestess, and was taking it home on the Titanic when the liner struck an iceberg and sank.

Sir Rider Haggard, the famous novelist, addressing the Hastings Rotary Club, said that the talk about Lord Carnarvon's death being due to magic was dangerous nonsense, and was stirring the rising tide of superstition. Could anyone believe that the Almighty would permit the spirit of the dead Pharaoh, who was only a man with a crown on his head, to murder people?

4

The Israelites in the promised land

IN CHAPTERS TWO AND THREE of this book you read about the societies of Sumer and Egypt. You will remember that settlers were attracted to both places because of the fertile land there. They could make farms and build villages, which later grew to become towns and cities.

Another group of people settled on land between Sumer and Egypt. This land was called Canaan and in ancient times it included most of present-day Israel and Syria. The people who settled there in about 1200 BC were the Israelites. They believed that Canaan was their 'promised land'.

From where did these people come? Who promised to give them the land? What happened to the people who lived in Canaan before they came? We can find the answers to these questions by studying archaeological evidence — the things the Israelites left behind — and the written evidence, such as the Old Testament of the Bible.

The Israelites were the ancestors of modern Jews, or people who belong to the Jewish religion. Today, Israel is the homeland of the Jews, although many Jewish people live in other parts of the world.

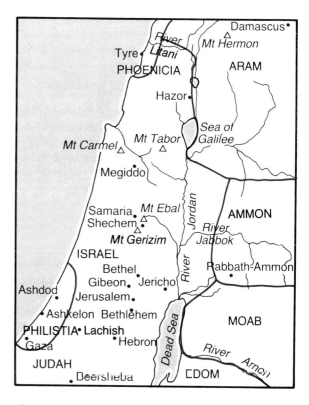

Fig. 4.1 Ancient Israel and Judah in about 1200 BC.

59

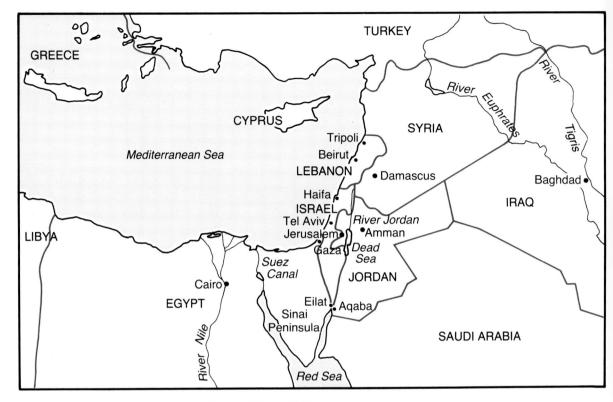

Fig. 4.2 The Middle East region today.

Time to understand

Look carefully at the two maps in Figs 4.1 and 4.2. They both show the same area but, as you can see, today's countries were known by different names in the ancient world.

1 What was Lebanon called about 3000 years ago?

2 Which countries have the same names today?

3 Does Israel have the same borders as it did in ancient times?

From Abraham to Moses

Abraham

The book called Genesis in the Old Testament of the Bible tells the traditional story of the origin, or beginning, of the Israelites. In Chapter 11 of Genesis we are introduced to Abraham. Abraham believed that God promised to give to the descendants of Abraham the land of Canaan and that they would become a great nation. In return, Abraham and his descendants had to promise to worship God (or Yahweh as the Israelites called Him) and to obey Him.

Abraham came from Ur in Mesopotamia, which you read about in Chapter Two. He probably travelled to Canaan between

2000 BC and 1950 BC. The stories of Abraham's adventures in Canaan tell us that his lifestyle was semi-nomadic. He did not own any land, but he travelled from place to place, probably grazing his sheep and cattle on the outskirts of settled areas. He had to buy land eventually to bury his wife Sarah. Clay tablets found at Mari, in Mesopotamia, tell us that many people at that time lived in this way. These people usually bred sheep and cattle and wandered between Mesopotamia and the Mediterranean coast. Sometimes they carried goods on donkeys and became traders.

Isaac and Rebekah

Abraham and Sarah had one son called Isaac. When Isaac had grown up Abraham sent a trusted servant back to Mesopotamia to find a wife for his son. The story of how the servant chose Rebekah tells us about everyday life at that time.

Abraham's servant and his camels were waiting outside the town of Nahor near the well. The servant was thirsty but had nothing with which he could draw water from the well. Rebekah, a beautiful young woman, came to draw water and he asked her to give him a drink. She did so and also drew water for his camels. The servant then gave her some jewellery and asked if there was room in her father's house for travellers. Rebekah assured him that there was.

The servant decided that she was the right bride for Isaac. Later that night he told her father and brother his story. They agreed that he could take Rebekah back to Canaan. What does this story tells us about life in about 1900 BC? You could first consider the things which seem unusual to you.

Isaac and Rebekah had two sons, Esau and Jacob. When Jacob grew up he believed that Yahweh told him to change his name to Israel. Israel had twelve sons and one daughter. According to tradition, the Israelites are sometimes called the sons of Israel.

Joseph in Egypt

Israel's favourite son, Joseph, was sold as a slave by his brothers to some passing traders. These brothers were very jealous of Israel's love for Joseph. Do you know the story of Joseph's coat of many colours? If not, you can read about it in the Old Testament Bible stories.

The traders took Joseph to Egypt where he became a slave for the Pharaoh. The Pharaoh noticed that Joseph was very capable and intelligent. Joseph was promoted to a high position in the Egyptian civil service.

While Joseph was in Egypt there was a famine which also affected Canaan. It was probably caused by a drought. In Egypt there was plenty of grain which had been stored from earlier harvests. Many people went to Egypt to buy food.

Israel sent ten of his sons to Egypt to buy grain. He kept the youngest, Benjamin, at home in case anything happened to the others. The brothers had to ask Joseph for the grain. He recognised them but they did not recognise him.

Joseph pretended that he thought they were spies. He asked them who they were. They explained and also mentioned their younger brother, Benjamin. Joseph gave them the grain but said they had to bring Benjamin to Egypt to prove they were not spies. Joseph's brothers, of course, did not understand what was happening.

When they returned to Egypt with Benjamin they asked for more grain. Joseph agreed but invented another reason to prevent them leaving Egypt. Benjamin was accused of stealing a silver cup.

Finally Joseph told his brothers who he was. The whole family was soon reunited. They lived in Egypt with Joseph.

According to the story the Israelites, as the descendants of Joseph and his brothers became known, remained in Egypt for a long time, perhaps hundreds of years. In the book of Exodus, in the Old Testament, we read that suddenly the Israelites became slaves of a new Pharaoh, who was worried about the number of Israelites and thought they were a threat to his power.

The Exodus

The story of how the Israelites left Egypt is called the *Exodus*. The leader of the Israelites was Moses. He asked the Pharaoh to let them return to their 'promised land'. At first the Pharaoh refused. The book of Exodus tells us that Yahweh then inflicted ten plagues on Egypt, one after another. Finally the Pharaoh agreed to let them go.

There are no records in Egyptian history either to contradict or to prove the story of the Exodus. This does not mean that it did not happen, but we cannot prove that it did.

According to the story, during the Israelites' journey back to Canaan, Moses gave them a set of laws. These laws were called the *Ten Commandments*. The Israelites believed that these commandments were given to Moses by Yahweh, during a meeting between them on Mt Sinai. These commandments, or laws, are the basis of many other laws in modern countries such as Australia, Great Britain, France and Germany.

When the Israelites reached Canaan, the promised land, they sent in spies to find out what was happening. The spies reported that many other groups of people were living there in strong, walled towns. These people included the native Canaanites, some Ammonites and some Hittites. Some of these groups had probably lived in Canaan for hundreds of years.

Most of the spies said that the Israelites would not be able to fight and win against these people. Two of them, Joshua and Caleb, said that the Israelites would be able to conquer the people living in the promised land. Moses decided to wait for forty years outside Canaan. Perhaps he thought that a new generation of Israelites would be stronger than a generation who had been slaves.

It is not possible to reconstruct the story of the conquest of the promised land accurately. There are many pieces missing in the 'jigsaw puzzle' of the origin of the Israelites. These pieces may never be discovered. Only a small part of the story told in the Old Testament may be proved by archaeology.

According to the book of Joshua, when the Israelites first entered Canaan they conquered Jericho and then a number of other towns. Archaeological digs have proved that around 1200 BC a number of towns in Canaan were destroyed, possibly because of an invasion. However, there is no evidence at Jericho to support the story.

Time to understand

The story of how the Israelites were made to work as slaves for the Pharaoh in Egypt is told in Exodus (Chapter 1, verses 8–14):

> Then a new king ascended the throne of Egypt, one who knew nothing of Joseph. He

said to his people, 'These Isráelites have become too many and too strong for us. We must take precautions to see that they do not increase any further; or we shall find that, if war breaks out, they will join the enemy and fight against us, and they will become masters of the country.' So they were made to work in gangs with officers set over them, to break their spirit with heavy labour. This is how Pharaoh's store cities, Pithom and Rameses, were built. But the more harshly they were treated, the more their numbers increased beyond all bounds, until the Egyptians came to loathe the sight of them. So they treated their Israelite slaves with ruthless severity, and made life bitter for them with cruel servitude, setting them to work on clay and brick-making, and all sorts of work in the fields. In short they made ruthless use of them as slaves in every kind of hard labour.

1 Although we do not know whether or not the Egyptians were also forced to work in this way, there is other evidence about work conditions in Egypt. Fig. 4.3 (over) is part of a wall painting from the tomb of an Egyptian official called Rekhmire.

    a Do you think there is an official in this wall painting? How can you tell?

    b What activities are taking place in this painting? Is there any similarity between these activities and those described in Exodus?

2 The following extract comes from a papyrus scroll dated about 1210 BC.

Total, 12 building jobs. Likewise, the men make bricks in their spells of duty, bringing them for work in the house. They make their quota of bricks daily.

    a What do you think 'spells of duty' are? What is a 'quota'?

    b Does this evidence suggest that bricks were made on building sites? How would workers manage this?

(*Clue*: Remember the main material used to make bricks.)

3 a Exodus tells us that the Israelites (or Hebrews) were forced not only to produce bricks but also to gather straw needed to make the bricks. Do you think that working as a slave in Egypt would have involved hard labour?

    b Imagine you are an Israelite working in a labour gang. Describe a typical working day.

The promised land

When the Israelites arrived in the promised land they found that the Canaanites who already lived there were quite prosperous. The Canaanites traded with Egypt and Mesopotamia and probably Greece and Crete as well. They had developed a system of writing. Their alphabet was probably an early form of our own alphabet.

For a long time Canaan had been part of the Egyptian empire. Egyptian soldiers kept the peace between the many small towns of the area. But when the empire became weak, there was no strong army to protect the land from invaders. It was around this time that the Israelites may have arrived.

Historians think that the population of Canaan was made up of many different types of people. Some of these people joined the Israelites to form the new nation of Israel. All the people who called themselves Israelites promised to worship Yahweh. They believed Yahweh was the only god. They called the land they conquered and inhabited Israel.

Fig. 4.3 A wall painting from the tomb of Rekhmire (Thebes).

Fig. 4.4 Bricks are made out of Nile mud in Egypt today.

The land was divided between twelve tribes (see Fig. 4.5). The tribe of Levi did not claim any land. Men of this tribe were always priests. They were supported by the other tribes.

The Israelites were sometimes attacked by Canaanites who had not been conquered when the Israelites first arrived. Sometimes they were attacked by groups of people living in territories outside Israel.

Each time Israel was attacked someone had to lead the army to defend the countryside. There was no king of Israel at that time. The book of Judges in the Old Testament contains a number of stories about people who became leaders of Israel.

One story tells how a man called Gideon led an Israelite army against the Midianites. The Midianites lived in the desert, east of Israel. Every year at harvest time they raided a part of Israel called Esdraelon. They stole much of each year's produce. Gideon and his army defeated the Midianites. After this, many people wanted Gideon to become king. He refused because he believed Yahweh was the king.

64

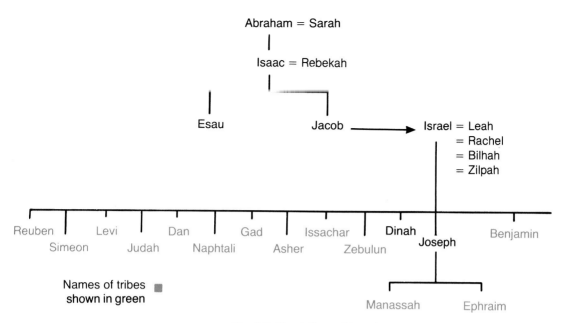

Fig. 4.5 The tribes of Israel.

Many years later another military leader became the first king of Israel. His name was Saul.

Time to understand

1 Many passages in the Old Testament suggest that farming in ancient Israel was common and well developed. Use the following biblical references to find out:

   a the crops and fruits that were grown,

   b the tools that were used,

   c the possible disasters that could have ruined crops.

He gave their harvest over to locusts
and their produce to the grubs;
He killed their vines with hailstones
and their figs with torrents of rain;

                       Psalm 78: 46–47

The Israelites had to go down to the Philistines for their ploughshares, mattocks, axes, and sickles to be sharpened. The charge was two-thirds of a shekel for ploughshares and mattocks, and one-third of a shekel for sharpening the axes and setting the goads.

                     1 Samuel 13: 20–22

I blasted you with black blight and red;
I laid waste your gardens and vineyards;
the locust devoured your fig-trees and your olives;
yet you did not come back to me.
This is the very word of the Lord.

                        Amos 4:9

And let them have daily without fail whatever they want, young bulls, rams, or lambs as whole-offerings for the God of heaven, or wheat, salt, wine, or oil, as the priests in Jerusalem demand. . .

                        Ezra 6:9

2 Use an encyclopaedia to find out the kinds of crops and fruits grown in Israel today. Is there any similarity between these and the ones referred to in the Old Testament? Why?

Fig. 4.6 The produce of Israel today.

The early kings of Israel

The people of Philistia — called the Philistines — were a constant threat to the security of the Israelites. The Philistine army was strong and well disciplined Its soldiers used iron rather than bronze weapons. In about 1050 BC the Israelites were defeated by the Philistines who then occupied much of Israel.

At this time there was a prophet called Samuel. The Israelites believed that Yahweh spoke to the prophets, who could then guide the rest of the people. Samuel said that Yahweh had chosen Saul, a young military commander, as the first king of Israel.

At first Saul was popular with the Israelites and he led them in successful battles against the Philistines. However, he was not able to conquer the Philistines once and for all.

Late in his reign, Saul seems to have become less popular. Samuel no longer supported him as king. Then a young soldier called David appeared on the scene.

Fig. 4.7 A Philistine and a Semite (possibly an Israelite) depicted in relief on the Pharaoh Rameses III's temple at Thebes.

There are many stories about David in the Old Testament. Although all of these stories may not be true, they do reveal that David was well liked and successful. Saul became extremely jealous of David, who eventually went into hiding in fear of his life.

When Saul died, after a disastrous battle against the Philistines, David appeared once again. He was first elected king over the tribe of Judah. Very soon, with the support of the prophet Samuel, he was elected king over all Israel. He led an army which defeated the Philistines.

Under David the kingdom of Israel grew strong and prosperous. Jerusalem became the capital of the new nation, united under a strong king. The conquest of the promised land was completed. Israelites controlled all the towns, and the

66

neighbouring territories of Ammon, Moab and Edom were all conquered by David's armies. Israel now possessed an empire.

When David died, his favourite son, Solomon, became king. Solomon reigned for many years and made a lot of changes. He changed the way the nation was governed and based his new form of government on the civil service in Egypt. He also made trading agreements with places such as Phoenicia.

During his reign Solomon built up the army so that Israel would become a stronger nation. In spite of this, some of the territory that Israel had conquered was lost again.

Solomon constructed many splendid palaces and other buildings. The temple that he built at Jerusalem for the worship of Yahweh was magnificent. Phoenician craftsmen helped Solomon to build this temple.

In order to pay for these buildings, as well as for his army, Solomon made the Israelites pay heavy taxes. He also forced many of them to work in labour gangs on his buildings.

Many Israelites resented these things. The main evidence for this resentment came after Solomon's death because when Solomon died Israel split into two separate kingdoms.

In the south the tribes of Benjamin and Judah were ruled by Solomon's son Rehoboam. The kingdom was called Judah. In the north the other ten tribes continued to be known as Israel.

Time to understand

1   Solomon built a huge temple in Jerusalem. There is a description of the temple in the First Book of Kings,

Chapter 6. A winged creature called a *cherub* (plural *cherubim*) is also described there. Cherubim are mentioned in many other parts of the Bible. Historians have tried to work out what the cherubim carved in the temple looked like. Here is the description:

> In the inner shrine he made two cherubim of wild olive, each ten cubits high. Each wing of the cherubim was five cubits long, and from wing-tip to wing-tip was ten cubits. Similarly the second cherub measured ten cubits; the two cherubim were alike in size and shape, and each ten cubits high. He put the cherubim within the shrine at the furthest recesses and their wings were outspread, so that a wing of the one cherub touched the wall on one side and a wing of the other touched the wall on the other side, and their other wings met in the middle; and he overlaid the cherubim with gold.
>
> 1 Kings 6:23–28

a   The temple was built largely by Phoenician craftsmen. Fig. 4.8 shows an ivory panel carved by a Phoenician craftsman.

Fig. 4.8 An ivory panel carved by a Phoenician craftsman.

Do you think it fits the description of a cherub? Why?

b   *Cherub* is a Hebrew word for a winged figure with a lion's body and woman's head. The Greek word is

Fig. 4.9 An artist's reconstruction of the exterior of the temple of Solomon.

Fig. 4.10 Tutankhamen's ecclesiastical throne and footstool.

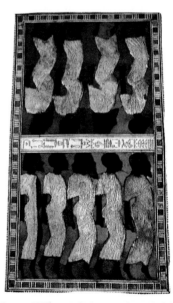

Fig. 4.11 The panels on the top of Tutankhamen's footstool.

68

sphinx. Where is a famous sphinx? Does it match the description in the Book of Kings?

c Use a dictionary to find the modern meaning of the word *cherub*. Is it anything like the description of the cherubim in Solomon's temple?

2 Do you remember that the land of Canaan was once part of the Egyptian empire? When the Israelites arrived there were probably many imported Egyptian objects in common use — objects such as pottery, jewellery, chairs and so on. This could mean that the Israelites adopted some Egyptian ideas and practices. Look carefully at Fig. 4.10 which shows a throne and its footstool. Both were found in Tutankhamen's tomb. Fig. 4.11 shows the top of the footstool. Now read the extract below from the book of Psalms in the Old Testament.

> The Lord says to my Lord: You shall sit at my right hand when I make your enemies the footstool under your feet.
>
> Psalm 110:1

a Describe the scene on the top of the footstool. Why do they all have their hands behind their backs?

b What are the possible nationalities of the people on the footstool? (Think of places and people that were once part of the empire.)

c What would be the reason for depicting these people on Tutankhamen's footstool?

d Psalm 110 is supposed to be about King David. What did the writer mean when he wrote that the Lord (Yahweh) would make David's enemies his footstool?

e Who lived first, David or Tutankhamen? Is it possible to say that the writer of Psalm 110 adapted an Egyptian idea?

Town and village life

The town and the village in Israel were *dependent* upon one another. This means that one could not exist without the other. In the towns lived tradesmen, merchants and people associated with the government. In the villages lived farmers who grew crops and raised animals on the land outside the towns.

The farmers sold their produce to the people who lived in the towns. The tradesmen in the towns sold their manufactured goods, such as tools, to the farmers. The people of the villages paid tax to the governor of the town. The townspeople defended the area in times of attack or invasion by an enemy.

Each town was located near a road or close to a water supply. If the town was near a road, merchants and traders were able to travel to and from the town easily. A water supply, such as a river or a spring, was necessary. Otherwise, water had to be carried to the town for everyday use.

Almost all the towns mentioned in the Old Testament were located on *tells*. Tells are mounds created by the remains of

Fig. 4.12 A reconstruction of the kitchen in a typical ancient Israeli house (see over).

earlier settlements. Other towns had been built on the same sites many years earlier. Why do you think this happened?

Towns were surrounded by strong walls to keep out invaders. Tall towers were built into the wall and from them defenders could fire arrows on the enemy.

Town gates were complicated constructions, as you can see from Fig. 4.15 on p. 74. A gate was the weakest spot in any wall. An enemy could set it on fire. On either side of a town gate were rooms in which armed men were stationed.

Inside the town walls were public buildings, storehouses for things like grain, workshops and houses. Houses were often built along the inside of the wall. These supported the wall.

There were industrial areas in most towns. Goods were not made in large factories as they are today. However, some towns specialised in the production of certain goods such as metal tools or silver work. The merchants of each town looked after trade with other towns.

Several small villages, of about fifteen houses each, were usually located around a main town such as Jericho or Lachish. These villages consisted of a group of houses clustered together but not protected by a wall. If the area was attacked, the villagers sheltered inside the walled town.

Farmland and vineyards were outside the village. Villagers would work each day in the fields and then return at night to the village. Most villagers wove their own cloth and made their own pottery. This meant that the villagers were almost self-sufficient.

Houses in both towns and villages were simple. Sleeping quarters were separate from the main part of the house where food was prepared and eaten. In 2 Kings 4:10 there is a brief description of a guest room used by the prophet Elisha. In it

were a bed, a table, a chair and an oil lamp. The ordinary people of town and village would not have had anything more than these.

The women, both mother and daughters, of each household ground wheat and barley to make flour. The uncrushed grain stood in large jars around the walls of the kitchen. Small clay ovens were used for cooking. On top of the oven there was usually a cooking pot as well. Sometimes there was a small hearth made of stones. Food could also be cooked over this open fire. During the winter food was cooked inside to help warm the house. In summer it was probably cooked and eaten in the courtyard.

Time to understand

This extract from Proverbs describes what was expected of women in ancient Israel. Proverbs was written by King Solomon.

A capable wife
Who can find a capable wife?
Her worth is far beyond coral.
Her husband's whole trust is in her,
and children are not lacking.
She repays him with good, not evil,
all her life long.
She chooses wool and flax
and toils at her work.
Like a ship laden with merchandise,
she brings home food from far off.
She rises while it is still night
and sets meat before her household.
After careful thought she buys a field
and plants a vineyard out of her earnings.
She sets about her duties with vigour
and braces herself for the work.
She sees that her business goes well,
and never puts out her lamp at night.
She holds the distaff in her hand,
and her fingers grasp the spindle.
She is open-handed to the wretched

and generous to the poor.
She has no fear for her household when it
snows,
for they are wrapped in two cloaks.
She makes her own coverings,
and clothing of fine linen and purple.
Her husband is well known in the city gate
when he takes his seat with the elders of
the land.
She weaves linen and sells it,
and supplies merchants with their sashes.
She is clothed in dignity and power
and can afford to laugh at tomorrow.
When she opens her mouth, it is to speak
wisely,
and loyalty is the theme of her teaching.
She keeps her eye on the doings of her
household
and does not eat the bread of idleness.
Her sons with one accord call her happy;
her husband too, and he sings her praises:
'Many a woman shows how capable she is;
but you excel them all.'
Charm is a delusion and beauty fleeting;
it is the God-fearing woman who is
honoured.
Extol her for the fruit of all her toil,
and let her labours bring her honour in the
city gate.

1   What kind of work was performed by
women?
2   Do women do all these things today?
Explain why.
3   According to this extract, why was a
hard-working woman thought to be better
than one who was beautiful?
4   Would you say that women played an
important part in life in ancient Israel?

Warfare

In ancient times, Israel was a link between
Egypt and Mesopotamia. To the west of
Israel was the Mediterranean Sea. But as
there were few suitable harbours on the
coast, trade by sea was limited. To the
east was the Syrian desert. Traders who
travelled between Mesopotamia or Syria
and Egypt naturally passed through Israel.
This was one of the reasons why the
Israelites were often attacked by the people
of neighbouring countries.

Whenever enemies attacked Israel they
tried to conquer the towns. We have
already seen that the towns were fortified,
or protected, by strong walls made of
stone and mud bricks.

The oldest town in Israel is Jericho.
Jericho was surrounded by huge walls and
a moat. There was also a tower 13 metres
high. The walls and the tower were built
long before the Israelites arrived. The
tower at Jericho dates from before 6000 BC.

Fig. 4.13 Remains of the stone tower at Jericho.

71

This means that the town itself, dating from about 9000 BC, is more than twice as old as the Great Pyramid at Giza in Egypt.

People who defended a town stood on top of the walls behind what are called 'crenellations'. Crenellations were raised sections and archers could shelter behind these while they fired arrows.

An enemy army normally placed a town under seige. This meant that the enemy army surrounded the town, and tried to break in. They put ladders against the walls and attempted to climb over the top. Naturally the people in the town tried to prevent this. The enemy concentrated on keeping defenders away from the part of the wall where they were climbing. How do you think they did this?

Sometimes enemy soldiers used a battering ram to make holes in the wall. The enemy soldiers could also tunnel underneath the wall. Sometimes they set the gate on fire.

Soldiers used spears, bows and arrows, swords, slings, javelins, axes and daggers. For protection, men wore helmets and carried shields. Sometimes they wore armour on other exposed parts of the body such as their legs.

Most soldiers fought on foot. Chariots were used when a battle was fought on an open plain. Chariots moved swiftly as they were drawn by two horses. In each chariot there was a driver, an archer and sometimes a shield bearer.

The people in a town under siege could hold out until they ran out of water or food, or until the enemy managed to break in. When an enemy army camped outside a town it took food and water from the surrounding countryside.

Most towns had a water supply within the town walls. Water was often stored in underground cisterns. These were cut into the rock and lined with lime plaster to

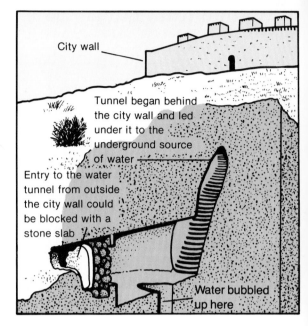

Fig. 4.14 A reconstruction of a hidden underground water system.

stop the water seeping out. Larger cisterns were called reservoirs. These had steps carved into the rock leading down to the water. The water stored in the underground cisterns and reservoirs had been drained off the ground after rain. Sometimes the water in them came from an underground spring. Townspeople often dug tunnels to reach an underground source of water.

Time to understand

In 701 BC the Assyrians attacked and conquered Lachish, an Israelite town. The Assyrians lived in upper Mesopotamia. They were trying to enlarge the land under their control. How do we know this happened?

There are four different sources of information or evidence. Two of these are written evidence and are printed on p.74.

Fig. 4.15 A reconstruction of the town of Lachish.

Fig. 4.16 A carved relief from Sennacherib's palace at Nineveh.

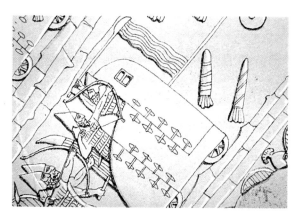

Fig. 4.17 An Assyrian battering ram.

The other information comes from digs at Lachish and at an ancient Assyrian town called Nineveh. The evidence provided by the digs shows that the two written accounts are about an actual event. The evidence also provides us with a lot of information about warfare in ancient Israel and Assyria.

The written evidence

In the fourteenth year of King Hezekiah, Sennacherib, King of Assyria, came up against all the fortified cities of Judah and took them.

II Kings 18:13

Sennacherib, king of the world, king of Assyria, sat on a throne while the booty of Lachish passed before him.
(*Inscription from Sennacherib's Palace, Nineveh.*)

1 Fig. 4.15 on p.73 shows an artist's reconstruction of the town of Lachish.
   a How many walls surrounded the town?
   b Why do you think there were so many towers?
   c Which wall was the most important? Why?

The archaeological evidence

There are two mounds at Nineveh. When the biggest mound was excavated the ruins of King Sennacherib's palace were found. The palace had been built of mud brick and covered with a thin stone facing. Many of the walls were covered with cuneiform writing or pictorial reliefs. The walls of one room were filled with scenes from the siege of Lachish.

2 Fig. 4.16 (p.73) shows part of a relief from the palace. The main gate of Lachish is in the centre. The artist has shown two stages of the battle here. On the left-hand side of the gate is a battering ram. This shows that the battle is in progress. On the right-hand side the conquered people of Lachish are marching out of the town, after the battle. There is no perspective in the relief so all the soldiers are shown in lines and are the same size.
   a List all the weapons used in this battle.
   b An Assyrian archer was always with another soldier. What did the other soldier do? Describe how the two worked together.

3 Fig. 4.17 (p.73) shows the details of a battering ram.
   a What materials could the battering ram be made of?
   b The soldier at the front end of the battering ram poured water from a large scoop. What does this tell us about some of the missiles fired from the walls of the town?

4 In Fig. 4.18 on p. 76 you can see the remains of a ramp built by the Assyrians against the walls of Lachish. Battering rams were dragged up these ramps. The ramp is made of large rocks. If you look again at Fig. 4.17 you will notice that the ramps are covered by another kind of material. What do you think this material is? Does this give us a clue as to why water was poured in front of the battering rams?

The prophets

The prophets were men who believed that Yahweh spoke directly to them. They then told the other Israelites whether Yahweh was angry or pleased. The Israelites believed that Yahweh became angry when His chosen people were not obeying His laws or had stopped worshipping Him. When Israel or Judah were attacked, the prophets said it was a punishment from Yahweh. Prophets also claimed to be able to *predict* that an invasion or disaster was coming.

Prophets sometimes lived together in groups. Often they sang or danced themselves into a frenzy so that they could 'communicate' with Yahweh. The Israelites usually believed the prophets. Sometimes kings asked them questions about important matters, such as whether the Israelites would be defeated by an invading army.

As well as groups of prophets there were also individual prophets. The names of these prophets are well known to both modern Jews and Christians. They include Samuel, Elijah, Elisha, Isaiah, Hosea and Amos. People of other religions in ancient times also believed what their prophets told them.

The Canaanites worshipped several gods and goddesses. In the First Book of Kings, Chapter 18, we can read the story of how the prophets of Baal competed against Elijah, an Israelite prophet. The competition was held to find out which was the true religion.

Time to understand

The extract below is taken from the Second Book of Kings, Chapter 6, verses 8 to 14. It is about a prophet called Elisha.

> Once, when the king of Aram was making war on Israel, he held a conference with his staff at which he said, 'I mean to attack in such and such a direction.' But the man of God warned the king of Israel: 'Take care to avoid this place, for the Aramaeans are going down that way.' So the king of Israel sent to the place about which the man of God had given him this warning; and the king took special precautions every time he

found himself near that place. The king of Aram was greatly perturbed at this and, summoning his staff, he said to them, 'Tell me, one of you, who has betrayed us to the king of Israel?' 'None of us, my lord king,' said one of his staff; 'but Elisha, the prophet in Israel, tells the king of Israel the very words you speak in your bedchamber.' 'Go and find out where he is,' said the king, 'and I will send and seize him.' He was told that the prophet was at Dothan, and he sent a strong force there with horses and chariots. They came by night and surrounded the city.

1 Using Fig. 4.1, describe where Aram was in relation to Israel.
2 How did the king of Israel find out about the plans of the Arameans, according to this extract?
3 Why do you think Elisha is called a man of God?
4 Why did the king of Aram want to capture Elisha?
5 Do you think there could be another explanation of why Elisha knew about the plans of the Arameans?

The decline of the Israelites in the promised land

After the death of Solomon, the Israelites divided themselves into two kingdoms. In the south the tribes of Judah and Benjamin called their territory Judah. In the north the other ten tribes called their territory Israel. Each of the kingdoms had its own king.

The history of the two kingdoms over the next 350 years is the story of how each kingdom struggled to be free and independent. Neither Judah nor Israel was strong enough to withstand attacks by the

Fig. 4.18 The mound containing the ruins of ancient Lachish, showing the ramp built by the Assyrians.

warlike people of neighbouring Mesopotamia.

In 721 BC Israel was conquered by the Assyrians who lived in upper Mesopotamia. The tribes of Judah managed to defend themselves against the Assyrians. But the Assyrians destroyed much of Judah's territory, burning crops and looting cities. Earlier in this chapter you studied the conquest of Lachish, a town in Judah, by the Assyrians. Judah was conquered in 587 BC by the Babylonians who lived in lower Mesopotamia.

Many of the Israelites were forced to leave their land and live in Mesopotamia. It was not until over fifty years later that some of the Israelites returned to their promised land.

Fig. 4.19 Statues of a Canaanite god (right) and goddess (left).

5

The Indus valley and beyond

THE ANCIENT PEOPLE of the Indus valley are something of a mystery. Until just over sixty years ago we knew nothing at all about them. In 1924 an English archaeologist, working with a team of Indians, discovered the remains of a civilisation that seemed to be about as old as the civilisations of Sumer and Egypt, which you read about in earlier chapters. The ruins of two large cities were found: Mohenjo-Daro and Harappa. Around these cities were clustered the remains of perhaps a hundred smaller villages and towns.

Mohenjo-Daro and Harappa were built around 2500 BC. They survived for about a thousand years and then they were abandoned and fell into ruins. Who built them? Why did they settle there? How did they live? And why were these cities abandoned? We do not know the answers to all these questions. Sometimes we have to guess, by comparing what has been found in the Indus valley with discoveries in Egypt, Sumer and other parts of the world. Some of the things found in the Indus valley have symbols on them — pictographs that must have had a meaning

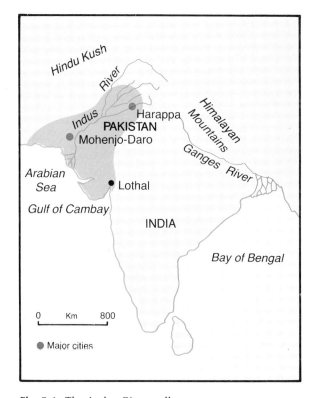

Fig. 5.1 The Indus River valley.

to the people who lived there so many thousands of years ago. But we have not been able to 'crack the code' of the Indus valley pictographs; we cannot read them.

Because of this, all our knowledge of these ancient people must come from the things they built and made.

The Indus River valley

Look at the map in Fig. 5.1. You can see that the Indus River flows through the modern country of Pakistan, to the west of India. Pakistan is a new country, less than fifty years old. Until 1947 it was part of India. Although Pakistan and India are now separate countries, for most of their history they have been joined. The Indus River rises in the mighty mountains of the Hindu Kush and flows south past the modern city of Hyderabad to the Arabian Sea.

If you know that the Indus, like the Nile, Tigris and Euphrates rivers, flooded regularly and that the land along its banks was rich and fertile, you should be able to make a guess about why people settled there so long ago. It may be that hunters from the eastern part of modern Iran crossed the mountains of modern Afghanistan, travelled down the Indus and settled near its banks. Perhaps hunters from the western part of Iran moved further west to settle in the Tigris–Euphrates valley and along the Nile. Use an atlas to find out if all this *might* have been possible.

Time to understand

Listed below are the *advantages* and *disadvantages* of the Indus River valley as a place for a settlement. Imagine you belong to a group of hunters who are trying to decide whether to settle there.

Have a group discussion about this important decision. What conclusion does your group come to?

Advantages
— The river valley is fertile because of the mud washed down by regular floods.
— The river is wide. People can travel along it in boats.
— There are fish in the river that can be used for food.
— The animals that live around the river can also be eaten.

Disadvantages
— To reach the valley, people have to cross high mountains, deserts and thick jungle.
— Wild animals live in the jungle. They can easily kill people armed only with spears, bows and arrows.
— The land around the river is swampy and marshy — a breeding ground for many diseases.
— When the river floods, it sweeps away people, houses and crops. The people must be buried, the houses rebuilt and the crops replanted. This destruction is regular and widespread.

The cities

The cities and villages of the Indus valley settlers were spread over about a million square kilometres. We know nothing about most of them because their ruins have not been studied. We do know, however, that Mohenjo-Daro and Harappa were much bigger than the other towns. Perhaps they were capital cities. We do not know whether they were both ruled by the same people or whether they were separate, independent cities, each with its own rulers. We do not even know whether both

Fig. 5.2 Mohenjo-Daro — an ancient city in ruins. The citadel is in the background.

Fig. 5.3 A street of Mohenjo-Daro.

cities were built at the same time. The cities were about 600 kilometres apart, separated by a barren desert.

By studying the ruins of these two main cities, archaeologists have learned that they were very well planned. The cities were divided into blocks, each about 400 metres long and 200 metres wide. The streets were wide and straight, and crossed each other at right angles to make the regular blocks. Each block was then broken up by narrow lanes. The entrances to the houses were from these lanes. There were no windows facing the wider streets, perhaps to keep the sun out and help cool the house. A person walking along the street would see only a row of blank walls.

The houses were made from clay bricks fired in a kiln. Most were two storeys high, although poorer families lived in small, one-storey houses with just two or three rooms. Wooden beams were put across the top of the walls. These were

then covered with clay which was pounded down to make a strong, flat roof. From the roof a brick drainpipe carried rainwater down into the sewer pipes below the street. Another pipe went from the toilet into the street drain. Every now and then manholes were built into the street so that the drains could be checked and cleaned.

Time to understand

1 Are the streets of your town or suburb laid out in a regular way? Do they cross each other at right angles and make regular blocks? Or are they set out in a different way? What are the advantages of having regular blocks in a city plan? Are there any disadvantages?

2 Fig. 5.4 (over) shows a cut-away plan of a house in Mohenjo-Daro. What rooms does

79

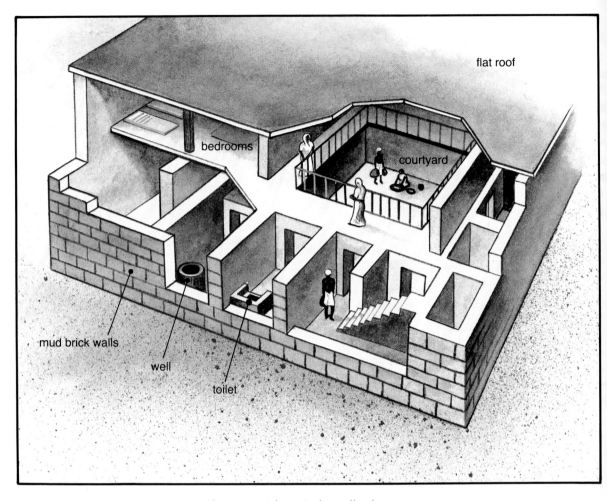

Fig. 5.4 Inside an Indus valley home.

this house have that are also part of your home? Why do you think this house has a flat roof? How do you think historians have been able to work out what houses from so long ago looked like? What can you learn about the people of Mohenjo-Daro by studying their homes?

The citadel

On the western side of both Mohenjo-Daro and Harappa was a citadel or fortress. Each stood on an artificial mound and was protected by a brick wall and towers. The citadel at Harappa was 450 metres long and 215 metres wide; the wall that surrounded it was 14 metres wide. Grim and forbidding, it looked over the city which stretched beneath it.

Near the citadel was a building that may have been barracks, and near the barracks was a row of huge granaries, each measuring 15 metres long and 6 metres wide. Close to the granaries were eighteen work platforms where workers threshed the grain and pounded it into flour, possibly watched by guards from the citadel.

At Mohenjo-Daro, another interesting building has been discovered near the citadel and granaries. It is the great bath, and you can see its ruins in the picture in Fig. 5.5. The bath was about 12 metres long and 7 metres wide. A wide flight of steps led down into the water and the whole building was enclosed by verandahs and arcades. Above the bath were small rooms that may have been cells. The bath itself was made waterproof with layers of mortar, bitumen and brick.

What can we learn from all this? Historians have put together all the clues they have found. From them they have worked out a possible explanation of life in the Indus valley cities. Here it is: The rulers of the Indus valley cities were powerful priests who lived in the barracks near the citadels. Farmers had to sell their crops to these priest-rulers. The grain was stored in the granaries and some people were either forced or employed to pound it into flour. Then, perhaps, it was sold or distributed to the people. The priests used the bath for ritual cleansing or purification — a custom that is still part of Indian life today.

If this explanation is true — and we are not sure that it is — the priests were obviously the most powerful people in the society of the Indus valley.

At work in the valley

Most of the people who settled in the Indus valley were farmers. In the rich silt left by floodwater they planted and grew wheat, barley, rice, vegetables and fruits. They grew sesame for its oil and cotton to make clothes. They kept cattle, buffalo, sheep and pigs. Oxen, horses and donkeys pulled their two-wheeled carts.

Archaeologists have found no traces of irrigation ditches like those discovered in Sumer and Egypt, but they believe that the people of the Indus must have used irrigation to help them farm in the hot, dry land.

Other Indus valley people worked in the city of Lothal, a port city about 600 kilometres south of Mohenjo-Daro. They made a huge dock on the Gulf of Cambay and built seagoing ships like those used by the Sumerians. From Lothal, traders set out for Sumer, Persia, southern India and Afghanistan. We know this because goods made in the Indus valley — especially the seals you can read about in the next section — have been found in all these places.

Those who lived and worked in the cities could not grow their own food. They may have been paid in grain from the granaries which the priests controlled.

Fig. 5.5 The ruins of the great bath at Mohenjo-Daro.

Time to understand

1 We might be quite wrong in our ideas about how the cities of the Indus valley were organised. Using all that you have read so far in this chapter, can you think of another explanation for the citadels, granaries and barracks of these cities? Do you have any other explanations for the great bath at Mohenjo-Daro?

2 Here are three *facts* about the cities of the Indus valley.

  a   They were all built on the same rectangular grid plan.

  b   The houses in each city were built to the same design. Even the bricks in different cities were the same size.

  c   The same weights and measures were used in all the cities.

Using these facts, what guesses could you make about the government of these cities? Do you think they *were* independent and separate? Or do you think one group of people controlled them all?

Fig. 5.6 A stone statue from the Indus valley. It has a beard and a cloak with a clover leaf pattern. It dates from about 2000 BC and may represent a priest.

Indus valley crafts

No one has yet found a royal grave in the Indus valley like those of Egypt and Sumer. Because of this, very few beautiful objects from the valley have survived. Fig. 5.6 shows one of the few stone sculptures to have been found. It is about 17 centimetres high and looks quite stern. Perhaps it represents one of the priest-rulers.

The most common objects found in the Indus valley are tiny stone seals, engraved with designs, animals and pictographs. The seals are only about 2.5 centimetres square and were probably used for stamping bags of grain and other goods. Perhaps each of the designs is the trademark of a particular merchant or grower. In Fig. 5.7 you can see one of these seals, engraved with pictographs as well as an animal picture. More than 250 of these symbols have been found but their meaning has not yet been worked out.

The potters of the Indus valley made a lot of toys and some of these have been

Fig. 5.7 A seal from the Indus valley. On it you can see a picture of an animal and the pictograph writing that has not yet been deciphered. The seal is typical of those found at Mohenjo-Daro and elsewhere in the Indus valley. Most of them show animals that would have been found in the area.

Fig. 5.8 Toys from the Indus valley.

discovered in the ruins of the cities. Model animals and carts seem to have been popular with the children of the valley. Some of the toys had holes in them so they could be pulled around on string.

Time to understand

1 You could make some seals like those found in the Indus valley. Divide some clay into pieces about 2.5 centimetres square. Using the picture in this book as a model, engrave your seals with animals and symbols as the ancient people of the Indus valley did. Dry your seals in the sun or fire them in your school's kiln. How hard is it to draw complicated pictures on to such a tiny object?

2 Think about the toys that children play with today. What are the most popular kinds of toys? If they were discovered in about four thousand years' time, what would they tell the finders about our world? Do you think they would give a fair picture of the world we live in now? Why?

3 Imagine you have 'cracked the code' of the Indus valley pictograph writing. Make up three or four inscriptions you have deciphered. Remember that they must fit in with what is already known about the Indus valley people.

4 If we *were* able to read the writing of the Indus valley, what sort of things would we be able to find out about the ancient civilisations there? That is, things that we do not know by studying the remains of cities like Mohenjo-Daro and Harappa.

Cities in ruins

Fig. 5.9 (over) shows a gruesome sight found by archaeologists in Mohenjo-Daro. The men, women and children had been stabbed or clubbed to death and their bodies had been left to rot where they fell.

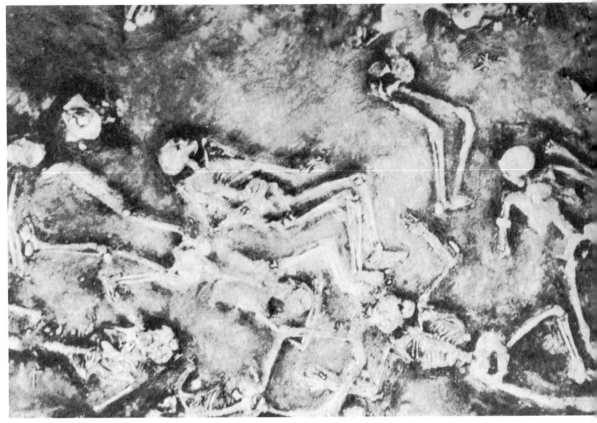

Fig. 5.9 Skeletons lie in the streets where once bodies fell. A grisly reminder of brutal murder at Mohenjo-Daro four thousand years ago.

The civilisation of the Indus River valley lasted only for a thousand years. It collapsed about 1500 BC and we do not really know why. The skeletons at Mohenjo-Daro indicate that the city's people were massacred by an invading enemy. But no other evidence has yet been found of violent attack in the other cities. Historians have thought of many reasons to explain the sudden collapse of the Indus valley society. The main ones are shown in the diagram in Fig. 5.10. Can you think of any others?

Time to understand

1 Look carefully at the possible reasons for the collapse of the civilisation of the Indus valley, shown in Fig. 5.10. Some of these suggested reasons are from *natural* causes; some are from *human* causes. Can you divide the suggested reasons into those caused by natural events and those caused by human beings?

2 What is soil erosion? Do you know what causes soil erosion? Could any of the things listed in Fig. 5.10 have caused soil erosion? Why? What would be the effect of bad soil erosion on people who had to grow their own food? Is it possible that

Perhaps, over hundreds of years, the climate changed and enough food could no longer be grown. The valley was once surrounded by jungle; now it is surrounded by desert.

Perhaps there were mighty floods that caused too much damage to repair.

Perhaps the people cut down all the trees to get wood to fuel the kilns to make bricks. This would help cause floods and make irrigation harder.

Perhaps a plague swept through the area and killed the people.

Perhaps the population grew too large for the supplies of food.

Perhaps the rulers became weaker and could no longer rule wisely or keep the granaries under their control.

Perhaps the cities were attacked and destroyed by a strong enemy — the Aryans, moving in from the mountains in the north.

Fig. 5.10 A society in ruins.

soil erosion was one of the reasons why the Indus valley civilisation collapsed?

3 Archaeologists digging in Mohenjo-Daro found an interesting thing. The further down they dug, the better built the city was. The buildings at the lower level were well made and the city was well planned, as we have seen in this chapter. Closer to the top, however, the houses were built of shoddy materials and were thrown together without any planning. These shacks were the homes of many people. It was as if the city had suddenly become very crowded and people had more to worry about than building fine homes.

Does this discovery give you any clues about the end of the city of Mohenjo-

Daro? Can you think of any explanations for the sudden decline in living conditions in the city?

The Aryans

We do not know why the Indus valley civilisation collapsed, but we do know that the next group of people to live in the valley were tough, warlike nomads called *Aryans*. Their armies were well organised and their iron weapons were much better than the copper and bronze weapons of the Indus valley people. They may have swept into the valley, massacring the people of Mohenjo-Daro and destroying the cities. Or perhaps they moved in at a time when the cities were already almost deserted and beginning to crumble.

The homeland of the Aryans was probably in southern Russia. From about 2500 BC onwards they moved, in waves, to other lands. They settled in Sumer and Egypt, Greece and Turkey. They moved into India around 1500 BC, and for nearly a thousand years after that, tribe after tribe of Aryan people crossed the mountain passes in the north-west to settle in what they called the 'land of the seven rivers'.

The first waves of Aryan invaders had no interest in settling down to a life of farming and building. They were warriors, fighting people led in battle by soldiers in light horse-drawn chariots. They destroyed but did not rebuild; they killed but did not settle.

From about 1000 BC, however, the Aryans began to settle down in the land they had conquered. Groups of tribes formed small kingdoms, each one ruled by a king and his council of warriors. The chief priest was the king's adviser. Later —

from about 600 BC — some of these kingdoms became larger and more powerful. Their kings and princes were often very rich, and wars were common as one kingdom tried to seize power from its neighbours.

Most of the Aryans lived in villages, sometimes marrying tribespeople they had conquered. The land was divided between the families in the village and everyone worked together to build the irrigation canals that were needed to bring water to the crops. Barley and wheat were the main crops; later, millet and rice were grown as well. Village houses were made from a wooden frame covered with walls of reeds and straw. Animals lived under the same roof as the family.

The Vedas

When the Aryans moved into the Indus valley, they did not have a written language. Poems, prayers, hymns and stories were passed from one generation to the next by word of mouth.

Many centuries later, these ancient poems and stories were written down in a language called *Sanskrit*. Four of these religious books have survived. They are called *Vedas*, coming from the Aryan word for knowledge. From the Vedas we can learn a great deal about Aryan religion. The Aryans worshipped many gods and believed that their gods could take many different forms, sometimes appearing as animals, for instance. To keep the gods happy, the people had to make sacrifices to them. Then the gods would help the people and grant them what they wanted. In the Vedas are many charms and spells the people could chant while they sacrificed an animal to the gods.

As time passed, the Aryans spread further south into India. They took their ideas and their way of life into the new land they settled. The religion of the Aryans developed into the religion we today call Hinduism. You can read more about this religion in the next section of this chapter.

Time to understand

The poem below is part of the 'Hymn to Night'. It comes from the Rigveda, the earliest of the Vedas. It might be as old as 1500 BC.

Explain in your own words what the poem is about. What can you learn from it about the people who made it up and passed it on until it was written down many hundreds of years later?

Hymn to Night

So vast, our Goddess Night, she rises,
star-eyes gazing everywhere;
all her finery of dress displayed.
Space high and low she fills, Eternal Night,
her beauty driving out the dark.
Close on the heels of sister Day
she treads. Let darkness run . . .
As you draw near, we turn for home
like birds that wing to nest.

Hinduism

Hinduism is the world's oldest religion. Unlike most other religions, it did not have one founder. Instead it grew out of the ideas and beliefs of the Aryan settlers in India, mixed up with the ideas of other groups of people. The name 'Hindu' comes from the Indus River — the name of India also comes from this river.

To an outsider, the most obvious thing about Hinduism is the division of society

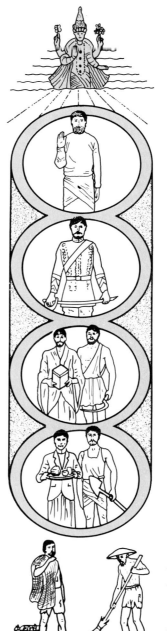

Gods and goddesses

Brahmins: Priests and scholars

Kshatriyas: Warriors and rulers — the noblemen

Vaisyas: Merchants and farmers, landowners and craftsmen

Sudras: Servants and workers, farm labourers and wage earners

Pariahs (outcastes): Their work was considered impure. They included gravediggers, butchers, hunters, fishermen, street sweepers and undertakers.

Fig. 5.11 The Hindu caste system.

87

into *castes*. The diagram in Fig. 5.11 shows how the caste system worked. At the top were the Brahmins, the priests and scholars whose work was to educate others. Then came the Kshatriyas, who were rulers and warriors, noblemen who governed others. Below them were the Vaisyas, farmers, merchants and craftspeople, those with land or skills of a special kind. The lowest caste was the Sudras, made up of labourers and servants, those who were born to serve others. Outside the caste system were the Pariahs, 'outcastes' or untouchables. These people worked in jobs that were thought to be unclean or impure. They were undertakers or gravediggers, hunters or fishermen, butchers or street sweepers.

According to strict Hindu ideas, it was impossible to change castes. You were born into a certain group and there you stayed until you died. You could not marry a person from a different caste, nor could you do the work of someone belonging to another caste.

We do not really know how the caste system began. Hindus believe that each caste sprang from a different part of Brahma, their chief god. Brahmins sprang from the mouth; the ruling caste from the arm; the farmers and merchants from the thigh; and the labourers from the foot.

Fig. 5.12 A painting from a Hindu temple in Calcutta, with the goddess Durga in the centre.

The outcastes did not come from the body of Brahma at all.

Brahma, as we have seen, is the chief god of the Hindus, the source of all life, the creator of everything. Hindus believe in two other important gods: Vishnu, the protector of living things, and Shiva, the god of destruction and death. A lot of Indian art shows pictures of these gods. They, and the other gods that Hindus worship, are all part of the Brahma.

Hindus believe that the human soul never dies. It is reborn many times in different bodies. This idea is called *reincarnation*. If a good person dies, his or her soul is reborn in the body of another good person, richer perhaps than the person who died. On the other hand, the soul of a bad person will be reborn into the body of someone poorer and less fortunate than the person who died. Perhaps the soul will even be reborn into the body of an animal. In one lifetime, one person may be a prince, another a beggar. In the next, this might be reversed. This idea helped Hindus to put up with the caste system. Even the poorest person in the lowest caste could believe that his or her next life would be better if they lived a good life and obeyed the gods.

Because they believe that all living things have a soul, the Hindus believe that all forms of life are sacred. Many do not eat meat because they think it is wrong to kill animals. They consider cows to be one of the most sacred things on earth: they give milk and help farmers with their work. To kill a cow and eat it would be considered a wicked crime. For this reason, some cattle are allowed to wander freely through many Indian villages, protected and fed by Hindus.

To ensure a better position in their next life, Hindus are expected to pray to their

Fig. 5.13 Hindus bathe in the Ganges River, as they have done for thousands of years. To Hindus, the Ganges is a sacred river and bathing in its waters is an ancient ritual.

gods, to offer sacrifices and to perform many rituals. These include reading the Vedas, or sacred writings, bathing their bodies in certain rivers (especially the holy Ganges River) and eating certain foods. Yoga is a way by which Hindus (and other people throughout the world) learn to control their bodies through exercises and to relax their minds.

Time to understand

The passage below comes from an ancient Hindu book. It tells how Hindu women should behave towards their husbands. Read the passage and answer the questions that follow.

> A woman has no other god on earth than her husband. The most excellent thing she can do is to obey him at all times. Her husband may be old, sick or bad mannered. He may be a drunkard or a gambler. He may live without honour. He may be deaf or blind or a criminal. Even so, his wife shall always think of him as her god. She shall serve him with all her might, obey him in all things, never criticise him and give him no cause for concern.
>
> If her husband laughs, she ought to laugh. If he weeps, she must weep too. If he feels like speaking, she will join in the conversation. When her husband sings, she must be in ecstasy. If he dances, she must watch him with delight. She must always be happy when he is around. There must be no gloom. Thus is the goodness of a woman's nature shown.

1 Using this passage as evidence, explain how a good Hindu woman was expected to behave when this book was written perhaps two thousand years ago.
2 Do you think these instructions are fair to women? What benefits, if any, might women have gained by behaving in the way set down in this ancient book? What disadvantages would women have experienced?
3 Do you think all Hindu women obeyed the rules set down in this book? Why?
4 Are married women expected to behave like this in our society today? Can you explain why women behave differently in our society than in ancient Hindu society?

Buddhism

By about 600 BC Hinduism was a powerful religion in India. It was especially popular with the rich people. Can you explain why? The Brahmins, or Hindu priests, were treated with great respect because they were the only ones who could understand (or pretend to understand) the Hindu teachings. Over the years these teachings had become more and more complicated. Ordinary people often did not know what they were expected to believe or what they should do to keep their gods happy.

Many people were unhappy about Hinduism and several religious leaders tried to change the religion to make it simpler and more meaningful to ordinary people. One who succeeded was Siddhartha Gautama, the founder of Buddhism.

The life of Gautama

Gautama was born about 500 BC, at about the same time that Confucius, another great religious leader, was born in China. Gautama was of the warrior caste, and his father ruled a small state in what is now the country of Nepal, in the foothills of the Himalayan mountains. Gautama was a rich and pampered child. According to legend, a wise man told his father when Gautama was born that Gautama would either become a powerful ruler or a religious leader. Gautama's father was determined that he should take his place as ruler of the kingdom, so he kept him within the palace walls, not allowing him to see the suffering of the outside world. In time, Gautama married and had a son.

Despite his happy life and luxurious surroundings, Gautama was not content. One day, so the story goes, he disobeyed his father and went outside the palace walls. In the town he saw four things that changed his life: a man crippled with old age; a man dying by the side of the road; a corpse; and a beggar holding up his bowl and asking for food. For the first time Gautama realised that the world was full of pain, suffering and death. He wanted to know why.

The Hindu priests in the palace could not tell him and, despite hours of thought, Gautama could find no answers to the questions that were bothering him. At the age of twenty-nine he made a momentous

Fig. 5.14 Villagers bring gifts to the tree under which Buddha sat and meditated until he became enlightened.

decision. He left his family, shaved his long hair, swapped his clothes for those of a poor man and began a new life as a wandering beggar.

The enlightenment

At first Gautama joined a group of Hindu teachers, or *yogi*, and listened to their ideas about the world. Then he joined a band of men who thought they would find the answers by denying themselves food and comforts. Gautama fasted until it was said that he could live on one bean a day. His stomach touched his spine, but still he was unhappy about his life.

90

Fig. 5.15 This wall painting from a cave at Ajanta in western India shows the young Gautama learning from other children. Which figure do you think is Gautama? How can you tell this scene took place before Gautama left the palace and went into the world?

Fig. 5.16 A Buddhist 'wheel of the law'. What do its eight spokes represent?

Finally, Gautama decided to try to control his mind by sitting quite still and concentrating his thoughts on one idea. He bathed, had a meal and sat down under a big tree, vowing not to leave until he understood why people had to suffer. He was tempted to give up and leave, but stayed as he said he would until, one night, his mind cleared and he understood the world as he never had before. It was like the bursting of a bubble. All doubt and uncertainty disappeared. From then on, Gautama felt that he understood the world completely.

Gautama had become 'enlightened' and became known as Buddha, the Enlightened One. For almost fifty years he wandered from place to place, teaching those who would listen to his ideas. He and his followers remained poor: they dressed in simple yellow robes and begged for their food. Buddha taught that people should not accept traditional religious ideas but that they should work out their own ideas. He disagreed with the complicated rituals of Hinduism. He believed that religion should be simple and practical. It is no wonder that his most devoted followers were people from the lower castes.

Buddha's teachings

Buddha taught his followers a set of rules for living. He believed that if they followed these rules they could become perfect. Then their souls could escape the constant rebirths that the Hindus believed in. They could rest forever in Nirvana, a state of peace.

Buddha believed that if people lived good, simple lives they would be happy. He made up eight rules to help people live good lives. These rules have been called the 'eight-fold path'. They are:

1 Right knowledge — the knowledge of truth;

2 Right intention — kindness and love towards others;

3 Right speech — truth and honesty;

4 Right conduct — never killing or harming living creatures;

5 Right work — being fair in one's work life;

6 Right effort — always trying to improve one's understanding;

7 Right thinking — thinking no evil of others;

8 Right concentration — thinking about important, not selfish things.

After Buddha

Because Buddha did not set down an exact list of religious beliefs, it was easy for his followers to split into different groups, each with different ideas about what Buddha meant. Today there are about 300 million Buddhists around the world. They worship many different kinds of Buddhism.

Buddha, you will remember, taught that it was wrong to worship statues of gods or build huge temples to honour them. He wanted a simple religion that ordinary people could be part of. It is strange that if you visit a Buddhist country today you will almost certainly find huge and ornate statues of Buddha and beautiful temples for Buddhists to worship in. As Buddhism spread, it became the religion of the rich as well as the poor. The simple ideas of Buddha were lost in people's wish to build statues and temples to honour the founder of their religion.

Fig. 5.17 A Buddhist temple in Burma.

Time to understand

1 Fig. 5.16 on p. 91 shows the Buddhist 'wheel of the law'. How many spokes does the wheel have? Can you suggest why?

2 Below are some of the teachings of Buddha. Explain what each one means. Are they at all like the teachings of any other religion you know of?

    a 'All that we are is the result of what we have thought. If a person speaks or acts with an evil thought, pain follows. If a person speaks or acts kindly, happiness follows.'

    b 'If a man does me wrong, I will return to him my ungrudging love. The more evil that comes from him, the more good shall come from me.'

    c 'There is no value in good actions that are done with the idea of winning praise. They must be done for their own sake.'

3 China was one of the countries to which Buddhism spread. Hundreds of years after the death of Buddha, a Chinese Buddhist called Xuan Zang made a long and dangerous journey across Asia to India. He wanted to gather Buddhist writings and take them back to China where they could be translated into Chinese and studied at the Buddhist monasteries there. Here is Xuan Zang's description of part of the journey:

Alone and deserted I crossed the sandy waste, finding my way only by looking out for heaps of bones. I suddenly saw hundreds of soldiers crossing the plain. Sometimes they came towards me, sometimes they halted. The soldiers were dressed in fur and felt. Then I saw camels and horses and the glittering of thousands of lances and fluttering of flags. Then everything changed into different shapes, sometimes far away, sometimes close, sometimes dissolving into nothing.

At first I thought they were robbers; then I realised they were demons.

a   Why do you think Chinese Buddhists wanted to collect Buddhist writings from India? How would this help them understand more about their religion?

b   Were the writings gathered by Xuan Zang written by Buddha himself? How do you know? (*Clue*: Read the section about Buddhism again.)

c   Do you think Xuan Zang really saw demons in front of him? Can you suggest why he thought he saw demons?

d   Use Xuan Zang's description to draw a picture of what he thought he saw before him.

e   The television program called *Monkey*·was based on a legend that grew up around the travels and adventures of Xuan Zang. Try to find out more about this legend by using books from your library.

6

Life in ancient China

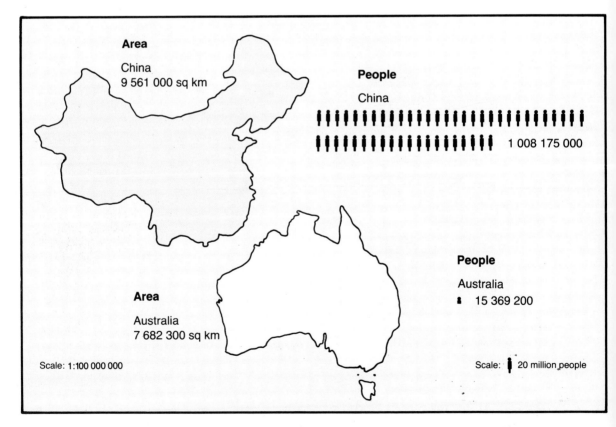

Area
China
9 561 000 sq km

People
China
1 008 175 000

People
Australia
▮ 15 369 200

Area
Australia
7 682 300 sq km

Scale: 1:100 000 000

Scale: ▮ 20 million people

Fig. 6.1 China and Australia: similar in area but vastly different in population.

CHINA, the world's third largest country, is home to a quarter of the world's people. Look carefully at the maps and diagrams in Fig. 6.1. What can you learn from them about the size and population of China compared with the size and population of Australia?

China's huge population has never been spread evenly throughout the country. Much of the land is mountainous; much of it is dry and barren. It is hard to grow food in these places. We have learned earlier in this book that ancient people settled in places where food could be grown easily. The most fertile part of China is the land around the Huanghe and Chang Jiang rivers. This is the North China Plain, and it was here that the first Chinese farmers settled. It is still the richest farming land in China.

People began growing crops in China around 5000 BC, just as people did in other parts of the world. Like these other early farmers, the Chinese settled on land made rich by the flooding of rivers. The land they chose was around the 'great bend' of the Huanghe River. You can see this in the map in Fig. 6.2. Soil — called 'loess' — had been blown here for millions of years. It was fine and yellow, up to 75 metres deep, and very fertile. The loess had another advantage, too, for when a

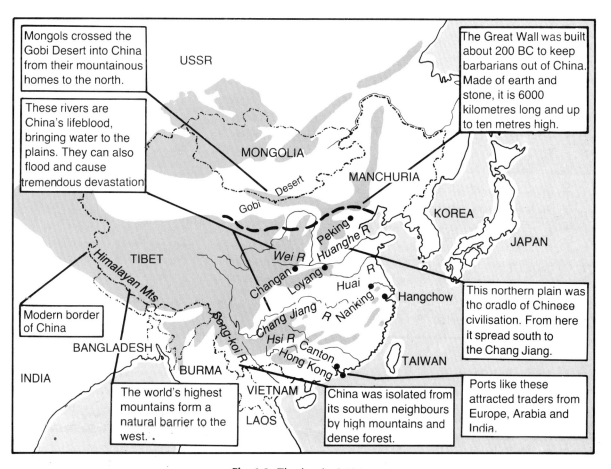

Fig. 6.2 The land of China.

hole was dug into it, it would not cave in. The early farmers could therefore make pit houses in the ground — an easy way to build a home that was warm in winter and cool in summer.

Banpo village

The largest village from this period in China's history was discovered in 1953. Its name is Banpo and people settled here about 4500 BC. How many years ago was that?

The village of Banpo was divided into three areas: one for living, one for burials and the other for pottery making. Babies were not buried in the grave area. Instead, their bodies were placed in pottery jars near the houses.

The living area of Banpo village was rectangular and surrounded by a ditch. In the middle was a large building, about 160 square metres. This was probably a meeting place, rather like a community hall today. You can see a reconstruction of this building in Fig. 6.3.

People's houses were much smaller. The floor was dug out below ground level (remember the loess!) and the walls were made of mud or straw over a framework of poles. The roof, supported on these poles, was made from thatch. In the middle of each hut was a fireplace and just outside the door was a deep pit where grain and vegetables could be stored.

Pottery must have been very important to the Banpo villagers, since part of their village was set aside just to make pots. Obviously those who were skilled potters were not expected to work in the fields. What does this tell us about the farming skills of the Banpo villagers?

Fig. 6.3 What the largest building in Banpo village may have looked like. Only the foundations and post holes were left in the ground and historians have guessed what the building was like from these clues.

Most of the pots that have been discovered at Banpo were made for everyday use: for cooking, storing grain, carrying water, collecting food, eating and drinking from, and so on. But a few of the pots were beautifully decorated with paint. In fact the people of Banpo village belong to what has been called the 'painted pottery' period of China's history because of their skill with brush and paint. Fish and animals were common decorations. Perhaps they were painted on the pots as good luck charms for fishermen and hunters. Other pots have been carved with squiggles and marks that were probably an early form of writing. Some of these marks were definitely numbers.

The people of Banpo grew mulberry trees and farmed silkworms. They kept dogs, pigs, chickens, sheep and goats, and used axes, hoes, fishing hooks, nets, knives, bows and arrows. They wove their clothes from hemp.

Time to understand

1 Banpo village was divided into three areas. Are modern towns and cities divided into areas? Why? Are they at all like the areas of Banpo?

2 Using the picture in Fig. 6.3 and the description in the text, draw a picture of what you think a house in Banpo would have looked like.

3 How important is pottery (or ceramic ware) in your life? How often in a day do you use goods made from pottery? Think about the ways pottery goods were used in Banpo. What materials are used to make these containers today? Why did the people of Banpo not use these materials?

4 Some of the best decorated pots have been found in the cemetery section of Banpo. Can you suggest why?

5 The diagrams in Fig. 6.4 show how a realistic fish pattern was changed over time in Banpo to produce an abstract design.

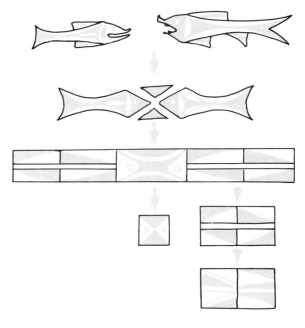

Fig. 6.4 From fish to abstract: changing patterns on Banpo pottery.

Fig. 6.5 The fish and abstract patterns on pottery from Banpo village.

You can see this happening on the pots shown in Fig. 6.5. What can you learn about the Banpo potters by studying these illustrations? Do you think they were skilled craftsmen? Draw or make a tracing of a natural object — a plant or animal — and try to convert it in stages into an abstract geometrical pattern. Would you say your pattern was 'artistic'? Do you think the Banpo patterns are 'artistic'?

Once upon a time . . .

As early farming villages like Banpo were abandoned and fell into ruins, their people were forgotten. The first history book written in China comes from about 100 BC. How many years was this after the Banpo settlement? The authors of this book set down all that was known or believed about China's past.

China, they said, was first ruled by twelve 'heavenly emperors', all brothers, who ruled for 18 000 years each. Then came eleven 'earthly emperors', also brothers, who ruled for another 18 000 years each. After them came nine 'human emperors' who reigned for 5000 years each. Then there were a number of other rulers, each of whom added something to Chinese knowledge. One taught people to build houses; one discovered fire; one taught humans how to tame animals and to fish with nets; one invented writing; one developed farming and medicine; and one organised raids against China's enemies, invented carts, worked out a system of measuring time and invented bricks. His wife taught the people how to make silk.

After many more rulers came Yu, who was honoured in the legends for his work in controlling floodwaters that had covered the land almost to the top of the mountains. The people insisted that Yu's son should follow him as ruler and so it was that Yu founded the first *dynasty* or ruling family in China's history. According to the legends, his family ruled China from 2205 BC until 1766 BC. This was known as the Xia dynasty.

There were seventeen rulers, or kings, in the Xia dynasty. It seems that the last of them was so cruel that the people revolted against him. The leader of this rebellion was Dang, a nobleman who began a new dynasty: the Shang. According to the old records, the Shang family ruled until 1122 BC.

Time to understand

1 What are legends? Are they true or untrue? How do we know that the accounts of China's first rulers are legends rather than facts? Do you think these legends could have been based on facts? Why?
2 Do you know of any other legends about early rulers or heroes in other countries? Are these legends based on facts at all?
3 Why was Yu thought to be such a hero? What does this tell us about life in ancient China?
4 Fig. 6.6 shows the symbols called 'yin' and 'yang'. According to the old Chinese histories, they were invented about 3000 BC by the same scholar who invented Chinese writing. The symbols represent opposite ideas that together create harmony and balance. 'Yin' was the female symbol, 'yang' the male symbol. They also stand for contrasting but balanced forces such as sun and moon, light and darkness, earth and heaven. The yin and yang symbols were later (about 1100 BC) included in a

Fig. 6.6 Yin and Yang.

famous Chinese book called *I Ching*, or the Book of Changes. Try to find out a little about this important early book.

An exciting discovery

According to Chinese ideas about medicine, some illnesses could be cured by using ground, or powdered, bones mixed with other substances. Certain bones were highly valued until quite recent times because they could be ground up for this purpose.

In 1899 farmers around the city of Anyang, not far from the sites of Banpo and other ancient villages, began digging up many broken pieces of polished bones and selling them to chemists to be ground into medicine. An antique dealer realised that they were very old and it was not long before archaeologists were working on the site. They dug out, pieced together, collected and studied thousands of bones — over 17 000 were discovered near Anyang and many more have been found in other places. What they learned from them changed their ideas about ancient China. Until then no one had really known whether the Shang dynasty, the one founded by Dang (according to the old books) really existed. The bones dug out at Anyang proved that it did.

It happened like this. Most of the bones that had been dug up were the shoulder bones of sheep, pigs, goats and cattle. Some were parts of the shells of tortoises. On these bones, ancient scribes had engraved questions about the future: questions like, 'Should an army be sent against so-and-so?' or 'Is tomorrow a good day to begin my journey?' or 'How can so-and-so be cured?' Hollows were then drilled into the bones and they were heated until they cracked. Trained 'fortune tellers' worked out from the cracks what advice the gods were giving to the questioner. It was rather like 'reading' tea leaves in the bottom of a cup to tell the future. The cracks could be 'read' only by those skilled in the art; to ordinary people they were mysterious and meaningless.

The symbols on these 'oracle bones' were not the same as the symbols used in modern Chinese writing. But there were some similarities and scholars were able to work out what they meant. They discovered that on the bones were the names of most of the Shang kings mentioned in the early history books. Even more exciting was the discovery that the place where the most bones were found, Anyang, was the last capital of the Shang

Fig. 6.7 Part of an oracle bone. This one is asking a question about hunting.

99

dynasty. By reading and studying the oracle bones and digging further into the ground, historians have been able to learn a great deal about this time in China's past.

Time to understand

1 Why do people want to know about the future before it happens? Would you like to know your future now? Why?

2 What other ways do you know by which people try to tell the future? Do any of them work? Do you think the Shang oracle bones would have worked? Why do you think so many of them were used? Does this prove that they did work? Or that they didn't work? Or does it prove neither?

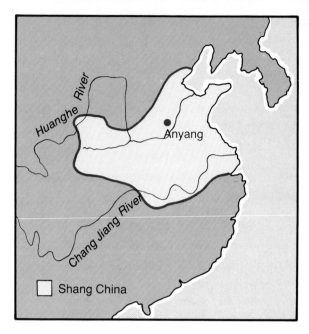

Fig. 6.8 Shang China. As you can see, the Shang rulers did not control all the land. The rest was ruled by the princes of other noble families.

Life in Shang times

The people of Shang China grew millet, wheat and rice, working their farms with hoes and other tools. They dug irrigation canals and used wheeled carts and horses to make their work easier. They wove their clothes from linen or, if they were richer, from silk.

At the centre of their cities was an area ringed by a wall and here were built the houses of important people. Around the city was a ring of smaller villages where farmers lived in their simple, pit-like houses. Like people in other parts of the world at this time, the Shang believed in an after-life. Their kings were buried in elaborate tombs, complete with tools and weapons, chariots and horses, clothes and jewellery, slaves and servants. One tomb

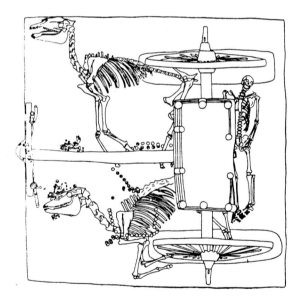

Fig. 6.9 A diagram of the remains of a Shang burial at Anyang. Only the skeletons of the charioteer and his horses remain, along with remnants of the chariot and its gear.

contained 164 human sacrifices, all killed to help the king in his future life.

These tombs were so large and elaborate that many thousands of people must have been needed to build them. Most of them were slaves, prisoners of war captured in one of the many battles the Shang rulers fought with their neighbours.

Until recently, scholars believed that the writing on Shang oracle bones was the oldest writing in China. The discoveries at Banpo have proved this to be wrong. Can you remember why? We do know, however, that the Shang made books from bamboo strips and pieces of wood and that they had developed a written language of several thousand symbols or characters. Like the cuneiform writing of Sumer, Shang writing began as pictographs and gradually changed into more abstract strokes.

During the Shang dynasty, Chinese people developed the art of using bronze to make weapons and tools such as spears, knives and arrows. Fig. 6.10 shows one of the beautiful bronze vessels made in Shang China. These vessels were made by pouring molten bronze (a mixture of tin and copper) between two pottery moulds, made in pieces, and then breaking the pottery away when the bronze had cooled. As you can see, some of the bronzeware was very highly decorated. The decorations were carved into the pottery moulds before the bronze was poured in, so they appeared in reverse on the hardened bronze.

The largest bronze object from the Shang period is a huge cauldron weighing about 1400 kilograms. It would have needed hundreds of craftsmen to make things like this. Towns grew up around the workshop areas where bronzeware was manufactured. Some of the objects were traded with other people, using cowrie

Fig. 6.10 A bronze vessel from Shang China. Elaborate vessels like this were used for religious ceremonies and many were buried with kings or other leaders.

shells from other parts of Asia as money. Some were specially made for the elaborate tombs of kings and were buried almost as soon as they were finished. Others — the smaller and simpler ones — were used in everyday life, sometimes replacing the pottery goods that had been used before the coming of bronze.

The end of the Shang

West of the Shang territory was an area ruled by the Zhou family. While the Shang kings were strong, the Zhou accepted them as powerful rulers and paid tribute to them. But the two groups never really trusted each other and in about 1122 BC a Zhou army defeated the last Shang king, who threw himself into the flames of his burning palace and died. According to histories written by Zhou supporters, this last Shang king was cruel and evil and deserved to die. The Zhou rulers were helped, so they said, by thousands of Shang slaves who revolted against their masters and joined the Zhou army. The new dynasty set up by Wu, the Zhou leader, lasted until 221 BC.

Western Zhou, 1100 BC–770 BC

The Zhou ruled for nine centuries. The first part of this period has been called 'western Zhou' because the Zhou capital was at Hao, south-west of the modern city of Xi'an. As you will read later in this section, the capital was moved in 770 BC further east to Louyang. From then until the end of Zhou rule has therefore been called the period of eastern Zhou.

The king

The Zhou king was supposed to have descended from the god of farming and was called the 'son of heaven' — a title given to all the Chinese emperors who came after him. He was both a king and a priest, and thus he had great responsibility. He was expected to be wise and good, to care for his people and protect them from enemies. People believed that the king's behaviour was reflected in the natural world. If the king was virtuous the crops grew and the people were happy. If the king was evil, the world too was bad and there might be drought, flood or famine. Remember that the king was supposed to be descended from the god of farming!

The king, therefore, had a right to rule only if he pleased the gods. If not, the gods showed their anger by causing trouble in the world. This 'right to rule' has been called a *mandate from heaven*. If you look up 'mandate' in a dictionary you will be able to understand this phrase. The Chinese believed that if a king was defeated by a rebel army he had lost his mandate from heaven. He was no longer fit to be king. The rebel leader now had the mandate from heaven and could start a new family dynasty.

Organising the land

One Zhou king said: 'All the land under heaven is my land; all the people on this land are my subjects.' He might have believed this to be true but it was obvious that one person could not rule all the land and all those subjects without help.

The system worked out by the Zhou kings was based on *rights* and *duties*. The king gave part of his land to his relatives or powerful noble families. They then had the *right* to use the land. They could make those who lived on the land work for them in whatever ways they chose. In return, the noblemen had many *duties*. They had to fight for the king when they were needed, to pay him in food, metals and jewels, and to appoint officials to govern the land. One of their most important duties was to collect taxes. The king demanded taxes to pay for the royal palace and for wars against his enemies.

This system of organising land and government is called the feudal system. Many hundreds of years later a similar system was used in Europe.

Everyday life

Most of the people were farmers, or peasants. Many were slaves. Often the lives of peasants were not much better than the lives of slaves. Peasants were forced to work on their master's land and to pay him dues in the form of part of their crop. When the king or noblemen wanted extra grain to feed their armies, the peasants had to work even harder to grow the extra grain. If the king or noblemen wanted more people to build palaces or tombs, canals or city walls, they sometimes called on the peasants, who had no choice but to obey their masters.

The powerful noble families all belonged to clans or family groups. They worshipped their ancestors, believing that the spirits of their ancestors, at the 'palace of the heavenly king', could answer questions and give advice on all kinds of matters. The people of Zhou China no longer believed that oracle bones would help them work out the future, but they still offered sacrifices to their ancestors and performed many rituals to ensure that the spirits of their ancestors were listening and caring for them. These sacrifices and rituals could be performed only by males. Because of this, a nobleman considered himself very unlucky if he had no sons.

Ordinary people had no clan names; nor did they worship their ancestors. Instead their gods were those of ancient times — the gods of wind and rain, thunder and stars, river and sun. Each village and even each family had its own special gods. Later, the clan names became more widespread and even humble villagers began worshipping their ancestors.

Fig. 6.11 The remains of a nobleman's chariot and horses, found in a tomb from the Zhou period. Compare this picture with the diagram in Fig. 6.9.

Attack from the north

The land in the north of China was too poor to grow crops. Here nomads moved from place to place with their herds, as they had done for thousands of years. Sometimes they threatened their farming neighbours to the south. In the eighth century BC the Zhou were attacked by a group of nomads called the Rong. To the Chinese the Rong were barbarians — as were any non-Chinese people. They looked with scorn at their straggling red hair, their green eyes and commented on their strange diet of meat and milk.

Barbarians they might have been, but the Rong (helped by some other enemies of the Zhou) managed to capture Hao, the Zhou capital, in 770 BC. The Zhou king was killed and his successor, Bing, was forced to move the capital further east to Louyang to escape from the attacks of the nomads.

Time to understand

1 Here is a translation of a poem written by a warrior in the Zhou army. Read it carefully and answer the questions below.

The spirits of the fallen

Grasping our great shields and wearing our
    hide armour,
Wheel-hub to wheel-hub locked, we battle
    hand to hand.
Our banners darken the sky; the enemy
    teem like clouds:
Through the hail of arrows the warriors
    press forward.
They dash on our lines; they trample our
    ranks down.
The left horse has fallen, the right one is
    wounded.
Bury the wheels in; tie up the horses!

Seize the jade drumstick and beat the
    sounding drum!
The time is against us: the gods are angry.
Now all lie dead, left on the field of battle.
They went out never more to return:
Far, far away they lie, on the level plain,
Their long swords at their belts, clasping
    their elmwood bows.
Head from body sundered: but their hearts
    could not be vanquished.
Both truly brave, and also truly noble;
Strong to the last, they could not be
    dishonoured.
Their bodies may have died, but their souls
    are living:
Heroes among the shades their valiant souls
    will be.

a   Tell the story of what happens in this poem.

b   What did the writer mean by the last line of the poem?

c   Do you know or can you find any poems in English that have the same ideas as this ancient Chinese poem? (*Clue*: Try to find some poems about the First World War.)

d   Using this poem and the photograph in Fig. 6.11, draw a series of pictures showing the events of the poem. You may be able to find pictures of ancient Chinese battle scenes in other books to help you make your pictures as accurate as possible. You could write out lines from the poem under each of your pictures to make a frieze for your classroom.

2 Here is part of another poem from the Zhou period. The 'big rat' is the tax collector. What does the poem mean? What does it tell us about Zhou China?

Big rat, big rat,
Do not eat my millet!
Three years I have served you,
But you will not care for me.
I am going to leave you

And go to that happy land;
Happy land, happy land,
Where I will find my place.

Eastern Zhou, 770 BC–221 BC

The period of the eastern Zhou was not peaceful. The Zhou kings had two main problems. First, there was always the threat of attacks from the nomadic tribes in the north. The nomads had tamed horses and could sweep down into China with terrifying speed and force. Second, the Zhou kings found that other rulers were no longer prepared to obey them without question. They still called themselves the sons of heaven but in fact, as time passed, the king of the Zhou was no more powerful than many other princes.

Battle after battle was fought between the rival princes and between groups of princes and the Zhou kings. Many thousands of peasants were forced to leave their fields and join their ruler's army. Some of the northern rulers even copied the nomads and put some of their soldiers on horseback. The Zhou kings did not win all these battles; in fact they became weaker and weaker. Could it be that they were losing their mandate from heaven?

Teachers and philosophers

Centuries of war and confusion forced some people to think carefully about the society in which they lived. Why was life so hard? Why did human beings fight each other? Was there a way to get rid of human problems? Was there a way of making people live in peace with each other? Why was the world as it was?

These were difficult questions indeed and most people had neither the time nor the energy to think about them. But the priests, who could read and write (unlike most people) found these questions interesting. The rulers employed the priests in their palaces to teach their children and help govern the kingdom. Some rulers even set up academies or schools, to which students and scholars came. These scholars often moved from court to court, offering their services to whoever paid them most and treated them with greatest respect.

One such wanderer was Confucius. You can read his story in the pictures in Fig. 6.12 (over).

Time to understand

As you learned from Fig. 6.12, according to tradition Confucius compiled books which contained his own ideas and the ideas he approved of from the past. Another source of information about Confucius's ideas is the *Analects*, probably compiled by people who agreed with him. Here are some extracts from the *Analects* which set down a few of the sayings of Confucius. Explain what each one means. Do you know any sayings in English with the same ideas? What can you learn about the ideas of Confucius from these sayings?

1 Having only coarse food to eat, plain water to drink and a bent arm for a pillow, one can still find happiness. Riches and honour gained by unrighteous means are to me as drifting clouds.
2 Were any prince to employ me, a good deal could be done, and in three years everything could be accomplished.
3 Those who are born wise are the highest type of people; those who become wise through learning come next; those who learn by overcoming dullness come after that.

Confucius was a government official who resigned because of all the evil and corruption he saw. He wandered from place to place, gathering scholars who were interested in his ideas.

Confucius believed that the disorder and unrest of his time could be overcome if each person knew his or her own proper place in society.

The young should respect and obey the old, wives should respect and obey their husbands, people should respect and obey their rulers. This would bring harmony back to the world.

Confucius believed in charity and good works, courtesy and politeness. Ritual and correct behaviour were important for they showed a person's inner goodness.

During his lifetime the ideas of Confucius were not always popular with government officials. Later emperors accepted them and Confucianism became China's official religion.

According to tradition, Confucius spent his last years writing down ancient works and his own thoughts. These classics, as they were called, were studied in China for two thousand years.

Fig. 6.12 Confucius, 551–479 BC.

Those who are dull but still won't learn are the lowest type of people.

4 The gentleman understands what is right; the inferior man understands what is profitable.

5 If a ruler himself is upright, all will go well without orders. But if he himself is not upright, even though he gives orders they will not be obeyed.

6 A government is good when those near are happy and those far off are attracted.

7 Do not do to others what you would not want done to yourself.

8 He who learns but does not think is lost; he who thinks but does not learn is in great danger.

The rise of Qin

Rival groups continued to fight for the control of China. Stronger kingdoms took over weaker ones until there were only six main states left in the struggle. The one that emerged as the strongest was the kingdom of Qin in the northwest.
The Qin people were prepared for war. They were organised into military bands based on family and clan groups. Then, 'as a silkworm devours a mulberry leaf', so the Qin armies devoured their enemies. In 221 BC the Zhou king was defeated. China had a new ruler and a new dynasty. The Qin ruler took the name Shi Huangdi, which means 'first emperor', and ordered that from then on his descendants were to be called 'second emperor', 'third emperor' and so on. However the kingdom lasted only for fifteen years — hardly longer than the reign of the first emperor himself.

The Qin dynasty, 221 BC—206 BC

The emperor and his chief adviser, Li Si were determined that enemies of the Qin family would not get a chance to start a rebellion. Li Si believed that he should do everything he could to keep absolute control in the hands of himself and the emperor.

The emperor ordered some members of the noble families to live near his capital city of Xianyang. This helped him and Li Si to keep an eye on what they were doing. The emperor made a law that all metal weapons except those belonging to his own soldiers had to be melted down. This made it even harder for people to rebel against him.

China was divided into districts and the emperor appointed governors to rule each one. He sent trusted soldiers to check up on the governors. He worked out an interesting way to make sure his generals did not make wars without his permission. Each general was given half a bronze model tiger split down the middle. The emperor kept the other half. A general was allowed to attack only when the emperor sent him the other half of his

Fig. 6.13 A tiger tally. The inscription says: 'This is the army tally; the right half is with the emperor; the left half is at Yang-ling.'

tiger. If he fought without both parts of the tiger he would be treated as a rebel and punished.

There were other ways to keep people in check, too. A new system of roads was built to make it easier for the emperor's troops to get to a place where trouble was brewing. The Chinese language was made simpler so that more people could read the emperor's orders. Coins, weights and measurements were made the same throughout the kingdom. There were even laws about the length of axles on carts. The new roads were fifty paces wide. If all the carts were the same width, their wheels would run along the same ruts. This stopped the roads from getting covered with ruts and made travel easier and quicker.

But still Li Si was not satisfied. In 213 BC he suggested to his emperor that the kingdom would never be safe as long as scholars were able to read books that gave them different ideas about how things should be organised. On Li Si's advice the emperor ordered that all books, except those about the Qin family, farming and medicine, should be burned. Some were hidden but most were destroyed. Scholars were questioned about their beliefs and

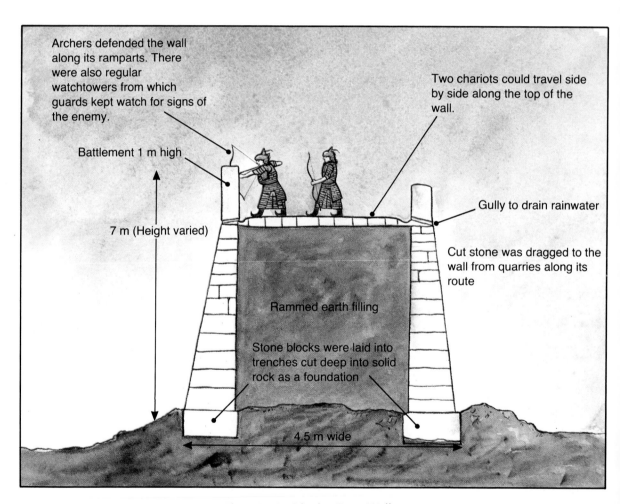

Archers defended the wall along its ramparts. There were also regular watchtowers from which guards kept watch for signs of the enemy.

Two chariots could travel side by side along the top of the wall.

Battlement 1 m high

Gully to drain rainwater

7 m (Height varied)

Cut stone was dragged to the wall from quarries along its route

Rammed earth filling

Stone blocks were laid into trenches cut deep into solid rock as a foundation

4.5 m wide

Fig. 6.14 Inside the Great Wall.

those who would not give up their ideas were killed. More than 400 Confucians were buried alive because they disagreed with the emperor.

The Great Wall

We have seen that China was often threatened by nomads from the north. Many small walls had been built at different times to try and keep these attackers back but none was really successful because they were too far apart and often poorly manned. Emperor Shi Huangdi decided that a great defence wall

Fig. 6.16a

Fig. 6.16b

Fig. 6.15 Part of the Great Wall today. The original wall has been rebuilt several times and little now remains of the wall built during the Qin dynasty.

Figs 6.16a, b, c Chinese soldiers made an extraordinary discovery in 1974. Near the site of Shi Huangdi's tomb they dug up a number of life-sized clay soldiers. Since then about 8000 figures have been found there. The soldiers, each with a different face, were lined up according to rank, and there were charioteers, archers and cavalry mounted on horseback. It was a complete army modelled from clay, ready to defend the emperor in his next life just as they had in this world (see over).

109

Fig. 6.16c See previous page.

would be made, joining up these smaller walls to provide protection once and for all. Thousands of men and women were taken from their villages to make the long journey to the north to build the wall. Among them were soldiers from the armies of the emperor's enemies, no longer able to fight because they had no weapons; criminals whose punishment was to build the wall; and villagers chosen at random by the governors and officials.

Think of the organisation needed to build a wall over 3200 kilometres long, and up to 7.5 metres high and 4.5 metres wide! Architects and builders had first to plan it, and surveyors had to peg out its path. Carts and wagons had to be built, tools had to be made and an army of peasants had to be sent far ahead of where the wall would go to plant and reap food for the workers. Stone had to be cut and shaped and dragged from the quarries to the wall.

The work was done in the worst of conditions: the wind howled from the northern grasslands; the sun beat down in the summer; in the winter snow and ice made life even worse. There were frequent attacks from the barbarians against whom the wall was being built. Food was always in short supply and thousands of workers died either from starvation or exhaustion. Their bodies were simply thrown into the wall, 'the longest graveyard in the world'.

Time to understand

1 During the Qin dynasty iron was used more and more for tools, weapons and implements. What sort of things could have been made from iron? Why do you think this was a better metal to use than bronze?

2 Why did Shi Huangdi go to so much trouble to organise his kingdom efficiently? Do you think any of his policies would have helped ordinary people to lead more comfortable lives?

3 Work in groups to make up a play with this beginning:

> The emperor's messengers ride into your village. All the villagers are rounded up to hear the latest orders, which are as follows: 'All books are to be burned. Anyone who does not hand over his books within thirty days will be branded on the face with a hot iron and sent to work on the Great Wall.' Some villagers want to hand over their books; others do not. What happens?

4 The Great Wall was built in less than fifteen years. What does this tell you about the organisation of the work?

The end of the Qin

The Qin dynasty was organised for war, not peace. The people were weighed down with heavy taxes and forced labour. Even though they may have worked in the fields all day, they rarely had enough to eat; even though they may have made cloth all night, they rarely had enough to wear. The emperor kept apart from his people, knowing that they hated him and fearing that someone, somewhere would kill him.

He died in 210 BC on a journey to the eastern part of his kingdom. His officials were very worried that the people would rise against the Qin dynasty if they knew the hated emperor had died. So they covered his body with rotting fish as it travelled in a cart back to the palace. As the body decomposed, people along the way believed it was the fish that smelled so bad. They did not realise the emperor's body lay underneath.

Time to understand

Si Xian, a historian from the dynasty that followed the Qin, described the burial of the hated emperor Shi Huangdi like this:

> The First Emperor was buried in Mount Li, which had been tunnelled and prepared for him in the early days of his reign. He organised 700 000 soldiers to bore down to the Three Springs. There they placed a stone tomb on a foundation of bronze. Vast numbers of rare objects and precious jewels were collected from around the kingdom and taken to the burial place. Craftsmen were ordered to make mechanical crossbows. These were put at the entrance so that if anyone entered they would fire automatically. Rivers of quicksilver were made. The stars of the sky were carved on the roof of the tomb; a map of the earth on its floor. Candles were made from walrus fat; these would last a long time.
>
> When the emperor had been buried, someone suggested that the workmen knew the wealth that was buried there. Therefore, as soon as the ceremony had been carried out the wall at the entrance to the tunnel was knocked down and the workmen were trapped inside. Trees and grass were then planted around so that the spot would look just like the rest of the mountain.

The mound covering this graveyard was once 166 metres high. Now, after two thousand years, it has worn away so that it is less than forty metres high. What can you learn about ancient China from Si Xian's description and the photographs of the 'entombed warriors' in Figs. 6.16a, b and c?

The last Qin emperor

The next emperor was, if anything, worse. In 209 BC he ordered another group of peasants to the frontier in the north to man the Wall. Nine hundred were held up on their way by floods. They knew they would be killed if they did not arrive on time. They had nothing to lose. Two of them killed the officer guarding them and appealed to the others to join them in a rebellion. Others, who had been forced to flee from their homes and live as outlaws, joined them. Scouts were sent out and a huge peasant army marched to the Qin palace. There they found that the noble families who had themselves been humiliated by the Qin would not help them. Zheng Seng, the peasants' leader, was murdered and the rebellion failed.

The struggle continued for another three years. Finally, in 206 BC, the Qin emperor was killed and his dynasty fell. He had lost his mandate from heaven and, according to

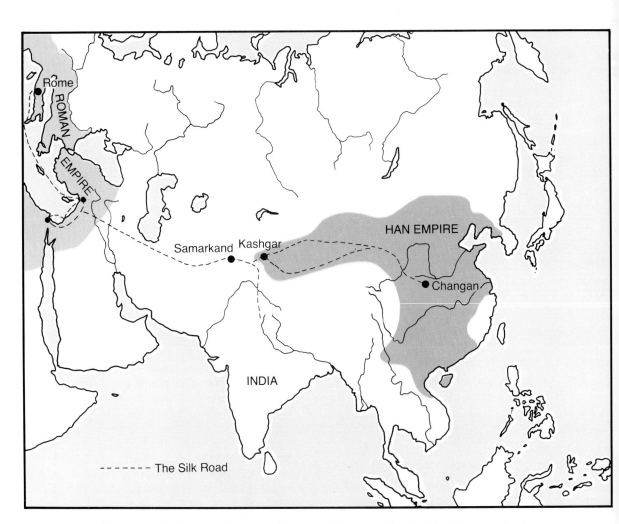

Fig. 6.17 The Han empire — the largest of those studied in this chapter. Was it also the greatest? The silk road was the route traders used as they travelled between the Han and Roman empires. Where do you think its name came from?

the rules, was no longer fit to govern.

Liu Bang, the rebel leader who finally defeated the Qin, came from the peasant class. The Han dynasty he founded was to last for over 400 years.

Time to understand

The Han dynasty was one of China's greatest: in fact the Chinese people were so proud of its achievements that they called themselves 'people of Han'. Many still do.

Much has been written about this period and you should be able to find out quite a lot about it for yourselves. Work in groups to do some research on each of the topics below. If you put all your findings together you will have a class book about the Han dynasty. Do you think the Chinese people are right to feel proud about this period in their history?

1   How Han China was governed
2   The discovery of paper
3   Si Xian, the Han historian
4   Zhang Xian, the explorer
5   Scholar officials and learning
6   The silk road to the west
7   Farming in Han times
8   Cities in Han times
9   Arts and craft
10 How Han China ended

7

Britain before the Romans

For ages and ages . . .

WHEN we are studying things that happened many, many thousands of years ago, it is often hard to remember just *when* these things happened. This is especially hard when we are learning about a long period of history. To help make it easier for people to understand when things happened, the past has been divided into *ages*. The time-line in Fig. 7.1 shows the ages into which the history of Britain has been divided before the Roman invasion in 43 AD.

In the Old Stone Age, Britain was joined to Europe by land because of lower sea levels and so the first people to live in Britain walked there from Europe. They were hunters who moved from place to place in search of the animals they killed for food and clothes. Their homes were caves. We know these people lived in Britain because some of their stone tools have been found there.

The people of the Middle Stone Age were hunters too but by this time the Ice Age was over and the weather had become warmer. You read about the Ice Age and its effects in Chapter One. Warmer weather brought new animals to Britain. So, instead of hunting great hairy mammoths and bisons, people hunted deer, wild cattle and pigs. The warmer weather increased the number and kinds of fish, so the people of the Middle Stone Age became expert fishermen as well as hunters. They learned to make better tools and fishing hooks, nets and spears. They started to use boats made from hollowed-out tree trunks.

In this chapter we shall be concentrating on the last three ages in the time-line: the New Stone Age, or *neolithic* period, the Bronze Age and the Iron Age.

The New Stone Age

Around 3000 BC new people began moving to Britain. By this time the sea level had risen and Britain had become an island, so these new arrivals crossed by boat from Europe to their new home. The

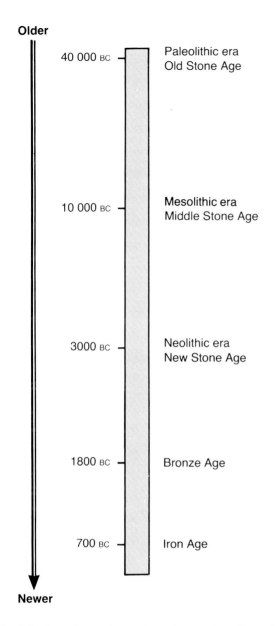

Older

40 000 BC — Paleolithic era
Old Stone Age

10 000 BC — Mesolithic era
Middle Stone Age

3000 BC — Neolithic era
New Stone Age

1800 BC — Bronze Age

700 BC — Iron Age

Newer

Fig. 7.1 From Stone Age to Iron Age: a time-line of British history.

newcomers were different from the people already in Britain, for they were farmers rather than hunters. They cleared the ground with stone axes and planted corn. They harvested it with sickles made of stone and ground it into flour by pounding it with a grindstone.

The people of the New Stone Age herded useful animals into pens and knew how to look after them so that they could be used for food and clothes whenever they were needed. They tamed sheep, cattle, pigs and goats, and used the wool and skins of these animals to make clothes. Like neolithic people in other parts of the world, those who lived in England knew how to make pottery. They also knew how to mine the flint they needed to make tools. Flint is a type of rock that could be easily fashioned into arrowheads and spearheads.

In parts of Britain today there is still evidence of neolithic settlement. From it we can learn quite a lot about the lives of the people of the New Stone Age.

Skara Brae

Skara Brae was a neolithic village in the Orkney Islands north of Scotland. The Orkneys are cold and windswept and the people of Skara Brae must have been very hardy indeed to survive there in their simple stone homes. Thousands of years ago, during a fierce storm, a sand dune covered the village. The people rushed around in panic, not knowing where to run. They left many of their precious goods strewn around their homes as they fled. In 1850 another storm hit the island and the sand dune that had covered the village and protected it for so many years was blown away. Beneath were the stone walls of the ancient village. A street linked the houses, which were shaped like rough circles and were probably once covered with roofs of timber and animal skins. Fig. 7.2 shows part of Skara Brae today.

Inside, the huts were furnished just as they were when the storm hit the village and destroyed it. Fig. 7.3 shows part of the inside of one house. The people of the settlement slept on stone beds, probably

115

Fig. 7.2 Skara Brae, a neolithic village in the Orkney Islands to the north of Scotland.

softened with a layer of heather. Can you see the stone dresser or cupboard in the photograph? Here the people kept their food, clothes and tools. The fireplace was on the floor and nearby was a watertight basin in which water could be stored. Rubbish was piled outside each hut until the whole village was almost buried in its own garbage. It must have been an uncomfortable, smelly place to live in, although the pile of rubbish probably helped to keep the wild winds out and make the village warmer.

Fig. 7.3 Inside a hut at Skara Brae.

Time to understand

1 The diagram in Fig. 7.4 is a plan of the village of Skara Brae as it was in neolithic times. Was it a large village? How many people do you think might have lived there? Why do you think all the houses were so close together?

Fig. 7.4 A plan of Skara Brae showing how the huts were linked by a narrow passageway.

2 The remains of pieces of meat were discovered in some of the beds at Skara Brae. Perhaps the villagers were eating a meal in bed as they sheltered from the wild storm outside. When the sand dune started covering the village, one woman was in such a rush to escape that her necklace broke as she squeezed through her narrow doorway. The beads were still there, scattered along the passageway as she ran, when the settlement was discovered thousands of years later.

Divide into groups and imagine you were the villagers of Skara Brae the day the storm came. Some could be farmers, others fishermen, some children and some women at home or out working with the men. Make up a play about the last day of your lives. What did you do when the storm began? When did you know it was going to be more dangerous than other storms? Where did you go to shelter? What happened when the sand dune began covering your village? Act out the play to the others in your class. Then you could put the best ideas together to make a play to act for other classes.

Windmill Hill

One of the interesting things about aerial photography — taking photos from the air — is that it sometimes shows us things that we cannot see easily from the ground. In Chapter One you read how archaeologists can learn about the past by studying aerial photographs.

Aerial photography helps us to see patterns in things — patterns that we cannot see clearly at ground level. The photograph in Fig. 7.5 is a good example of this. It shows Windmill Hill in southern England, one of many neolithic camps where people gathered to round up animals and enjoy feasts. In the photograph you can see part of three circular ditches dug around the highest part of a hill. The earth from the ditches was built up into banks. Spaces were left between the banks and ditches. The animals were herded through these gaps to the top of the hill and then hurdles or

Fig. 7.5 Windmill Hill from the air.

barriers were put up across the gaps to stop the animals getting out again.

It seems that every autumn the people of a clan or large family group met at a place like Windmill Hill to round up their animals and kill many of them for food to keep them going through the winter. The meat was smoked in their fires. For the rest of the year the families split up so that each had its own grazing lands. We can tell that round-up time was feast time because of all the animal bones lying around the fires that were built there to cook and smoke the meat.

Not far from Windmill Hill, at West Kennet, is a large grave. This type of grave is called a *long barrow*. You can see a photograph of its entrance in Fig. 7.6. It is one of many neolithic tombs found in Britain. The huge stones from which this and other long barrows were built were probably dragged to the site on rollers made from tree trunks. Inside the barrow was a long passage and on both sides of the passage were burial rooms lined with stone. The entrance, as you can see, was lined with large stone slabs, with a particularly big slab acting as a door. The earth dug out from the barrow was

Fig. 7.6 The entrance to West Kennet barrow, showing the stones lined up around the entrance and the huge stone at the 'doorway'. This stone is four metres high.

put over the top to make a huge mound. About thirty adults and children were buried in the long barrow.

Time to understand

People in the New Stone Age believed in gods and goddesses. Little has remained to tell us about the religious beliefs of the New Stone Age people in Britain, but we do know that they built great stone circles which were probably linked with their religion. These circles are scattered in many parts of Britain. In many places only a few stones remain today, because through the ages people have used them to build houses or walls. From the air, however, we can get a good idea of the original shape of the stone circles because the banks and ditches that were built as a kind of wall around the stone circles can still be seen.

Avebury is a village about a kilometre away from the long barrow at West Kennet. Fig. 7.8 shows what the village looks like today. Can you see the unusual circle around the modern village?

About 5000 years ago a great temple was built at Avebury by neolithic people. It may have been a temple to the sun. You can see what this monument once looked like by studying the drawing in Fig. 7.7. The bank was 425 metres across and the ditch inside it was once 10 metres deep. The bank and ditch enclosed an area of more than 11 hectares. Use the drawing to write a description of the temple at Avebury. You could also make a model of it with papier-mache and small stones. Do you think we are right in thinking that Avebury and other stone circles are religious monuments? Why? Can you think of any other reasons why they might have been built?

Fig. 7.7 Avebury about 5000 years ago. The ditch may have been filled with water to emphasise that the temple was separated from the area around it.

Fig. 7.8 Avebury today. Part of the modern village is inside the ancient circle. What remnants can you see of the neolithic monument?

The Bronze Age

Around 1800 BC new people started crossing from Europe to Britain. Some carried with them knives, daggers, brooches and ornaments made from the metal called bronze. It was this change from stone to bronze that gave the period its name: the Bronze Age. Of course, for many people things did not change at all, at least for some time. They kept on using their tools of stone, farming their land and grazing their animals as they always had. But bronze was easier to work and shape than stone and over the years people learned how to use it to make their lives more comfortable.

Most people could not make bronze for themselves. Instead, they bought their bronze implements from travelling bronzesmiths. The bronzesmiths bought tin and copper from traders. When they were ready to make something out of bronze, they first had to melt the tin and copper together in a clay pot set in a very hot fire. When the tin and copper had melted together to make bronze, the hot liquid was poured into moulds the shape of axeheads, spearheads or whatever the smith wanted to

Fig. 7.9 What a farm may have looked like in the Bronze Age.

make. When the tools were hard, they were sharpened with a heavy stone hammer.

Bronze Age people lived in family groups called clans. The chieftains of these clans were obviously richer than the ordinary farmers. They and their families wore ornaments of bronze and gold — bracelets, necklaces, brooches and buttons. These people drank from cups made from bronze and stored water in bronze buckets.

Farming

The drawing in Fig. 7.9 shows what a farm in the Bronze Age may have looked like. The houses were huts made from wood and dried mud with thatched roofs. You can see from the picture that the houses were surrounded by fences. The fences kept the animals in at night. Outside the enclosures, farmers ploughed fields with simple ploughs pulled by two oxen. The people of the Bronze Age were the first to use ploughs like this. Ploughs made their work easier and made it possible for them to grow more food for themselves and their animals. In the land beyond the ploughed fields the people gathered wood and berries. Here, too, their animals grazed on the summer grasses.

Stonehenge

The most famous monument from the Bronze Age is Stonehenge, on the Salisbury Plain in southern England. Like the stone circles of neolithic times, Stonehenge was a religious building, perhaps a temple or sanctuary in which people praised and worshipped their gods. In fact, Stonehenge was started in neolithic times. Perhaps as early as 2600 BC a ditch and bank were built. Inside the ditch was a circle of small pits, many of which contained the ashes of people who had been cremated. Four or five hundred years later, an avenue of earth banks was built from the monument to the river Avon, about a kilometre away. Sixty bluestones, each weighing about four tonnes, were brought to the site from south Wales, many kilometres away. They were placed in a double circle inside the bank and ditch.

Two hundred years later more stones were taken to Stonehenge. Some of them can still be seen there today. These blocks, which were dragged from a quarry more than 30 kilometres away, weighed up to 50 tonnes each. Some were as high as 7 metres. Eighty of these stones were carefully shaped so that they would fit

Fig. 7.10 Part of Stonehenge today. Compare this with the diagram in Fig. 7.12. Which parts can you see in the modern picture?

finished. The biggest stones were set up inside the circle, with the largest in the centre and the smaller pairs forming a horseshoe shape around them. The stones were placed so that on midsummer morning the first rays of the morning sun would fall between them. Most of the bluestones from the old temple were put back in a circle inside the new stone circle. The biggest bluestones were placed in a horseshoe shape inside the new horseshoe.

Fig. 7.11 The building of Stonehenge. The top drawing shows how the circle was marked out. Below you can see how an upright stone was shaped into a point at the top and how the lintels were chipped away to make holes into which the upright stones could fit. The bottom picture shows how each lintel was shaped and moulded so that together they would form a circle.

together in the way the people wanted. The diagrams in Fig. 7.11 show you how this was done.

The diagram in Fig. 7.12 shows what Stonehenge looked like when it was

Time to understand

There is a lot that we do not know about Stonehenge. Here are some questions and ideas about this ancient monument. Discuss each one and see if you can think of some answers to problems that have puzzled people for many years.

1 How were the lintels put on top of the standing stones? Did the builders use platforms of logs, perhaps? Or did they make ramps of earth leading to the top of the stones? Did they build Stonehenge in winter and use packed snow as a way of reaching the top of the stone circle? Legends tell of giants who could move stones with magic powers. Could they have built Stonehenge? Draw some diagrams of possible ways of getting the lintels on top of the standing stones.

2 How were the bluestones brought from Wales? Use an atlas to find the Prescelly Mountains in south Wales, where the stones came from, and the Salisbury Plain in England, where Stonehenge was built. What do you think were the most likely ways the stones would have been taken to Stonehenge? What does this tell us about this group of people in the Bronze Age?

3 Look at the picture of the Lion Gate at Mycenae in Chapter Nine (Fig. 9.7 on p. 154). In what way is the Lion Gate like

Fig. 7.12 Stonehenge in the Bronze Age. Can you see the upright stones topped with lintels? The horseshoe of lintel-topped stones inside? The circle of smaller bluestones? The horseshoe of bluestones inside the circle?

Stonehenge? The Lion Gate was built at about the same time as Stonehenge. Did the people who built Stonehenge influence the building of the Lion Gate? Or did those who built the Lion Gate travel to Britain and help with the design and building of Stonehenge? A carving of a Greek dagger has been found on one of the stone blocks of Stonehenge. Does this throw any light on the mystery?

4 Why was Stonehenge built? Computers have shown that the circles of Stonehenge can be used to give an accurate calculation of the movements of the sun, moon and stars during the year. Stonehenge can be used to predict eclipses. If Stonehenge is an ancient calendar, the people who built it must have had an extremely good understanding of astronomy and mathematics.

The Iron Age: Celtic Britain

Greek traders had a name for the tribes of people living in the forests around the Danube River. They called them 'Keltoi', and from this has come our word 'Celt' to describe these people. The Celts were the next group to invade Britain. They took with them an important new metal: iron. The Celtic period is therefore part of the Iron Age.

The Celts were not one people. They were a group of races who spoke a similar language and had similar customs. The map in Fig. 7.14 (over) shows how the Celts expanded from their early homes in central Europe east, west and across the channel into Britain. Many Celts still live in Britain. They are descended from two main tribes: the Britons, who settled in Wales and Cornwall, and the Gaels, who settled in Ireland and Scotland. The Gaelic Celts were among the first to go to Britain — perhaps as early as the eighth century BC. They were later pushed into the remote regions of Ireland and Scotland by the Britons, who invaded in about 500 BC.

What the Celts looked like

The Celts were tall people, strong and fit. They looked quite fearsome to their enemies partly because of their hairstyles. Warriors soaked their hair in water mixed with chalk to make it thick and fair. When it dried, it was stiff. Most Celtic men wore moustaches. One Roman wrote that they let their moustaches grow so long and straggly that their food was always getting tangled up in them.

Fig. 7.13 A bronze mirror, decorated with swirling, flowing patterns.

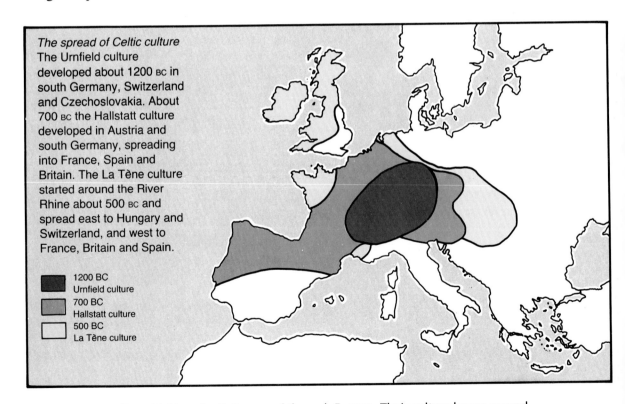

The spread of Celtic culture
The Urnfield culture developed about 1200 BC in south Germany, Switzerland and Czechoslovakia. About 700 BC the Hallstatt culture developed in Austria and south Germany, spreading into France, Spain and Britain. The La Tène culture started around the River Rhine about 500 BC and spread east to Hungary and Switzerland, and west to France, Britain and Spain.

- 1200 BC Urnfield culture
- 700 BC Hallstatt culture
- 500 BC La Tène culture

Fig. 7.14 How the Celts spread through Europe. Their culture began around 1200 BC in central Europe and from there spread east, west and north. The Celts were never a united people.

Celtic women wore their hair long, either flowing or braided and pinned with gold or bronze pins. Fashionable women dyed their eyebrows black and put berry juice on their face to darken their lips and cheeks. Fig. 7.13 shows a bronze mirror used by Celtic women. One side was highly polished. The back, as you can see, was decorated with a swirling pattern.

The Celts seemed to like bright colours. Their trousers, cloaks and gowns were often decorated with contrasting threads woven into the material in geometric patterns. Checks were popular. They were also fond of jewellery. Many brooches, cloak pins, armlets and necklaces have been discovered by archaeologists.

Time to understand

Use the description of the Celts in this section to draw a picture of a Celtic family.

Living in tribes

The Celts lived in tribes, each ruled by its own king or queen. There were often battles between different tribes, and the chief of a small tribe often had to give hostages to the chief of a stronger tribe to make sure that his people were not attacked. Each tribe was made up of a number of large families, or kins. Each kin had the responsibility of making sure that its members did not break the tribe's laws. If someone in one kin committed a crime against a member of another kin — stealing, for example, or even murder — he or she was fined by the tribe. The fine depended on the crime and on the importance of the family in the tribe. Every freeman had his value or 'honour

price'. It was paid by the kin of the wrongdoer to the kin of the victim.

The diagram in Fig. 7.15 (over) shows how Celtic society was organised. The warriors, druids, craftsmen and farmers were all freemen. They could attend the tribe's meetings and were allowed to be part of a kin. The serfs and slaves, on the other hand, were not freemen. Serfs were the descendants of tribes that had once been conquered. They were allowed to farm a small patch of land but could not attend assemblies or belong to a kin. Slaves were usually prisoners of war. They had even fewer rights than the serfs.

The druids had a special part to play in society. They were the Celtic priests. Their name may have come from a Celtic word meaning 'knowledge of the oak', for the Celts believed that the oak tree was sacred. The druids chanted prayers at religious ceremonies and made sacrifices to the gods and goddesses. There may have been human sacrifices as well as animals. Some of the druids lived with the chiefs and warriors; others lived in separate sanctuaries in the forests.

Only the sons of noblemen could become druids. It took many years for them to learn all the secrets of the tribe's religion. All the knowledge was passed on by word of mouth; nothing was written down. As well as looking after the religion of the tribe, the druids also handed down the tribal laws. Because the people were afraid of them, the druids held great power in the tribe.

The Celts believed that it was good fortune to cut off the head of a captured enemy and keep it around them. Sometimes they put the heads on posts which they kept in their homes or carried with them into battle; sometimes they embalmed the heads and displayed them in their shrines.

A hill-fort

Celtic Britain was not a peaceful place. We have seen that tribes often fought each other. Later, they had to defend themselves against the mighty Roman army. The Celts built defended settlements on the tops of hills where they could live in safety when threatened by an enemy. The photograph in Fig. 7.17 (p. 128) shows

King or Queen

Warriors

Druids

Craftsmen

Farmers

Serfs and slaves

Fig. 7.15 A Celtic tribe. Each tribe was made up of a number of families.

what remains of Maiden Castle, a hill-fort in Dorset in southern England. It was built on the site of a much earlier neolithic camp. The banks, or ramparts, of a hill-fort were built of stone, often brought to the site in loads. These ramparts were up to 10 metres thick and were sometimes built around a framework of wooden posts set in holes dug out with picks made from iron or deer antlers. Maiden Castle covered an area of more than 18 hectares

and, as you can see, was protected by three ramparts and ditches. The ditches were 6 metres deep and up to 15 metres wide.

Time to understand

1 The drawing in Fig. 7.16 shows what a Celtic hill-fort probably looked like. Use the picture and what you know of the

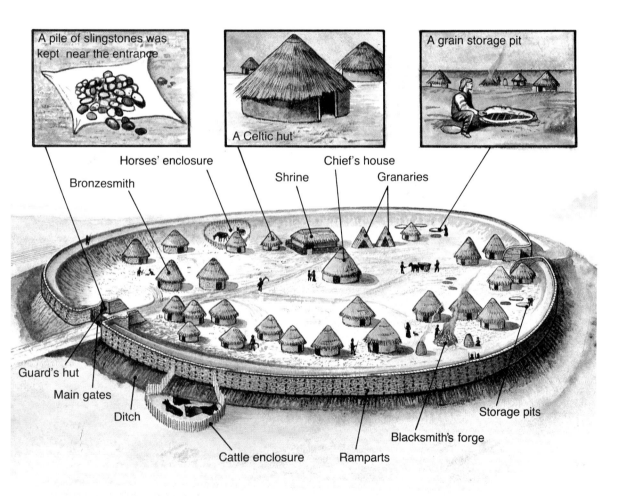

A pile of slingstones was kept near the entrance

A Celtic hut

A grain storage pit

Horses' enclosure

Bronzesmith

Shrine

Chief's house

Granaries

Guard's hut

Main gates

Ditch

Cattle enclosure

Ramparts

Blacksmith's forge

Storage pits

Fig. 7.16 A Celtic hill-fort.

Celts to answer the questions below.

a Where was grain stored in the hill-fort? Why did the Celts need to store grain in the fort? How was the grain cooked?

b Write a description of Celtic homes, using the evidence of this picture. Can you guess what they were made from?

c Why do you think the chief's house was in the centre of the hill-fort?

d Why was a bronzesmith's hut built in the hill-fort? What sort of things would the bronzesmith have made?

e Why was a blacksmith's forge part of the hill-fort? What sort of things would the blacksmith have made?

f Why do you think a shrine was built in the hill-fort?

g What do you think would have been the weakest point of a hill-fort? How did the Celts try to defend this point?

h How did the ditch help the Celts defend the hill-fort?

i How do you think the people inside the hill-fort got supplies of fresh water for themselves and their animals? Would this have been a problem when the hill-fort was being attacked?

j If you were an enemy of the tribe of Celts who built this hill-fort, how would you attack it? What problems would you have to face? Do you think your attack would be successful? Why?

2 Archaeologists have found whole skeletons of pigs, sheep and cows buried in pits in Celtic hill-forts. They were not killed for food because if this were so their bones would have been scattered. Can you suggest why these animals were killed and buried?

Fig. 7.17 Maiden Castle from the air today. The inside bank is about a kilometre around. Can you see the maze-like entrances at the left and right of the photograph? How would these help the defenders of the hill-fort?

Fig. 7.18 A Roman arrow head still embedded in an enemy's backbone. This man was killed when the Romans attacked Maiden Castle soon after 43 AD. The archaeologist who discovered the bones wrote that the arrow had entered the body from below the heart and that the victim had been finished off with a cut on the head.

Celtic art and craft

The Celts used iron to make their tools and weapons because it was a strong, hard metal. But they still used bronze for decoration and to make things that had to be carried about. The shield in Fig. 7.20 (over) was made from bronze and gold. Chiefs and nobles wore jewellery made of gold and electrum, a mixture of silver and gold. Among the most beautiful ornaments made by the Celts were thick neck-rings called torcs. These were made of twisted strands of metal with hollow, decorated ends were worn around the neck.

The Celts were obviously gifted metalworkers. They loved geometric patterns, abstract designs and strange animal and human shapes. They also produced many other kinds of art. The illustrations in Figs 7.19–7.22 will give you some idea of their skill.

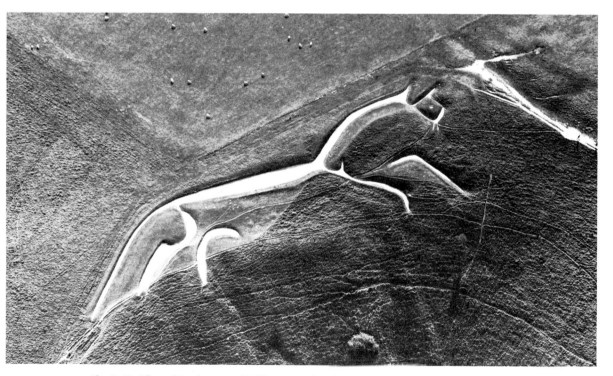

Fig. 7.19 The white horse of Uffington. This figure was drawn in chalk on the downs, probably in the first century BC. It is 120 metres long from nose to tail. The horse — or is it a dragon? — is hard to see from the ground but stands out from the air. Could it have been a signal to the ancient gods?

Telling stories

We have already learned that the laws of the Celts were passed down from one generation to another. In the same way their stories and legends were passed on. Poets or *bards* told these stories at feasts and ceremonies. The favourite stories were about great men of the past. One of the most famous of these was Cuchullain, champion warrior of the Ulster people in Ireland. According to legend, he defended the tribe single-handedly against an enemy army.

Time to understand

The diagram in Fig. 7.22 shows a few Celtic 'whirligigs'. These designs were often put together to make a much larger pattern. They were carved into stone or moulded on to bronze ornaments, jewellery or shields. Use these whirligigs to design your own Celtic design. You may be able to get

Fig. 7.20 The Battersea shield, made by the Celts in the late Iron Age. This shield was found in the Thames River at Battersea in London. The patterns were hammered onto the shield from the back and decorated with small enamelled studs.

Fig. 7.21 An electrum torque made of eight wire cables, each made up of eight separate strands.

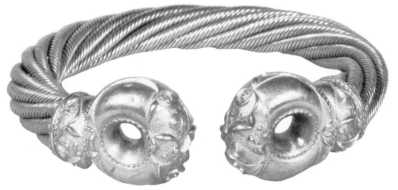

some ideas about patterns to use by looking carefully at the Celtic objects in this chapter.

The end of a world

From about 500 BC to 250 BC the Celts were the most powerful people in Europe. They stretched from Russia in the east to Spain in the west. But in the third century BC the Romans defeated the Celts in northern Italy. As the Romans became more powerful they expanded into other parts of Europe, conquering the Celts and taking over their land.

In 43 AD the Romans attacked Britain. Some of the Celts — the Belgae — fought bitterly against the invaders but other tribes who had themselves been attacked by the Belgae fought on the side of the Romans. South-east England was soon conquered by the Romans but many Celts fled to Ireland, Wales and Scotland. These areas were never fully conquered by the Romans.

Fig. 7.22 Some patterns from Celtic art.

Time to understand

1 A few Celts have become famous for their part in defending their country against the Roman invasions. Two of these people were Caratacus and Boudicca (sometimes spelt Boadicea).

Find out more about these two Celts by looking up their names in an encyclopaedia or other reference book. What did they do to try to save their people?

2 Welsh and Gaelic are Celtic languages. Both are still spoken in the British Isles today. Where do you think these languages are spoken? Why?

The rise and fall of Minoan Crete

So the story goes . . .

OUT IN THE DARK blue sea there lies a land called Crete, a rich and lovely land, washed by waves on every side, densely peopled and boasting ninety cities . . . One of the ninety towns is a great city called Knossos, and there, for nine years, King Minos ruled and enjoyed the friendship of almighty Zeus.

Under the palace of Knossos, so the story goes, there is a labyrinth, or maze — the home of the fearsome minotaur, half-man and half-bull. The labyrinth has been so well made by King Minos's chief craftsman, Daedalus, that no one has ever found out how to escape from it. The minotaur, it seems, is indestructible.

Minos is a powerful king and with his strong navy he controls the waters around Crete. He conquers the city of Athens in Greece and demands that each year the Athenians send him seven young men and seven young women to be sacrificed to the minotaur. This is a constant reminder of his strength and power.

In the third year Theseus, the prince of Athens, volunteers to go to Crete as one of the young men to be sacrificed to the minotaur. He vows to kill the minotaur and break the power of King Minos. They sail from Athens in a black-sailed ship, a symbol of the death they are going to meet. Theseus promises his father, Aegeus, that if he kills the minotaur he will set a white sail for the return voyage.

When Theseus enters the palace at Knossos, Ariadne, the daughter of King Minos, falls in love with him. She and Daedalus together work out a plan to save his life. Theseus volunteers to be the first to enter the labyrinth and face the minotaur. Ariadne gives him a ball of thread which Theseus ties to the entrance of the labyrinth and unwinds as he goes through its twisting passages.

At last he faces the minotaur. As it charges towards him, bellowing with rage, Theseus strikes it over the heart with his fist. Time and again he does this until the mighty creature begins to weaken. Finally Theseus seizes it by the horns and pulls its neck back until the bones break. The minotaur lies dead.

Theseus follows the thread back to the entrance of the labyrinth. He and Ariadne, with the other Athenians, sail from Crete in the dead of night. They stop to rest on the island of Naxos but there their good fortune runs out. The god Dionysius falls in love with Ariadne and carries her off as she sleeps. In triumph he hurls her crown into the sky, where it still shines as a group of stars.

Theseus is heartbroken and forgets to hoist the white sail. His father Aegeus, watching from the cliffs, sees the ship coming back with its black sail and throws himself into the water below.

This story comes from an old Greek legend. The words at the beginning of the chapter are translated from the *Odyssey*, an epic poem by Homer, one of the greatest ancient Greek poets. Only a hundred years ago few people would have believed that Crete was once 'densely populated . . . boasting ninety cities'. Crete today is still a beautiful island, but it is an island of villages and small towns. Its people are mainly farmers, and sheep and goat grazers, not city dwellers.

Today we know that Homer was right. Crete *was* once an island of great palaces and cities. We know too that four or five thousand years ago it was a centre of civilisation, similar in many ways to Sumer and Egypt. We know that around 1400 BC this society was struck down by great disasters. It vanished almost without trace. Only the legends kept alive the idea that Crete was once a force to be reckoned with and that its people lived in a way unknown to most other people of the time.

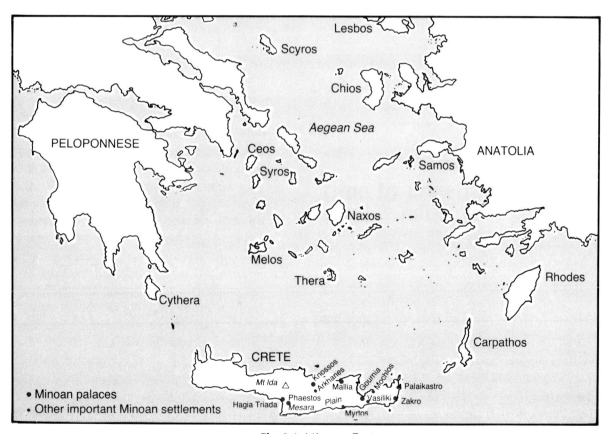

Fig. 8.1 Minoan Crete.

Time to understand

1 According to the legend, King Minos's craftsman, Daedalus, helped Ariadne in her plan to save Theseus from the minotaur. When King Minos realised this, he imprisoned Daedalus and his son Icarus to stop them leaving Crete. Daedalus, however, was a brilliant engineer and he invented a clever way of escape.

Use a book of Greek legends to find out how Daedalus and Icarus escaped from Crete. What happened to each of them after they had made their escape?

Fig. 8.2 Theseus and the minotaur.

2 The sea between Greece and western Asia is called the Aegean Sea. Can you guess why? (Read the story again!)

3 Do people still make up stories about strange monsters and beasts? Are today's monsters at all like the minotaur? Why?

4 Draw a comic strip to illustrate the story of Theseus and the minotaur.

In the beginning

The first known people to live on the island of Crete were neolithic or New Stone Age people who settled there about 6000 BC. They grew crops, fished in the waters around the island and grazed sheep, cattle and goats. Like other neolithic

Fig. 8.3 The ruins of the palace of Knossos (see pp. 137–140)

Fig. 8.4 Columns at the entrance to the Hall of the Shields at Knossos (see pp. 137–140). They taper from top to bottom. The columns were made from wood, and the tree-trunks were put in upside down. Perhaps it was to stop them from sprouting again!

135

people, they lived in mud-brick houses. Gradually they developed skills in making pottery, building, spinning and weaving.

After perhaps 3000 years, the Cretans were joined by a new group of migrants, in about 3000 BC. These newcomers, who had probably travelled from western Asia, brought with them the skill of working with metal: copper, bronze, silver and gold. We have seen in other chapters how important this skill was in the way a group of people developed. The newcomers also brought links with their homeland and other parts of the world. The population grew quickly and metal tools replaced the older stone ones. Drills, chisels, saws and nails made building easier, and craftsmen such as goldsmiths, jewellers and bronzesmiths began producing beautiful objects.

This Bronze Age civilisation flourished in Crete for almost two thousand years. During this time roads and bridges were built and Cretan merchants sailed to many parts of the known world. Cities were built: Phaestos, Mallia, Knossos and Zakro, for example. The largest and most powerful of these cities was Knossos. The kings of Knossos not only ruled their own people but also had power over the other kings.

The civilisation of Bronze Age Crete has been called the 'Minoan' civilisation, after the legendary King Minos. Around 1700 BC a violent earthquake hit the island and destroyed most of its buildings. New and grander buildings were built in their place. The ruins of many of these buildings have now been discovered and explored, and from them we can learn a great deal about the achievements of Minoan Crete. One of the most important pieces of evidence is what remains of the palace of Knossos, rebuilt after the earthquake on the site of an earlier palace. Before looking more closely at this palace, it is worth learning how it came to be found.

Time to understand

Find Crete in a modern atlas. Can you see the western coast of Asia? How do you think the Bronze Age newcomers got to Crete?

Rediscovering the past

Few civilisations were so completely lost as Minoan Crete. Even in the eighth century BC, when Homer was writing, it was a land of legends. Until the end of the nineteenth century, the Crete of King Minos was thought to be nothing more than a myth.

The man who brought the past to life was Sir Arthur Evans, an English archaeologist. He became interested in Crete when he was shown some small seal engraved with drawings and symbols. He believed that this was the writing of an ancient people and that those people once lived in Crete. Evans was rich enough to be able to buy the rights to dig on the hill where he believed the palace of Knossos once stood. In 1900 he began work there.

Within a few days of digging, his team had discovered fragments of painted pottery and clay. Sometimes they were only as large as the palm of a hand but they had not lost their colour and could be put together to make vases and jars. In the same way, fragments of plaster were matched up to make frescoes or wall paintings. Day after day they discovered more of the great palace. The architect with the expedition became more and more confused. There seemed to be no plan to it; it was like a great honeycomb.

Sir Arthur Evans worked on Crete until 1936. He discovered not only a buried city but a whole lost civilisation. With his own funds he restored part of the palace of Knossos to what it probably looked like in Minoan times. Later archaeologists working in Crete have found and excavated several other sites of Minoan civilisation on the island. The work is still going on; there may be much more to learn.

The palace of Knossos

The palace at Knossos covered more than a hectare. It was built on the side of a hill and some parts were four storeys high while other parts were only two storeys. The walls were made of unbaked brick, and wood was sometimes used for the columns, doors and window frames. The roof was flat and supported by high pillars. The plastered walls were often decorated with colourful frescoes.

The rooms were built around a central courtyard, 60 metres long and 30 metres wide. There were areas for living in, for storage, for workshops, for official business and for worship. It was almost a whole city in itself.

Fig. 8.5 A reconstruction of the west wing of the palace of Knossos — one small part of a mighty building.

Fig. 8.6 The throne room of King Minos. The gypsum throne was flanked by stone benches where the king's advisers sat as they discussed state matters.

Fig. 8.7 The storerooms at the palace. Grain, wine, oil and precious stones were stored in the rectangular bins below ground level.

Fig. 8.8 Painted dolphins on a wall of the queen's quarters in the palace. Can you suggest why the Cretans often painted these and other sea-creatures?

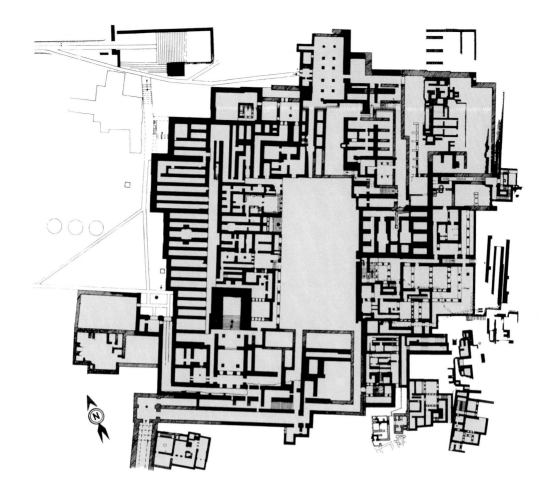

Fig. 8.9 A plan of the palace of Knossos.

The northern part of the palace was the manufacturing centre where the artists and craftsmen worked. West of the central court were the throne rooms and shrines. The king was the high priest as well as ruler, and with these two positions you can imagine that he was a very powerful man. There were long storage rooms here too. The people paid their taxes in grain, oil and wine and all these goods were stored in the palace. They were kept in large pottery jars, sometimes taller than the people who made them. The photograph in Fig. 8.7 shows a few of these jars that were discovered by Arthur Evans. In the east were the royal apartments, which were approached by a great staircase.

There were several sunken bathrooms in the palace. Their walls were beautifully decorated, often with pictures of dolphins. There were no taps on the deep baths, so they were probably filled by servants. There were no plugholes either, so the servants must have had to bale out the water when the king and his family had finished their baths. Some of the water for the baths and flushing toilets came from natural springs; some came from rainwater and was collected from gutters in the roof. Pipes ran under the floors and there were

139

Fig. 8.10 Models of Minoan houses, about five centimetres high, made from glazed pottery.

manhole covers to allow servants to check the system regularly.

You can see from the diagram in Fig. 8.9 that the palace at Knossos was built rather like a maze, with hundreds of linked halls, corridors, rooms, courts, balconies and terraced gardens. In fact, the word 'labyrinth' may have come from the palace itself. Many of the walls were decorated with paintings of the double axe or *labrys*, the symbol of the Cretan mother goddess. There is a picture of this double axe in Fig. 8.14.

Time to understand

1 Many people believe that the palace at Knossos was one of the most imaginative and original buildings ever built. Use the photographs and diagrams in this section to explain why.
2 'The palace at Knossos was home, warehouse, parliament house and temple all in one.' What does this mean?

Life in Minoan Crete

Minoan Crete was at its best in the sixteenth and fifteenth centuries BC. At its peak Knossos and the harbour port nearby may have been the home of 100 000 people. Most of them lived crowded together like bees in a hive. Their houses were small with flat roofs and tiny windows. Richer people lived in country mansions, which were rather like smaller and simpler versions of the royal palaces.

Time to understand

Fig. 8.10 shows some tiny clay tablets showing pictures of Cretan houses. They are only 5 centimetres high. On paper or cardboard the same size as these tablets, draw a series of pictures showing some house styles of today. Are they at all like the houses of Minoan Crete?

Food

The Cretans of Minoan times ate pretty much the same sort of food as they do today. There was pork, mutton and goat meat, fish and wild game such as hares, ducks and partridges. Bread was made from wheat and barley grown on the island, and milk and cheese came from sheep and goats. Fruit, nuts, olives and honey were plentiful. Cooking was done over charcoal grates. The royal family and nobles used fine pottery eating and cooking utensils; the poor made do with much simpler things.

Clothes

Cretan women wore long, colourful flounced dresses with tight bodices. Their breasts were left bare. Sometimes patterns made with gold leaf were sewn onto the dresses. Their hair was always elaborately done, and they wore beads and jewels around their necks and wrists. They must have spent a lot of time putting on their make-up and curling their hair. Men wore a kilt or loincloth, tight belt and sandals or high leather boots. They were bare-chested, except in cooler weather when they put on a cape.

Religion

The Cretans worshipped their gods at shrines either in the royal palaces or outside high on the island's mountains or in sacred caves. In cracks in the walls of some caves great stores of goods have been found: weapons, double axes and ornaments. These were gifts to the gods.

The chief gods of the Cretans were a mother goddess and a young god who was probably her son. The mother goddess was often shown with snakes, flowers or birds beside her. The statues in Fig. 8.13 (over) may show the mother goddess, or perhaps one of her priestesses.

Recreation

The Minoans loved spectacles and shows. Bull leaping was a favourite amusement, but tumbling and acrobatics, boxing and wrestling were all popular too. Musicians, acrobats, dancers and jugglers lived at the palace. There was even a paved area surrounded by seats where they performed for the nobility. At times such as the beginning of spring there were festivals where young people sang and danced to the accompaniment of pipes and lyres.

The Minoans also enjoyed board games. Some of the boards they played on were beautifully made and inlaid with gold and jewels. One found at Knossos measured about a metre by half a metre.

Imagine . . .

The people of Knossos have gathered around the great court in the palace. The king and royal family are in their place of honour. Nobles, craftsmen, farmers and children have made their way to the palace from all over the island. There are so many people that the stands cannot fit them all and they spill out on to the area around. They are excited and restless while they wait for the sport to begin.

At last a group of tall young men and women enter the ring. They carry no weapons. A bull is released among them. Confused by the noise and the crowds, it turns this way and that. One of the young men lures it towards him. As the bull rushes at him, its head down charging, the youth stands without moving. Just as he is about to be gored he seizes the bull's horns and holds them as he springs over the angry bull. This performance is

Fig. 8.11 This wall painting at Knossos shows the Cretan sport of bull-leaping. The girl on the left is grasping the bull's horns ready to somersault; the youth is making his somersault and the girl on the right steadies the acrobats as they land. The first bull-leapers were princes and princesses; later slaves and common people performed for the royal family.

Fig. 8.12 This fresco at the north entrance to the palace shows a charging bull.

Fig. 8.13 These statues, about thirty centimetres high, were found in the ruins of Knossos. The larger one has a snake curling around its arms and stretching towards its tiara. The smaller statue is holding a snake in each hand. The figures probably represent the snake goddess, or possibly the earth mother.

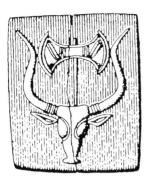

Fig. 8.14 The two symbols of Minoan Crete — the bull's head and the double axe — engraved on a stone seal at Knossos.

Fig. 8.17 A ceremonial cup, or rhyton, shaped like the head of a bull. The horns were of gold, the eyes of rock crystal and the muzzle of mother-of-pearl.

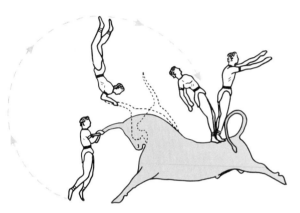

Fig. 8.15 How young Cretans leapt bulls?

Fig. 8.16 A gold pendant, showing two bees sucking a drop of honey, from a Cretan necklace.

Fig. 8.18 A fresco from the southern entrance showing servants carrying ceremonial cups into the palace at Knossos.

repeated several times as others lure the bull towards them and wait until the last moment before they leap over its back. One young woman misses. The bull's horns go straight into her chest and a stream of blood gushes out. There is nothing anyone can do to save her.

The game is nearly over. The bull is tired and confused. When the last leaper has left the ring it is captured and bound in nets. Servants drag it to the king who rises up and slays it with his double axe. The bull is dead and the double axe is put on top of its head as a symbol of the victory.

Time to understand

Think again about the legend of Theseus and the minotaur at the beginning of this chapter. Using what you have learnt about the palace at Knossos and the Cretan sport of bull leaping, suggest how this legend may have come about.

Art

Minoan artists were very skilled, as you can see from the illustrations in this chapter. They were particularly clever at portraying the world of nature — the animals, plants and flowers of their land, and the fish and sea creatures of the waters around their island. Some of the best artworks made in Minoan Crete were small bronze figures, gold jewellery, stone vases and jars, and ivory carvings. We have seen already that the frescoes or wall paintings in the palace at Knossos give us a good idea of palace life.

A mystery

When Arthur Evans was digging in the ruins of Knossos he came upon a mystery picture. He found ten fragments of painting that together seemed to make up a picture of a person gathering crocus flowers. You can see the bits of painting he found in Fig. 8.19, with the dotted lines showing where the rest of the painting probably fitted. But the person was blue.

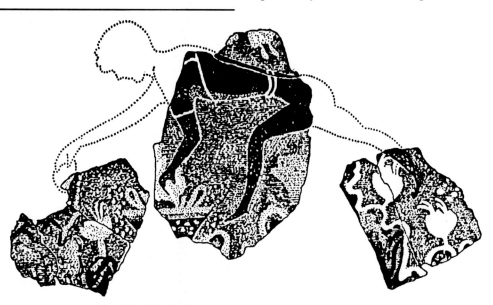

Fig. 8.19 The 'saffron gatherer': boy or monkey?

It was a rule in Minoan art that men were always painted reddish brown and women were always painted white. So where did this blue person come from?

When Evans looked more closely at the picture he found that it was hard to distinguish the hand from the foot. Also, the figure was crouching as if moving on all fours. Perhaps it was not a human after all.

Another fresco solved the puzzle. On this one the blue figure was definitely a monkey. The Cretans kept monkeys as pets. Evans had found a painting, not of a person picking flowers but of a monkey taking a walk in the garden.

Writing

Like other people of the time — the Sumerians, for instance — the Cretans used signets and seals to mark their belongings. The stone seals, which were often carefully carved, were pressed into wet clay to make an impression. The clay tag was attached to the string of a bundle or jar of goods. When it dried, the jar or bundle was labelled with the owner's or trader's name. It seems, too, that people in Crete wore little seals around their wrists, rather like an identity tag. These were all carved differently, some with pictures, some with more abstract designs.

The first Minoan writing was in the form of picture symbols or hieroglyphics. Sir Arthur Evans found other kinds of writing on Crete as well. He discovered clay tablets marked with lines and curves.

Archaeologists could not decipher these tablets, but they were able to divide the writing into two kinds. They called the first kind *Linear A*. This was the earliest writing and very few examples of it have been found. No one has yet been able to decipher it.

The second kind of writing was called *Linear B*. About 3000 pieces of Linear B writing have been found, dating to about 1400 BC. In Crete, they have been found only in the ruins of the palace at Knossos. However, tablets marked with Linear B signs have also been discovered in parts of Greece. It seems that this language was an early kind of Greek. The fact that the same Linear B marks have been found in Crete and Greece shows that at one time Greek people lived in Crete. Perhaps they invaded the island and lived there as conquerors. Can you think of any other explanations?

The Linear B tablets were studied by many people for many years. Finally in 1953 the code was broken by an English architect called Michael Ventris. In 1936, when he was a 14-year-old schoolboy, Ventris had heard Arthur Evans give a lecture about Linear B. He was fascinated by the puzzle and four years later came up with a possible solution. He was wrong but

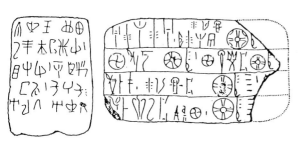

Fig. 8.20 Linear A (on the left); and Linear B (right). Linear A, the older writing, has not yet been deciphered. Can you see any similarities between the scripts?

kept working at it until he finally deciphered the writing.

The result was very disappointing. All the tablets so far translated contain lists of sheep, copper, corn and other goods. They are all official records: lists that were made by palace officials in their daily work. For example, they record deliveries to the palace ('Imported white textiles with red borders — 35') and who had paid their taxes. There are no stories or poems, nothing to show us what the Cretans felt about life.

Time to understand

1 Do you know what captions are? Most of the illustrations in this book have captions explaining what they are and telling a little bit about them. It has been said that the world of Minoan Crete is like a book of pictures whose captions cannot be read. What does this mean? Do you think it is a good explanation of the way we have learnt about Minoan Crete?

2 Fig. 8.21 shows one side of a clay disc found in the palace ruins of the Cretan city of Phaestos. The disc is two centimetres thick and has a diameter of 16 centimetres. On it, as you can see, are a series of pictures and signs. No one has yet been able to work out the meaning of this writing. The signs begin on the outside of the disc and go round in a spiral, rather like the grooves on a record.

Look carefully at the Phaestos disc.

a Some of the marks are pictures that can be recognised quite easily. Can you find them?

b Some of the pictures and signs appear more than once. Which ones are they? Does this give you any clues to the meaning of these marks?

Fig. 8.21 The Phaestos disc.

3 Do you have any ideas about why this strange writing was stamped into clay?
4 Make up your own disc, using a mixture of pictographs and signs. Give enough clues that others have a chance of reading your message. Try it out on your classmates.

Death and burial

The Cretans never burnt the bodies of dead people. Instead they buried them in graves, usually with some of their possessions. Both men and women were buried with pottery; men also had weapons while women were buried with their jewellery. People were buried in a crouching position, with their knees tucked up towards the chin. Sometimes the body was laid on the floor of a grave; sometimes it was crammed into a pottery jar.

In the early days, the Cretans built large round tombs in which several hundred people were buried. Later on it became more common to use smaller tombs cut into the side of a hillside. Only two or three people were buried in each of these tombs. Often their bodies were put into pottery bathtubs or coffins.

Time to understand

Using all that you have learnt so far about Minoan Crete, explain what evidence we have that it was a wealthy society.

The rest of the world

The wealth of Crete came from its trading power. A couple of kilometres from Knossos was the port city of Amnisos. Here the Cretan fleet was based. The high-prowed Minoan boats were about 12 metres long, and had both oars and sails. About thirty oarsmen rowed on each side.

In these ships traders sailed around the Aegean Sea and beyond. They sailed to Spain, western Asia and Mesopotamia to buy tin, copper and silver for metalworking. They bought gold and pearls from Egypt and ivory from north Africa. From the Greek islands they bought marble and obsidian, lead and silver. The Cretans sold in return grain, timber, dye, olive oil, wine, pottery and textiles. Some examples of Cretan craftwork have been found as far away as Egypt and Italy.

Fig. 8.22 The charred walls of a storeroom at Knossos. The height and position of the black marks indicate that a strong wind was blowing when the fire was burning.

Time to understand

Crete lies between three continents. What are they? How would Crete's position help to make it a good trading country?

The end of Minoan Crete

The Minoans seem to have enjoyed their life. They made and loved beautiful things, and had time for fun as well as work. Because they lived on an island and had a strong fleet, they were reasonably safe from attack. Their palaces were not heavily fortified, which indicates that the people did not fear attack from outside the island. There are only a few pictures of soldiers or battles in their paintings or on their vases. One fresco shows some African men dressed as soldiers. But they are badly armed and seem to be dancing rather than marching. Perhaps they were kept for ceremonies and special occasions to serve as the palace guard.

Two things seem to have combined to cause the end of Minoan Crete. The first was the rise in Greece of the Mycenaeans — a warlike group of people who became stronger than the Cretans. You will learn more about these people in the next chapter of this book. Large groups of Mycenaean warriors began raiding the island of Crete, attacking the palaces and plundering what they could.

Then, in about 1450 BC, catastrophe struck. A volcano erupted on the island of Thera (now called Santorini), about a hundred kilometres north of Crete. Millions of cubic metres of hot rock and poisonous ash were hurled into the air and much of it fell to earth on Crete. Fires started on the island and raged through the palace. Great tidal waves smashed into the island, partly destroying the palace at Knossos and completely destroying many of the island's other palaces and homes. At the same time, it seems, there was a mighty earthquake (like the one that destroyed the first palace of Knossos). One archaeologist digging at Knossos wrote:

> The throne room was found in a state of complete confusion. A great oil jar lay overturned in one corner, ritual vessels were . . . being used when the disaster came. It looks as if the king had hurried here to undergo too late some last ceremony in the hopes of saving his people.

It was too late. The bull within the earth — the earthquake — had shattered Knossos forever. A splendid building had become a smouldering heap of rubble. In the fire the palace documents on their clay tablets were baked hard, to become a permanent record of the people who had once lived there.

The picture in Fig. 8.22 is a clue to the destruction of Knossos. It shows part of a storeroom in the palace. Can you see the black marks on the walls? These were made by fire, caused when the oil in the storage jars caught alight. The height and position of the marks tell archaeologists that the fire happened on a windy day when the wind was blowing from the south. Strong southerly winds blow in Crete only in the springtime. We know, then, that the fire that helped to destroy the palace broke out on a windy spring day.

When Knossos was rebuilt it was occupied by Mycenaeans, not Cretans. The old ways lingered on but by this time Crete was simply a colony of Mycenae, not a culture in its own right. When the Mycenaean world itself collapsed, so did the culture of Crete. Soon it was no more than a memory.

Time to understand

1 An earthquake and volcano hit the island of Krakatoa in 1883. Use reference books or an encyclopaedia to find out what happened. The catastrophe that hit Crete was four times as violent as the eruption on Krakatoa.

2 The palace of Knossos was built right across a *fault* in the earth's crust. Do you know what a *fault* is? How does this help to explain the end of Minoan Crete?

3 Arthur Evans experienced an earthquake when he was digging at Knossos in 1926. He wrote: 'It is something to have heard with one's own ears the bellowing of the bull beneath the earth who, according to a primitive belief, tosses it on his horns.' What do you think of Evans' description of the earthquake? Do you think 'the bull beneath the earth' is a good way to explain how an earthquake sounds? Do you think this might have had anything to do with the beginning of the legend about Theseus and the minotaur? Do you think it might have anything to do with the Cretan sport of bull leaping?

4 Here are three facts about Linear B, the Cretan writing which you read about earlier in this chapter.

    a Archaeologists have found Linear B writing in many parts of Greece as well as Crete.

    b In Crete, Linear B writing was found only in the palace of Knossos.

    c In Crete it dates from about 1500 BC.

What can you learn about Greece and Crete from these three facts? Do your conclusions help to explain the beginnings of the legend of Theseus and his journey to Crete to defeat King Minos?

9

Hoplites and philosophers: the ancient Greeks

AT THE WEDDING of Peleus and Thetis, Eris, goddess of quarrels, rolled a golden apple between Hera, Athene and Aphrodite. On it was written 'For the fairest', and the three goddesses asked Zeus to choose which of them was meant. He refused. He said that only a mortal could make an unbiased choice, and that the man to do it was Paris, prince of Troy. Hermes took the goddesses to Mount Ida near Troy, where Paris was tending cattle. At first, Paris refused to judge. He suggested that the goddesses divide the apple equally between them. But Hermes threatened him with a thunderbolt, and he agreed to judge. One by one the goddesses appeared before him, and each offered him a bribe to place her first. Hera offered royal power; Athene offered wisdom; Aphrodite offered Queen Helen of Sparta, the most beautiful woman in the world. Paris chose Aphrodite, and Hera and Athene flew back to Olympus in a rage and began to plan trouble for Paris and doom for Troy.

Paris went to his father Priam and asked for a fast ship. Aphrodite gave him safe journey to Sparta, and Eros buried an arrow of love for him deep in Helen's heart. She eloped with Paris; to prevent pursuit they avoided the direct route home and instead reached Troy by way of Egypt, Phoenicia and Cyprus, a voyage which lasted several months.

This story was written over two and a half thousand years ago in ancient Greece. In fact, it is only the beginning of the story. The main characters in this part of the story are gods and goddesses. There are only two mortals, or human beings — Paris and Helen. In some ways the gods and goddesses seem to act like human beings. What human qualities do they have in the story?

The ancient Greeks believed that there were two main differences between gods and mortals. Gods, they believed were *immortal*. In other words, they never died. The Greeks also thought that the gods controlled the lives of human beings.

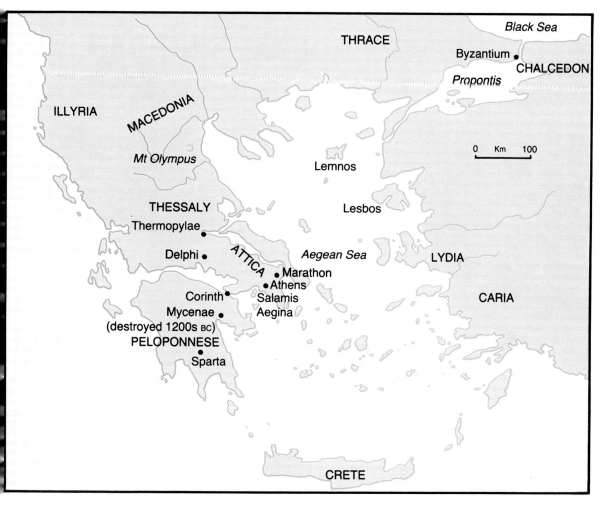

Fig. 9.1 The ancient Greek world.

You have just read the beginning of the long story of the Trojan War. It began as a game among the gods and became a war among human beings.

According to the story, Helen was married to Menelaus, who was the king of Sparta in southern Greece. When she eloped with Paris, Menelaus and his brother Agamemnon, the king of Mycenae, led a huge army against the town of Troy in Anatolia where Paris lived. The story of the war between the Greeks and the Trojans, known as the Trojan War, was written down by the poet Homer. Homer did not invent the story about the Trojan War. He simply wrote it down. The story had probably been told for hundreds of years. This kind of oral story-telling is called *oral tradition*.

For a long time, historians believed that Homer's *Iliad* was only a story. However, just over a hundred years ago a German archaeologist called Heinrich Schliemann discovered the town of Troy in Turkey.

Fig. 9.2 Heinrich Schliemann.

1200 BC. Each town was built around a *citadel*, or fortress. Inside the citadel was the king's palace. If the town was attacked the townspeople were able to gather inside the citadel for protection.

According to Homer, Mycenae was founded by Perseus. Perseus asked a family of giants called the Cyclopes to build the walls for him. Many of the walls of Mycenae still stand. They are built of huge blocks of stone. Archaeologists have called them *cyclopean* walls after the legendary giants.

Much of what we know about Mycenae has come from the graves or tombs there. Some are the tombs of noblemen and their families. Often, personal possessions such as mirrors, jewellery, cups and knives were buried with the people of Mycenae. Royal graves contained gold and treasure. Unlike the tombs of ancient Egypt, many Mycenaean tombs had not been robbed.

Was it just a legend?

Heinrich Schliemann had read the *Iliad* when he was young. When he was in his early forties he became an archaeologist and decided to look for Troy. The site he chose to excavate was a mound called Hisarlik in Turkey. His guess proved right. The mound contained nine levels, or strata. Each level was once a settlement, town or city. One of these strata could be the Troy of the *Iliad*.

One of the other cities mentioned in Homer's *Iliad* was Mycenae. After digging at Troy, Schliemann excavated Mycenae, in southern Greece. Can you see Mycenae in the map in Fig. 9.1?

Mycenae was one of a number of small, independent towns in Greece in about

The evidence

The period of time from about 1600 BC to about 1200 BC is called the Bronze Age. What other Bronze Age people have you read about in this book? During the Bronze Age Mycenae and other towns, such as Tiryns, were strong and prosperous. The people who lived in Greece at that time were Achaeans.

In the *Iliad*, the Achaean Greeks defeated the Trojans. After the Trojan war, Troy was destroyed. The evidence from the mound, Hisarlik, suggests that around 1200 BC Troy was destroyed by a fire. Do you think that the *Iliad* was based on real events?

Here is some more evidence. The excavations of places such as Mycenae and

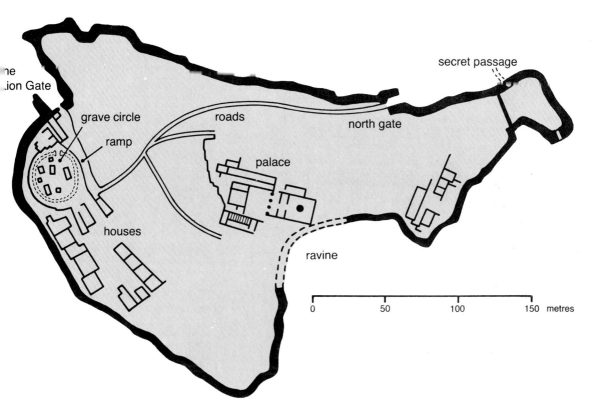

Fig. 9.3 A groundplan of Mycenae. The walls followed the natural line of the hill. Can you estimate how long the walls were? Was Mycenae a large city?

Tiryns have shown that a number of towns in Greece were destroyed around the same time in 1200 BC. We do not know why this happened. Do you think it is possible that the destruction of Troy and the destruction of Mycenae were connected in some way? Perhaps Troy was destroyed by Mycenacans whose unguarded town was destroyed by another group of people. Perhaps Troy and Mycenae were destroyed by the same group of people. It is a puzzle still to be solved.

Fig. 9.4 The Burial Circle at Mycenae: the double fence of stone slabs has been called Grave Circle A. In tombs were the skeletons of men, women and children. The women's skeletons were covered with thin gold discs. We know from Mycenaean paintings that these were originally sewn onto their dresses. There were many gold bracelets and necklaces in the tombs as well. Most of the men had swords or daggers.

153

Mycenae

Greece in the Bronze Age

Fig. 9.5 During the Bronze Age the kings of Mycenae ruled from their citadel on a spur between two mountains. The citadel was protected by massive walls. Inside the walls were the palace and houses for court officials. Outside were the houses of other people such as craftsmen and traders. The main entrance to the citadel was through the Lion Gate. Just inside the Lion Gate were six royal graves surrounded by a double row of stone slabs. These graves have provided archaeologists with information about life in ancient Mycenae. ▷

Fig. 9.6 The citadel: inside the citadel there were buildings for storing food. For example, there was a granary where storage jars with wheat and barley were found. The palace was right at the top of the hill, with a spacious court, throne room, bedrooms, bathroom and shrine.

Fig. 9.7 The Lion Gate: the Lion Gate still stands. On either side of the gateway are two huge upright slabs of stone. Above these is a horizontal stone slab known as a lintel. Above the lintel there is an arch so that the weight of the wall above it will come down to the ground rather than press on the lintel and break it. The gateway is four metres wide and probably had a gate in Mycenean times. Above the lintel is a triangular block of stone carved with a lion on either side of the column. Do you think these mean ◁ anything?

Fig. 9.8 The Treasury of Atreus: this tomb has been named after the father of Agamemnon. It is called a 'beehive tomb' because its shape resembles that of a natural beehive. First a hole was dug from the top of the hill. Then the hole was lined with stone blocks, each jutting out a little beyond the block below it. In this way a dome shape was formed. The treasure of the tomb was never found.
▽

Fig. 9.9 Gold death mask: when Schliemann first discovered this gold death mask he thought he was looking at a portrait of Agamemnon. In fact, the faces of five of the people buried in the tombs had been covered with gold death masks. We do not know who they were.

The end of Mycenae

In about 1200 BC people known as the Dorians began to arrive in Greece. We do not know where the Dorians came from but we do know that they were different from the Achaean Greeks.

The Dorians had no form of writing, whereas the Mycenaean Greeks wrote a form of early Greek, called Linear B, which, as you read in the last chapter, was also the language of the Cretans. However, the Dorians used iron weapons rather than the bronze weapons used by the Myceneans. Iron weapons were much stronger than bronze.

The Dorians conquered most of Greece and forced the people who were already living there to become their slaves or to migrate to other lands. Some towns managed to resist them. Some may not have been attacked. The period from 1200 BC to 800 BC is sometimes called the Dark Age of Greek history. This is because very few records from that period of time have been discovered. This means that the picture of life during the period is unclear.

Time to understand

Many stories from ancient Greece were written about *heroes*. These men tried to win respect and admiration, and to be remembered by later generations. They were usually strong and handsome, intelligent and quick-witted. The *Iliad* and the *Odyssey* tell the stories of the heroes. Achilles is a good example of a Greek hero. Read the following extracts about the Trojan War from the *Iliad* before answering the questions below.

Fig. 9.10 Achilles, the Greek hero.

Achilles' father, Peleus, told his son, 'always to strive for the first place and outdo other men.' Agamemnon, king of Mycenae, insulted Achilles:

This cut Achilles to the quick. In his shaggy breast, his heart was torn between two courses, whether to draw his sharp sword from his side, thrust his way through the crowd, and kill King Agamemnon, or to control this angry impulse.

Several Greek warriors tried to persuade Achilles to join in the battle against the Trojans. He had refused because Agamemnon had insulted him:

> 'Conquer your pride, Achilles. You have no right to be so stubborn. The very gods for all their excellence and majesty and power, are capable of being swayed.'

When Achilles heard that his friend, Patroclus, had been killed by the Trojans he decided to join the battle:

> There he stood and cried aloud, while in the distance Pallas Athene raised the war-cry too. The Trojans were utterly confounded. Achilles' cry was as piercing as the trumpet call that rings out when a city is beset by murderous enemies and their hearts turned to water when they heard that brazen voice.

Achilles had to fight Hector, the brother of Paris, outside the walls of Troy:

> Achilles drew near him, looking like the god of war in his flashing helmet . . . and the bronze on his body glowed like a blazing fire or the rising sun. Hector looked up, saw him, and began to tremble. He no longer had the heart to stand his ground; he left the gate and ran away in terror.

1 Why did Achilles not join in the battle at first?
2 Why did he change his mind?
3 How would you describe Achilles, the warrior?
4 What is meant by the words 'the bronze on his body'? Why do you think it 'glowed'?
5 Look up the meaning of the word *hero* in a dictionary. Does Achilles fit the modern definition of a hero? Why?
6 Find out the kinds of weapons used by the Greeks and the Trojans in this battle. You can do this by reading the story of the *Iliad*, or by using a reference book on Mycenae or Troy.

The city-states of ancient Greece

From about 800 BC the Greeks began to write records of their lives. Both these written records and the archaeological evidence help us to understand that by 800 BC there were a number of separate communities dotted throughout Greece. These communities were called *city-states*.

Each city-state (called a *polis* in Greek) had developed from a small settlement, perhaps just a few families or clans. To protect themselves in time of war the people in a settlement built an *acropolis*. An acropolis was very similar to a citadel. (Do you remember reading about the one at Mycenae?) Sometimes it was a natural outcrop of rock or sometimes just a hilltop. The acropolis was fortified, or surrounded by a wall. When the city-state was attacked, everyone was protected on the acropolis.

A city-state usually consisted of an acropolis, around which developed a town, as well as the surrounding farmland. Each city-state was independent. This meant that the people grew their own crops, made their own pottery, developed their own form of government and made their own laws. Sometimes they traded with people in another city-state. Sometimes two neighbouring city-states fought over land and power.

How did these separate city-states develop? Greece is a very mountainous country. A city-state was usually separated from its neighbours by mountains. In 800 BC travel between two city-states was slow. The few roads and mountain passes were often steep and high. Sometimes it was easier to sail along the coast than travel overland.

Most of the people who lived in the city-states were the descendants of either the

Dorians or the Achaeans. One of these Dorian city-states became famous for its strong, courageous soldiers. This city-state was called Sparta.

Time to understand

Most ancient Greeks thought of themselves as either Athenians or Spartans or Corinthians or Megarians, and so on. They belonged to their own city-state, not to a larger area called 'Greece'. However, they had several things in common. They spoke the same language, wore similar clothes and worshipped the same gods.

Fig. 9.11 shows the ancient Greek alphabet. Many of these letters are used today as symbols in mathematics. As well many words that are used today come from ancient Greek words.

1 These English words were originally Greek. Do you know what they mean? Using Fig. 9.11 as a guide, write them out in ancient Greek.

    a   drama
    b   isosceles
    c   canon
    d   paralysis
    e   comma
    f   iris
    g   parenthesis

As it was written in Ancient Greece	As it is written today	Names of the Greek letters	The nearest English letters
A	A	alpha	A (either as in *cat* or *cart*)
B	B	beta	B
Λ	Γ	gamma	G (as in *go*)
Δ	Δ	delta	D
E	E	epsilon	E (as in *red*)
I	Z	zeta	Z
H	H	eta	E (like the *a* in say)
Θ	Θ	theta	Th (as in *thick*)
I	I	iota	I
K	K	kappa	K
L	Λ	lamda	L
M	M	mu	M
N	N	nu	N
ΧϚ or ΧΣ	Ξ	xi	X (as in *axe*)
O	O	omicron	O (as in *hot*)
Γ	Π	pi	P
P or P	P	rho	R
Ɛ or Ϛ	Σ	sigma	S
T	T	tau	T
V	Y	upsilon	U (either as in *look* or *Hugh*)
Φ	Φ	phi	Ph, F
X	X	khi	Kh, Ch
ΦϚ or ΦΣ	Ψ	psi	Ps
Ω	Ω	omega	O (as in *home*)

Fig. 9.11 The Greek alphabet.

h climax

i horizon

j catastrophe

2 The words written below in Greek are all the names of gods, goddesses or heroes. Translate their names into English.

a ΖΕΥΣ

b ΠΟΣΕΙ△ΩΝ

c ʽΗΡΑ

d ΠΕΡΣΕΦΟΝΗ

e ΑΡΗΣ

f ΑΦΡΟ△ΙΤΗ

g ΕΚΤΩΡ

h △ΗΜΗΤΗΡ

i ΗΡΑΚ△ΗΣ

j ΑΘΗΝΗ

Life in Sparta

> Forward, sons of Sparta, holding your shields in front of you, wield your spears like men. Do not spare your lives: cowardice is not a Spartan virtue.

These words were spoken by a Spartan poet to inspire soldiers. When he wrote 'cowardice is not a Spartan virtue', the poet meant that Spartan soldiers never retreated from a battlefield (or at least, they were not supposed to!). They fought until they won or died.

Spartan women told their husbands and sons, as they went to battle: 'Come home *with* your shield or *on* it.' In other words, a Spartan killed in battle was carried from the battlefield on his shield.

Why were Spartan soldiers so brave? Were they as strong as others thought they were? Some of the answers to these questions are found in books written by the ancient Greeks themselves. Other ancient writers, such as the Romans, also wrote about Greece. Because of this the picture we have of life in ancient Greece is much clearer than our picture of other societies you have studied earlier in this book. Many of the books written in ancient Greek have been translated into English and other European languages. There is also plenty of archaeological evidence.

Fig. 9.12 A Spartan hoplite or foot soldier.

159

Spartan men

According to the Roman writer Plutarch, any Spartan baby who appeared to be sickly or deformed was left at the foot of Mount Taygetus to die. This, of course, may not be true. However, it tells us about the kind of life the Spartan baby was about to face.

If the child was a boy he went to school at the age of seven. This school was not like the primary school you probably attended. The boy lived at the school. It was like an army barracks.

The seven-year-old began to train in athletics, gymnastics and music. The whole purpose of education in Sparta was to produce strong soldiers. Because of this Spartan boys were taught just a little reading and writing, if they were taught at all.

At the age of ten a Spartan boy entered athletic and musical competitions. Music probably consisted of dancing and singing in groups or choruses.

At about your age (11–13 years) a Spartan boy began the next stage of his schooling. This stage was very uncomfortable and difficult by today's standards. Remember, as well, that he had been living away from his family since the age of seven.

At this secondary stage the young Spartan's hair was cut very short. He was allowed to wear only one piece of clothing in both summer and winter. This meant he went barefoot as well. He practised athletic exercises naked. He slept in the barracks on a bed of rushes he had gathered from a river.

Plutarch tells us that the boys were given a small ration of food to encourage them to steal from nearby gardens. The twist to this story is that the boy who was caught stealing was punished severely — not for stealing but for being caught! Plutarch has probably exaggerated this part of a Spartan boy's education. Boys may have had to forage or hunt for food on camps just as today's boy scouts are taught how to set up camp and survive in the bush.

All these hardships were supposed to make the young Spartan strong and fearless. When he was eighteen he attempted his army entrance. If he failed he was in disgrace. If he passed he could enter the lowest rank of the army.

By the age of twenty-four a young man had completed his military training and could become a regular soldier. He was expected to marry at this time and begin a family. Even so, he did not live with his family. He still lived in the barracks.

At thirty he became a full Spartan citizen provided he had successfully completed all the stages of his education and military training. He was then allowed to live with his family. He also grew his hair long to show that he had reached manhood.

Even though he lived with his family, a Spartan citizen still ate his meals at the barracks with the other men. Each man contributed a share of the food. Most of his time was spent keeping up his physical fitness, supervising the education of younger Spartans or helping to govern Sparta.

Spartan men were always ready to go to war. So who looked after the farms, grew the crops and made the pottery? The people who did these things were not called Spartan citizens. They did not train for the army or help to govern Sparta. You will read more about these people later in this chapter.

Time to understand

1 How well did Spartans fight? What kind of weapons did they use? Did they wear armour? Read this account and answer the questions below.

> The Spartans now began to sing their war songs, reminding each other of the glorious actions in which they had all shared. They knew that confidence born of experience is more reliable than any stirred up by fine words on the spur of the moment. Then the armies closed in. The Argives and their allies rushed forward in a violent fury, but the Spartans moved slowly to the measured music of a band of pipers. This is not done for any religious reason, but to make sure they keep in step while they're advancing and to stop the whole formation disintegrating, as so often happens when large armies move into the attack.

a   Music was part of the Spartans' education. Why did the Spartans sing before a battle? How was music used as the battle began?

b   Have you ever seen an army regiment marching? How do they keep in step with one another?

c   Do you think it was a good idea for the Spartans to keep in step? Why?

2 Most Greek foot-soldiers (or *hoplites* as they were called) had similar equipment. Fig. 9.14 (over) is an Athenian painting of two soldiers playing a board game. Fig. 9.12 shows how a modern artist has imagined a Spartan hoplite looked. The artist has based his drawing on paintings and written descriptions.

a   Name the weapons used by hoplites.

b   How could a hoplite defend himself? What other protection did he have?

Fig. 9.13 Spartan soldiers advancing in formation.

Fig. 9.14 Two soldiers playing a board game.

Spartan women

Spartan girls were also educated. They were trained in athletics so that they grew fit and strong. Yet Spartan women did not fight in battles. Instead, the Spartans believed that strong women would bear strong children.

Unlike the boys who lived in barracks, girls stayed at home while they were growing up. They learnt how to look after and organise a home.

Spartan women were famous for their beauty. (Do you remember Queen Helen?) Their beauty was natural — the law did not allow them to use such luxuries as cosmetics, jewellery and perfumed oil.

Helots and the perioeci

The Spartan citizens you have just read about were descended from the Dorians. The people they conquered became *helots*.

Every Spartan citizen was given some land on which he could grow crops. He used these crops to support his family and to contribute food to the common meals at the barracks. As Spartan men spent all their time either training or fighting, helots worked their farms. Although they were not paid for their work, helots were allowed to keep any crops that were left after the Spartans and their families had taken what they needed.

Some helots served in the army. Usually a Spartan soldier had two or three helots with him.

Sometimes the helots rebelled against the Spartans. These revolts were always crushed brutally. This was one of the reasons why the Spartans were always ready for war.

Another group of people were the *perioeci*. They worked as traders and craftsmen, as the Spartans had no time for these occupations. The perioeci were free people but had to serve in the army if they were needed.

Life in Athens

Life in ancient Athens was different from life in ancient Sparta. Athenian men were educated, but not only as soldiers. They did not spend most of their time training in the army. They were proud of their city-state and so, of course, would defend it against enemy attack. Because of their pride they built temples decorated with sculpture to honour the gods and make Athens beautiful. They worked hard governing Athens and planning new laws to make life as fair as they believed possible. They enjoyed the theatre and public festivals. They wrote history and studied philosophy.

We have a much clearer picture of life in Athens than of life in Sparta. The reason for this is that Athenians decorated their pottery with scenes of everyday life and scenes from mythology. As you know pottery was used widely in ancient societies. Many pots, cups, vases and jars made in ancient Athens have survived. The vivid scenes shown on them are almost like photographs of the lives of Athenian men, women and children.

Athenian boys and men

> As long as a child is occupied with a rattle nothing else in the house will get broken.

An Athenian writer gave this advice to parents. In ancient Athens, children were treated much the same as children today. They played with toy soldiers, dolls, horses on wheels, marbles and balls. Until they were able to read, their parents told them stories about gods, goddesses and heroes such as Achilles and Heracles.

Until he was about six or seven years old an Athenian boy was looked after at home by his mother and a nurse, who was probably a slave. He then started school. Schools were run by private teachers, who were paid by the parents.

Each boy was taken to school by a trusted family slave called a *paidagogus*. The paidagogus went to all the boy's lessons to make sure he behaved.

Athenian boys studied reading, writing, arithmetic, geometry, music, poetry, gymnastics and games. These were not all taught in the same school. Usually reading, writing, arithmetic and geometry were taught in one school, while music and poetry were taught somewhere else. Gymnastics and games were taught in another school called a *palaestra*.

All gymnastic exercises were performed naked. Before exercising, the pupils bathed, rubbed themselves down with oil and then sprinkled themselves with fine powder or dust. Just as today an athlete 'warms up', so boys began their training sessions by loosening up their muscles. Then they practised running, jumping, wrestling, boxing and discus and javelin throwing. After a training session, the boys scraped all the oil, dust and sweat from their bodies before having a shower.

Fig. 9.15 Terracotta toys: a boy riding a goose and a doll with movable arms.

Boys who misbehaved were punished by their teachers and trainers, who used sticks or leather sandals to beat them. Teachers were usually shown on vase paintings holding a stick or a branch of narthex (a plant like flax).

Competitions in music, athletics and poetry recitation were the only ways of testing how much boys had learned. There were no examinations like the ones you do today. If a competitor was successful, both he and his teacher or trainer received a prize.

Fig. 9.16 A music teacher and pupils. Who is the man on the far right?

Boys from poor families usually finished their schooling at fourteen. Boys from wealthy families continued their education for four more years. Sometimes they studied extra subjects such as astronomy and public speaking.

When he turned eighteen the young Athenian began his military training. First he had to promise never to desert his comrades in battle and never to let Athens down. After a year of training he was given a shield and a sword by the government. He then spent the next year patrolling and guarding the borders of Attica. Attica was the territory around Athens.

At twenty the young man became a full Athenian citizen. He could then help in the governing of Athens while earning his living.

Athenian men also kept themselves fit. The government built public gymnasia, which were large open-air sports grounds.

Here Athenian men could continue to train. A good athlete competed in organised games, such as those held at Olympia.

Time to understand

The story below tells us how one Athenian father organised his daughter's marriage. It also tells us much about Athenian life, which really was 'a man's world'. Only men attended dinner parties (like the one described in the story), unless it was a wedding banquet.

Kleisthenes had a daughter called Agariste, and he was anxious to marry her to the finest man in the whole of Greece. So during the Olympic Games, shortly after winning a crown in the four-horse chariot-race, he had a public announcement made that anyone who thought himself good

165

enough to become Kleisthenes' son-in-law should present himself at Sikyon before sixty days were up. In one year from then, Kleisthenes would formally celebrate the wedding.

A great crowd of suitors came — everyone in Greece with a family or reputation to be proud of. Kleisthenes kept them busy with wrestling and racing, and built an arena specially for this purpose.

When the sixty-day period was over, and all the suitors had arrived, Kleisthenes made his enquiries. First he asked each of them his name and place of origin. Then he spent a whole year examining them, and finding out about their abilities, upbringing, temper and way of life. His method was to interview each of them individually and in the others' company, and give the younger ones tests in gymnastics. But the supreme test was their behaviour at meal-times: for throughout their stay Kleisthenes entertained them very lavishly and expensively.

The suitors from Athens came out best in all this testing, and best of them was Hippokleides, son of Tisander. Kleisthenes liked him not only for his own abilities, but also because he was related to one of the oldest families of Corinth.

At last the day came for Kleisthenes to announce the name of his chosen son-in-law, and celebrate the marriage. One hundred oxen were sacrificed, and all the people of Sikyon were invited to join the suitors at a banquet. After dinner the suitors competed with each other in poetry and public speaking, and as the evening wore on, Hippokleides, who was doing better — and drinking more — than anyone else, asked the flute-player to play for him, and began to dance.

Hippokleides thought his own dancing was magnificent, but Kleisthenes wasn't quite so pleased — especially when Hippokleides called for a table and climbed up on to it. First he did a Spartan dance, then some Athenian ones, and ended up by standing on his head and waving his legs in the air.

The Spartan and Athenian dances were bad enough, but the leg-waving was too much for Kleisthenes, who lost his temper and said: 'Hippokleides, you've just danced away your marriage.' 'So what?' said Hippokleides. 'See if Hippokleides cares!'

This answer soon became a proverb — but Kleisthenes married his daughter to Megakles, another of the suitors from Athens.

1 What is a *suitor*? Why did so many suitors accept Kleisthenes' invitation?
2 How do we know that Kleisthenes was wealthy?
3 How did Kleisthenes examine the suitors? Do you think he valued a good education? Why?
4 Is there anything in this story to suggest that the suitors from Athens were better educated than the others?
5 Why did Hippokleides behave as he did? Do you think Kleisthenes approved of this? Why?
6 The phrase 'See if Hippokleides cares' became a proverb. What is a proverb? When would this proverb be used? Can you think of any similar proverbs used today?

A man's world?

Most of the records from ancient Athens describe the activities of Athenian men. Athenian women were highly regarded, but they were not called citizens. They did not take an active part in the business or the government of Athens.

Only the sons of free Athenians could become Athenian citizens. When a young man had completed his education and military training he became a citizen. He could then take an active part in the affairs of Athens.

Slaves

There were many slaves, both male and female, in ancient Athens. In fact, about 30 per cent of the total population were slaves. These people had either been bought at slave markets or captured as prisoners of war.

Household slaves did most of the housework, such as cleaning and cooking. Slaves accompanied the mistress of the house when she went shopping in the *agora*, or market place. Most household slaves were well treated. They took part in religious ceremonies and some slaves became 'part of the family'.

A slave was regarded as part of the citizen's property, just like his house and other possessions. Because of this, a slave could go out to work to earn money for his master. Sometimes the slave was able to keep some of his wages, and lucky slaves were able to save enough to buy their freedom.

At work

Almost all the evidence from ancient Athens suggests that an Athenian citizen spent only part of the day 'at work', or earning his living. 'At work', he could have been many things — perhaps a merchant, a potter, a metal worker, a sculptor, a sandal maker or an architect.

Athenians got up early to take advantage of the daylight hours. Breakfast was often just a hunk of bread dipped in wine. Most of the day's work took place in the morning. The agora bustled with activity as traders arrived with their goods, fishermen brought their day's catch and craftsmen opened their shops. Slaves and free Athenians worked together.

Business stopped at noon for a simple midday meal. In the afternoon citizens went to the gymnasium or a barber's shop to prepare themselves for the evening.

Fig. 9.17 A mistress and her slave, depicted on a vase used for holding perfume.

Dinners and parties

Athenian men usually ate their meals with their families. However, dinner parties were common. These were a social event, attended by men only.

Fig. 9.18 Two guests are entertained at a dinner party.

When the guests arrived for a dinner party, slaves took off their sandals and washed their feet. The guests then lay back on couches. Slaves brought in tables laden with food such as fish, oysters, meat, poultry, bread, fruit, olives and cheese.

Once the meal was over, the guests washed their hands in bowls of water brought in by slaves. They did this because all food was eaten without cutlery. Then they began drinking. The wine they drank was always mixed with water.

Each guest contributed something towards the entertainment. Some asked riddles; some told funny stories; some played the lyre. Sometimes flute girls, who were probably slaves, were hired to entertain the guests.

Governing Athens

Every Athenian citizen was a member of the Assembly. Mass meetings of the Assembly were held about once a fortnight on the Pynx, a hill outside Athens. At these meetings the citizens voted on things such as whether Athens should go to war with another city-state or whether a new temple should be built. This kind of government is called *democracy* because the people (*demos* in Greek) made the decisions themselves. Many countries, such as the USA, Australia and Britain have democratic forms of government today. The main difference is that today people elect representatives to make decisions for them because the populations of these countries are so much bigger than that of ancient Athens. The Athenians developed this system of government.

As well as voting in the Assembly, an Athenian citizen could help in the day-to-day running of Athens as a member of the city's Council, as a magistrate or as a minor official. To do this a citizen had to take time off work. While he was working as, for example, a magistrate in charge of organising a festival, he was paid a wage from the Athenian treasury.

Another way a citizen helped in the running of Athens was to serve as a juror in the law courts. Each year 6000 men volunteered to serve on the jury. Every time a case was to be heard, a jury was chosen from the 6000 volunteers. Juries were large and could vary in size from 201 to 2001 jurors. The juries judged whether the person accused of a crime was guilty or innocent. They also decided on the punishment. Men were paid for each day they served on a jury just as people on jury duty today are paid.

Time to understand

Greek clothes were much simpler than the clothes we wear today. In fact, the Greeks did not need tailors or dressmakers to cut or sew their clothes. Clothes were simply draped or hung on a person's body. To make garments look different, a Greek man or woman could tie or pin the cloth in various ways. Cloth was made of wool which had been bought in the market place, then spun and made at home. It was dyed various colours using natural dyes from plants and minerals.

1. Figs 9.19 and 9.20 show different ways of putting on a *chiton*, or tunic. The cloth was pinned and then tied. Explain in words how a chiton was worn by men and by women.

2. Figs 9.21 and 9.22 show some other ways of wearing chitons and cloaks, which were worn in cool weather. Explain how these were draped or fastened. You may do this either by drawing or in words.

Athenian girls and women

Athenian girls were educated, but not to the same extent as boys. Girls stayed at home with their mothers, learning to look after the house. 'Looking after the house' included caring for the children, preparing meals, weaving cloth, making and mending clothes and generally keeping things well ordered.

Most housework was done by slaves, and even quite poor families had slaves. Girls from wealthy families probably learnt to read and write. They were also taught to dance and perhaps play a musical instrument.

Fig. 9.19 A woman's chiton.

Fig. 9.20 A man's chiton.

Fig. 9.21 Men's clothes

Fig. 9.22 Women's clothes.

Fathers usually arranged marriages for their daughters. Do you remember how Kleisthenes chose a husband for Agariste? Sometimes a girl was married at the age of fourteen. She would then have to organise her own home so the education given to her by her mother was very important.

Only a well-respected, middle-aged woman was allowed to go out of the house on her own. Younger women were always accompanied by a slave. 'Going out' was usually a visit to a friend's or a relative's house. Women did not go to a gymnasium or even to athletic games. They were allowed to attend big religious festivals, perhaps even the drama festivals. They could also visit shrines to worship one of the gods or goddesses.

Time to understand

Fig. 9.25 (p. 172) shows the groundplan of a typical Greek house. There were usually two storeys. When the man of the house

170

Covered walkway
Here athletes could practise track events even if it was raining or very hot.

Grove
Usually a gymnasium was built near a group of trees. Here athletes rested after training or men gathered to talk or simply watch the athletes.

Dressing room
This was where the Athenians left their clothes before rubbing themselves down with oil and sprinkling themselves with powder.

Shower room
Some gymnasiums contained showers where athletes could wash after scraping off the oil and dirt with a *strigil*, a curved bronze scraper. Sometimes they had to make do with a swim in a nearby stream.

A paidotribe
A *paidotribe*, or trainer, is always shown holding a forked stick as a sign of his position. Umpires at games held a branch.

Jumping pit
Long jumping was an event at organised athletic games. Jumpers held weights to help them jump further.

Shops
Athletes bought powder and oil as well as refreshments.

Boxing room
Punch-balls were suspended from the ceiling for boxers to use while they were training.

Palaestra
This was an open courtyard covered with fine sand. Here men could practise wrestling or boxing.

Discus and javelin throwing areas
These two field events originated in ancient Greece. Javelin throwing also helped train men to use spears successfully in battle.

Fig. 9.23 The gymnasium.

Fig. 9.24 Two women weaving.

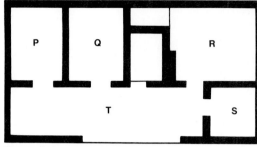

Second storey

First storey

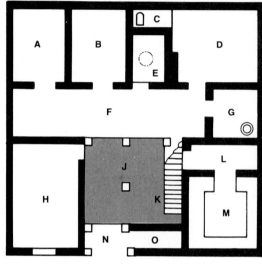

entertained his friends, the women stayed in their 'quarters', which were often upstairs. When a female visitor came to the house, she would not visit the 'men's quarters', which was usually the dining room.

1 First of all, copy the plan of the house into your notebook or folder as accurately as you can.

2 Now, using the list of furniture opposite and the description of a 'well-organised house' that follows, draw shapes to represent furniture in each room on your plan. You will need to consider:

— how each room was used;

— whether things were to be stored in the room;

— how many people were likely to use the room (i.e. there should not be too much furniture in each room).

A Livingroom/workroom
B Slaves' bedroom
C Bathroom with terracotta tub
D Kitchen
E Open fire for cooking
F Covered portico
G Storeroom
H Shop (pressing and selling of olive oil)
J Open courtyard with altar in the middle
K Steps to upper storey
L Anteroom
M Men's dining room
N Entrance to house
O Porter's lodge
P, Q Women's bedrooms
R, S Men's bedrooms
T Hallway

Fig. 9.25 Groundplan of a Greek house. The second storey is to fit above rooms A,B,D,F,G. (C and E are uncovered.)

172

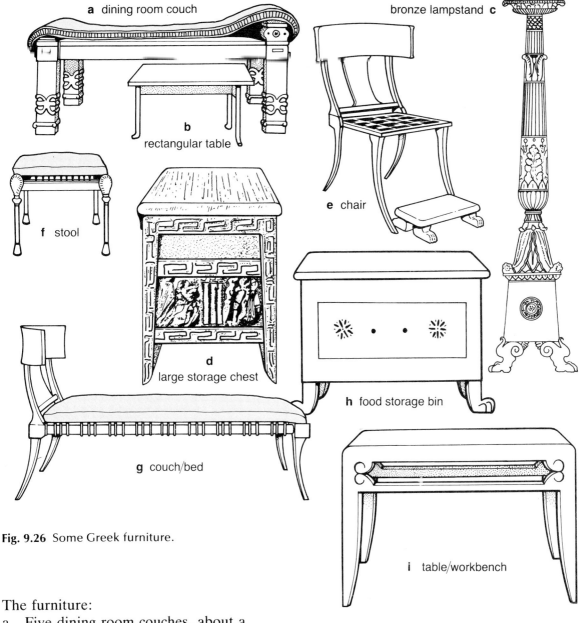

Fig. 9.26 Some Greek furniture.

a dining room couch
b rectangular table
bronze lampstand c
e chair
f stool
d large storage chest
h food storage bin
g couch/bed
i table/workbench

The furniture:

a Five dining room couches, about a metre wide and perhaps 2 metres long
b Five rectangular tables, which are stored under the couches when not in use
c Six bronze lampstands
d Six large storage chests
e Three chairs
f Six stools
g Six couches or beds
h Five kitchen storage chests
i Two workbenches/tables
j Four wall shelves (not illustrated)
k One loom (see Fig. 9.24)

The well-organised house

Our house is not decorated in an ornate manner, each room is built the right shape and size for whatever is to go in it, and you can tell the purpose of each room just by looking at it. The master bedroom, for example, in the securest part of the house, contains the most valuable carpets and furniture; the driest rooms are used as grain-stores; the coolest rooms store wine; the brightest rooms contain the ornaments and furniture that are seen to best advantage in daylight. The living-quarters are carefully planned to be cool in summer, warm in winter; the house is designed so that we get maximum sunlight in winter, maximum shade in summer.

Our furniture, too, is placed where it will be of most use. Objects required for sacrifice are all collected together; my wife's best clothes, and my own armour and best clothes, are kept with the bed-linen; clothes for male and female slaves are kept in the appropriate rooms. Another store is for weapons, and another for wool-carding equipment; in another are the kitchen utensils, in another serving-dishes, in another bath utensils; in another the baking-dishes are kept, and in another the cutlery and table settings. Everything is carefully separated into things needed for special occasions and things used every day. Each month's stores and supplies are kept separately from the entire year's stock; in this way there is less danger of running out of anything without noticing.

The things each slave uses every day for cooking, baking or spinning, are kept by the individual slaves, and they are shown how to put them away and keep them safe. But everything used less often, for banquets or for entertaining guests, we leave in the charge of our housekeeper. She knows the place of each object and keeps written accounts, remembering who used each object last, and making sure it's returned to its proper place as soon as she gets it back.

'The gods are everywhere'

The Greeks believed that gods and goddesses controlled not only the lives of human beings but also things like thunder, lightning, rain, a good harvest and so on. Natural events were explained by myths. When thunder rolled the Greeks said that Zeus, the chief of the gods, was angry and hurling his thunderbolt. When a storm wrecked a ship, Poseidon, the god of the sea, was angry.

The Greeks worshipped their gods and goddesses so that their daily lives would run smoothly. For example, to make sure of a good harvest, Greeks would make sacrifices to the goddess Demeter before they planted their crops.

The main gods and goddesses were thought to live on the misty summit of Mount Olympus. Zeus was head of the gods. Each god or goddess looked after a particular aspect of life on earth (see Fig. 9.27). There were also a number of less important gods.

The gods were worshipped in stately temples. Everyone in a city-state attended the elaborate ceremonies and festivals which were held in honour of the gods. Usually these began with a procession through the city to the temple. In the procession there were priests and priestesses, animals for sacrifice, and men and women carrying fruit and flowers. The animals were sacrificed to the god outside the temple. The ceremony ended with the worshippers eating the roasted meat of the sacrificed animals.

A religious festival sometimes lasted several days. After the opening ceremony games and competitions were held. One of the greatest festivals in Athens was the Panathenaea which celebrated the birthday of Athena, the patron goddess of Athens.

Fig. 9.27 The main Greek gods and goddesses.

175

Fig. 9.28 The Athenian Acropolis today.

Most religious festivals in Athens took place on the Acropolis. The Acropolis was a large natural outcrop of rock. On it were temples and sanctuaries, including the Parthenon. Even though it is in ruins, the Parthenon is still thought to be one of the most beautiful buildings in the world.

Time to understand

Persephone was the beautiful daughter of Demeter, goddess of the harvest. Hades, god of the underworld, fell in love with her. He asked his brother, Zeus, for permission to marry her. Zeus agreed but Demeter could not bear to think of Persephone living beneath the earth in the dark underworld.

One day Persephone was picking flowers in a field. She bent over to pick a particularly beautiful bloom. As she did, the earth opened and Hades appeared from the underworld. He was riding in a chariot pulled by black horses. Hades grabbed Persephone and carried her off to the underworld.

The gaping hole in the earth closed. No one seemed to know what had happened

to Persephone. Demeter searched for nine days and nights. Finally the sun, Helios, told her what had happened, and that Zeus approved of it.

Demeter then disguised herself as a beggar woman. She refused to have anything more to do with Zeus. Crops were poor and plants and trees withered. The earth was barren and people were starving. Finally Zeus sent another goddess to Demeter to beg her to bring the trees and plants back to life. Demeter agreed on the condition that Persephone returned from the underworld.

Finally, it was agreed between Zeus, Hades and Demeter that Persephone should spend six months of each year with her mother, Demeter, and six months with her husband, Hades, in the underworld. When she was with her mother, crops and plants grew and then the harvest was abundant. When she returned to the underworld plantlife began to wither and seemed to die.

1 This myth was used by the Greeks to explain a cycle in nature. What is this cycle? Can you give its scientific explanation?
2 Think of another cycle or an event in nature, for example an earthquake or a volcanic eruption. Can you make up a myth to explain this?

Two great festivals

The Olympic Games

Today, athletes from all over the world compete at the Olympic Games. The very first Olympic Games were held over 2000 years ago in 776 BC at Olympia in Greece. They were held in honour of Zeus, chief

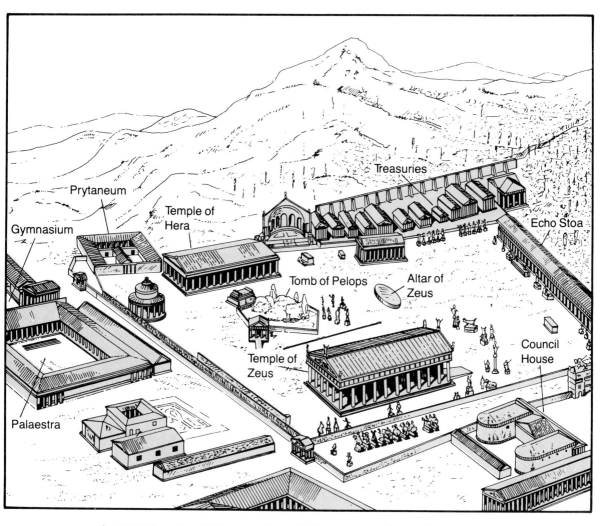

Fig. 9.29 The site of Olympia about 2000 years ago. The stadium and the hippodrome were to the east of this group of temples and sanctuaries.

of the gods. The original Olympic Games were, in fact, a religious festival. Athletes from all over Greece went to Olympia to take part in the games.

Olympia was not a city-state but a group of temples and sports grounds. The city-state of Elis was in charge of organising the games. Each year messengers from Elis travelled through Greece inviting athletes and spectators to Olympia. They also announced a sacred truce. This meant that any arguments or wars between the city-states would be forgotten for the time

being, so that the games could be held in peace.

During the games Olympia came alive. As well as athletes and spectators, there were entertainers such as acrobats and story-tellers. Visitors to the games could also listen to philosophers arguing or men reciting verses by famous poets.

The games were held in mid-summer and lasted for five days. On the first day the fitness of the athletes was tested. A pig was sacrificed to Zeus and all the athletes, standing in front of a statue of Zeus,

177

Fig. 9.30 The slaughter of a pig at the beginning of the games.

swore that they had trained for ten months.

The opening event was a spectacular chariot race in the hippodrome. Many of the competitors never finished the twelve double laps. Imagine forty chariots, each drawn by four horses, thundering down to the turning post. In the turn several chariots collide. In a cloud of dust wheels fly off axles, drivers are thrown in the air and horses struggle to be free of their strangling yokes.

Other events were held in the stadium and included sprinting, discus and javelin throwing, boxing, wrestling, long jumping and horse racing. Another event was the *pankration*. This sport combined wrestling and boxing. It was very dangerous as kicking and strangling were allowed. Umpires watched contestants closely to make sure there was no biting, gouging of eyes or finger breaking.

On the third day, which was always the day of the full moon, everyone watched a huge sacrifice to Zeus. This was the most important event of the festival. All the competitors and representatives of every city-state walked in a procession to the altar of Zeus. It was a very solemn ceremony.

At the end of every event the victor was announced. At Olympia he was crowned with a wreath made of wild olive, and he was usually given a valuable reward when he returned to his city-state. Victors celebrated with feasting and drinking in the evening after a victory.

All athletes were amateurs. Earlier in this chapter you read about gymnasiums in Athens. Other city-states also built gymnasiums where men could train to compete in athletic competitions.

The festival at Olympia is the best known of the Greek games. Other games were held every four years at Delphi and every two years at Argolis and Corinth.

Time to understand

1 Look carefully at Fig. 9.32, which is a plan of a stadium. Runners sprinted up the field, made a left-hand turn and ran back to the starting line. Which runner had the most difficult run? Why?

2 Fig. 9.31 is a detail of the starting line. Each runner stood behind a starting gate or husplex. How did a starter begin a race? What could go wrong at the beginning of a race? How are races begun today?

3 Fig. 9.23 on p. 171 shows men practising for the events which made up the Pentathlon, which is an important contest at the Olympics today. How many events make up the Pentathlon and what are they? What kind of athletes enter the Pentathlon?

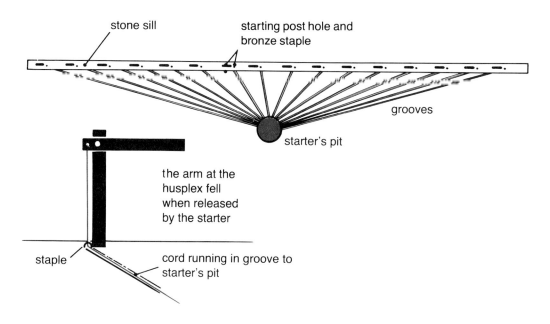

Fig. 9.31 The starting line for a foot race with a starting post, or *husplex*, inset.

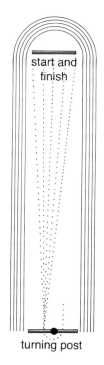

Fig. 9.32 Plan of a stadium.

Drama festivals

No one really knows when the first play was performed in ancient Greece. However, in 534 BC the name of the first actor, Thespis, was recorded. Today, actors are sometimes called *thespians*.

Plays were performed at drama festivals. In Athens, there were three main festivals each year. They were held in honour of Dionysus, the god of wine. Every citizen was expected to attend. Otherwise Dionysus would be offended. You might remember what happened at the beginning of the Trojan War when two goddesses were offended.

At the beginning of each festival, animals were sacrificed and ceremonies were performed. Then the plays began in one of the huge theatres which could seat thousands of people.

Drama festivals were actually competitions. Prizes were awarded to the writers of the best plays. Sometimes five

179

Fig. 9.33 The theatre of Epidaurus today.

plays were performed in a single day. A festival lasted several days.

There were two main kinds of plays. The first was called tragedy. The stories or plots were taken from mythology or history. They were usually sad. The other was comedy. These plays were just good fun. Often the characters were meant to represent prominent people living in Athens at the time.

All the plays that have survived from ancient Greece were written by Athenians. We know that other city-states also held drama festivals from the number of theatres scattered throughout Greece.

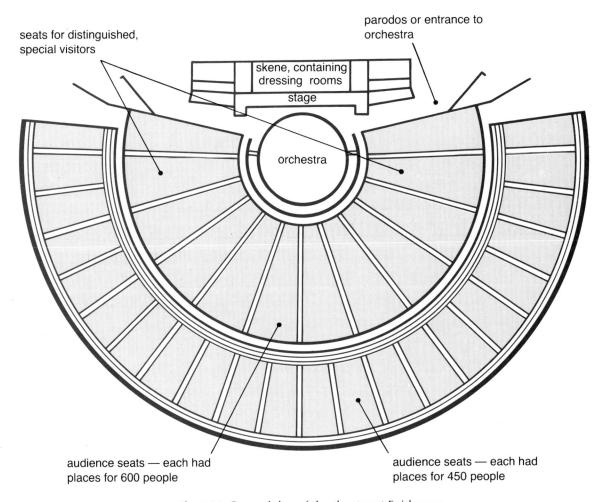

Fig. 9.34 Groundplan of the theatre at Epidaurus.

180

No more than three actors and a chorus of about fifteen people were needed to perform a play. Each actor played a number of different parts. He simply changed his mask and costume when he acted the part of a different person. Women were not allowed to take part in plays. If one of the characters in a play was female, the actor wore a mask to show that he was playing the part of a woman.

Masks were often larger than life so that people sitting at the back of the theatre could recognise the character clearly. Each mask showed a different expression. If the play was a tragedy the expression was usually sorrowful. In a comedy the masks were very exaggerated and made people laugh.

Fig. 9.35 A marble carving of an ancient Greek theatrical mask (top), and a terracotta model of an actor in a mask (bottom).

Costumes were simple but dramatic. Actors wore built-up shoes, again so that people could see what was happening from the back of the theatre. You can imagine that if you were wearing a heavy plaster mask, a large flowing costume and built-up shoes, it would be difficult to move. Because of this, there was not very much action in Greek plays. Most of the action was simply narrated or spoken of, except in comedies.

The chorus was an important part of each play. The members of the chorus chanted and danced in front of the stage in the orchestra. They sometimes filled in gaps in the story which could not be shown on stage. They also explained the action to the audience.

The training of a chorus for a particular play was very expensive. Wealthy Athenian citizens usually paid for a chorus. The *choregus*, or citizen financing a chorus, was given a prize as well if the play was a success. Actors were paid by the government.

The audience at a play often became very involved. Sometimes people wept at a tragedy or swayed to the music and chanting of a chorus. If the audience disliked a play or thought the acting was poor they whistled or threw things at the actors.

Each theatre was designed so that even the people sitting right at the back of the theatre could hear clearly everything spoken on stage. This is still noticeable today in the surviving Greek theatres.

Time to understand

1 Fig. 9.34 shows a plan of the theatre at Epidaurus. Use the key to answer the following questions.

a How many people could the theatre hold?

b How many seats were reserved for distinguished guests? What kind of people do you think these were?

c What is the meaning of the word 'orchestra' today? Do you see any similarities between that meaning and the original use of the word?

d The stage is small compared to the orchestra. Can you explain why?

e The front of the skene formed the background for most plays. What else could be used to add atmosphere to plays?

2 The following methods were used to create sound effects. Can you imagine what each sound effect was supposed to be?

a pebbles rolled gently in a pottery bowl,

b two wooden bowls clapped together,

c a round stone rolled down a tunnel which ran underneath the seats.

The Golden Age of Athens

During the fifth century BC Athens became the most glorious and beautiful city-state in Greece. The people of Athens were proud and confident. This period has been called the Golden Age of Athens.

Athens was the cultural centre of Greece from about 475 BC until about 425 BC. These two dates coincide with two wars in which Athens was involved. You will learn more about these wars later in this chapter.

Government and empire

As you read earlier in this chapter, the people of Athens governed themselves with a form of government called democracy. The most influential job any man could hold in the government was that of *strategos*, or general. Each year ten generals were elected. If necessary, a general had to lead part of the army in battle. He also could put proposals or ideas to the Assembly of the people. If the people accepted the idea, it became law.

Pericles was a very clever general. Year after year he was elected. Most people accepted his ideas as right for Athens. Pericles therefore became the unofficial leader of Athens. Under his leadership Athens gained an empire. This empire included most of the islands in the Aegean Sea, a number of city-states in Asia Minor and some in northern Greece.

Athens agreed to protect the places within the empire from attack by other states. These places had to pay for Athens' protection by giving *tribute*. Tribute was usually money or ships. This made Athens strong and wealthy.

Architecture

Some of Athens' finest buildings were erected during the Golden Age. The Parthenon was one of the largest Greek temples ever built. It was dedicated to Athena, patron goddess of Athens. It stood (and still stands in ruins) on top of the Acropolis, and could be seen from great distances, even out to sea.

The Parthenon is a good example of Greek architecture. It is very simple and graceful. Its design was carefully worked out by Ictinus, an architect, so that it appeared perfect.

Sometimes the horizontal lines of a building look as though they are sagging when viewed from a distance. To correct this optical illusion, Ictinus made sure all the horizontals, such as the platform and

Fig. 9.36 The Parthenon today.

Fig. 9.37 A sculptor painting a statue. Most sculptures were painted in ancient Greece.

steps were built on a slightly arched curve. Yet, not a single block of stone is curved.

The Parthenon was decorated with exquisite sculpture. The most famous is a frieze which went around the whole building just above the top of the columns. It depicts the procession during Athena's festival, the Panathenaea. Children, old men, young girls, horses, sheep and cattle are all carved in perfect detail. Most of the sculpture has been removed from the Parthenon so that it can be preserved in museums.

Arts and sciences

Other arts and sciences flourished in the Golden Age of Athens. Drama became so important that a special magistrate was in charge of organising festivals. Herodotus and Thucydides wrote history books. Hippocrates founded a school of medicine. He is called the 'father of medicine', just as Herodotus has been called the 'father of history'.

Another 'father' was Socrates, a philosopher. Philosophy means love of wisdom. Socrates lived in Athens from approximately 470–399 BC. He taught that people should look for the truth of everything. His way of teaching was to ask questions. He had a large following of disciples. Some men also opposed him.

There was no police force to catch criminals in Athens. If someone was suspected of committing a crime, another citizen took him to the law courts to accuse him of the crime. This happened to Socrates. He was accused of corrupting the young men of Athens and making the gods angry. The jury judging the case was bribed by Socrates' enemies. He was found guilty and sentenced to death.

One of Socrates' disciples was Plato. Plato wrote down everything he could remember about Socrates' teaching. The books that Plato wrote about Socrates are part of our heritage from ancient Greece.

The Greeks abroad

One of the most important Greek gods was Poseidon, god of the sea. Greek sailors hoped that Poseidon would give them a safe voyage across the Aegean Sea to the east or the Adriatic Sea to the west.

Greek seamen were usually merchants and traders. They carried goods to and from Greece. In fact, the Greeks needed to import certain foods, such as corn, in order to survive.

The mountainous countryside of Greece produced very few crops. The soil was poor and there was not much rain. The main crops were grapes and olives. The most common farm animal was the goat, which could eat anything anywhere. Cattle and sheep were not common by today's standards. This meant that very few were killed for food. The sacrifice of a cow or sheep to the gods was really a sacrifice. This may help explain why after the

sacrifice all the spectators ate the roast meat. It was a special occasion, not only because it was a way of worshipping the gods but also because it was a rare chance to eat meat.

As the population of city-states grew, there was less food to go around. One solution to this problem was to send some of the people to live in other countries.

The Greeks who travelled overseas rarely came home. They spent the rest of their lives in the new settlement, or colony, they had formed. Very often these colonies became prosperous city-states, similar in many ways to the city-states back in Greece.

This movement of Greeks overseas is called *colonisation*. The two main areas of

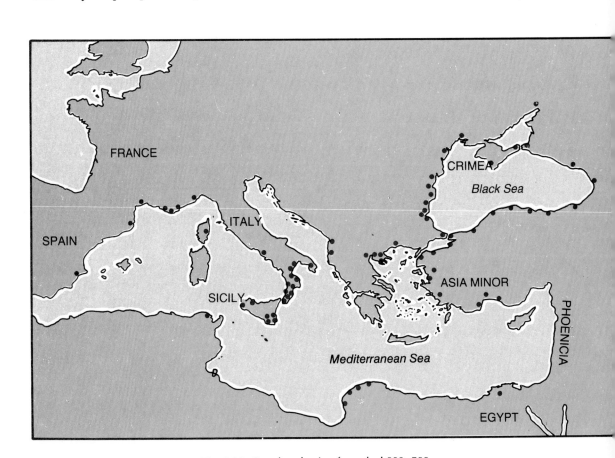

Fig. 9.38 Greek colonies founded 800–500 BC.

colonisation were in the east, to the coast of Asia Minor and the Black Sea and in the west, to Italy. When the Greeks founded colonies they took with them their culture, traditions, language and art. In fact, the colonies remained Greek. Usually the city-state that sent out the colonists was called the mother city. The colony and the mother city usually traded with one another. They also supported one another in times of war.

Time to understand

Read the following story about a Greek ship called the *Argo* that was almost wrecked in a storm at sea.

When they reached the narrow, winding straits, walled in by cliffs, they felt the current swirling against them, and were filled with a great fear. Their ears rang with the grinding and crashing of the rocks, and the endless roar of water against the cliffs. They rounded a bend, and saw the rocks opening ahead of them. Their hearts sank but there was no choice but to go on, straight for the gap between the rocks.

Suddenly the rocks rushed at one another, and met with a thunderous crash. A storm of foam and white spray leaped up, and the sea groaned and thundered till the sky echoed. *Argo* was snatched by the current and whirled round in a helpless circle.

Then without warning the rocks parted again, and the captain ran down the gangway between the rowing-benches, shouting to his crew to row as hard as they could. Eagerly they obeyed him, but the current was still too strong. Their oars bent like bows, but they were swept back three metres for every two they travelled.

Then another huge wave rushed down on them, and *Argo* rolled end-on and plunged through the rolling water. She was washed back between the clashing rocks, and

wedged there unable to move. The current ebbed and flowed, and the rocks rumbled and roared on either side, but *Argo* was stuck fast.

That was when Athene came down and took a hand. She thrust the solid rock aside, freed *Argo* and sent her speeding through the channel. On the ship flew, winged like an arrow — but even so, as the rocks crashed shut, they snapped off the very tip of the superstructure at the stern. Apart from that, they were safely through — and Athene soared back up to heaven, her task complete.

1 How do you think the Greeks would explain this terrible storm at sea?
2 According to the story, why was the ship freed?
3 Can you think of another possible explanation for the freeing of the ship?
4 Rough seas and shipwrecks were two of the problems the Greek colonists had to face. Make a list of some of the other difficulties they had to overcome. Can you guess what sort of people went to new homes overseas?
5 The story of the *Argo* comes from Greek mythology. According to the myths, the ship's commander was called Jason and its crew were called Argonauts. Find a book of Greek myths in your library and read the story of Jason and the Argonauts. What were they searching for? Why? Did they find it?

The Greeks at war

In the year 490 BC a huge army, sailing in 600 ships, crossed the Aegean Sea to Greece. Darius, the great Persian king, had come to attack Athens.

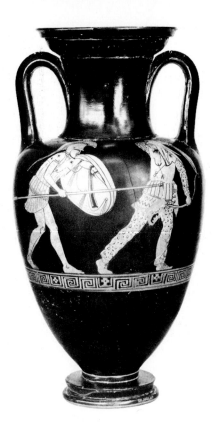

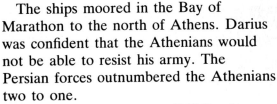

Fig. 9.39 A Greek hoplite and a Persian archer.

Fig. 9.40 Xerxes' bridge of boats.

The ships moored in the Bay of Marathon to the north of Athens. Darius was confident that the Athenians would not be able to resist his army. The Persian forces outnumbered the Athenians two to one.

To Darius' horror over 6000 Persian soldiers died in a single day's fighting. Athens lost fewer than 200 men. The rest of the Persian army retreated to their ships and soon were making their way back across the Aegean. The Athenians were triumphant because their freedom was assured.

Ten years later Xerxes, the next king of Persia, marched a bigger army across Thrace, down through Macedonia and into northern Greece. The Persian navy sailed close to the coast, following the army's march. Xerxes wanted revenge.

The story of the Persian invasion of Greece is told in great detail by the Greek historian Herodotus. Sometimes he exaggerates details in order to make a good story.

Herodotus said that when Xerxes' army arrived at the Hellespont they constructed a bridge of boats lashed together with strong cables. They then built a road on the floating bridge across the narrow strait of water. Herodotus goes on to say that when a storm destroyed the bridge, Xerxes ordered some soldiers to whip the water of the Hellespont to punish it!

The Persians were defeated by the Greeks who had united to protect their homeland. Never before had the Greeks fought a common enemy together.

Xerxes' army and navy were much bigger than the combined forces of the Greeks. How did the Greeks win?

All the accounts of the Persian wars tell the same story. The Greeks were fighting for their freedom. The Athenians had a strong navy. In land battles the Spartans proved to be as good as their reputation.

At the narrow mountain pass of Thermopylae in northern Greece the Spartans held back the Persian army for several days. A traitor showed the Persians another way over the mountains. A small band of three hundred Spartans continued to fight, even though they were attacked from both sides. The battle was a victory for the Persians but the bravery of the Spartans inspired the rest of Greece.

The Athenians contributed the most to the combined Greek navy, which was moored in the straits of water between the mainland and the island of Salamis. They knew the Persians would sail there after their victory at Thermopylae.

The Persian ships were much larger than the small Greek *triremes*. The Greeks tricked the Persians into believing that they were retreating and the Persians sailed into the narrow straits of Salamis. When most of the huge Persian fleet had crowded into the straits, the Greek fleet turned around. They used the rams on the front of their triremes to sink many Persian ships.

The defeat of the Persian navy at Salamis was decisive. The surviving ships quickly retreated across the Aegean Sea. Xerxes himself left his land forces and went back to Persia. The final battle on Greek shores was another Greek victory. At Plataea the skill and bravery of the Spartan soldiers won over the Persian army.

The Greek states had united to defeat a common enemy. However, after the Persian wars, rivalry between the city-states became very strong. Over the next fifty years this rivalry, jealousy and fear caused the city-states to divide into two groups. One was led by Sparta, the other by Athens. Eventually, a war broke out between these two groups.

This war, called the Peloponnesian War, lasted almost thirty years. Athens and the city-states on its side were defeated by Sparta and its allies. Athens was never quite the same again. By 400 BC the Golden Age was over.

Time to understand

Fig. 9.41 shows a Greek warship, or trireme. This has been reconstructed from descriptions in literature and archaelogical evidence. A trireme was rowed by 170 oarsmen.

1 Describe how these oarsmen were arranged.

2 The hulls were painted with pitch to make them appear black. What is pitch? Why did the Greeks use pitch? Could they have used some other material?

3 The ram on the front was often covered with metal. This was used to knock holes in the sides of other ships. When could this happen? Draw a diagram to illustrate your answer.

4 What could go wrong when a trireme was attacking another ship? How do you think this was prevented?

5 Fig. 9.42 shows a defensive position which could be adopted by triremes. Could any of these ships be attacked? Why or why not? What could possibly break up this formation?

6 Here is a description of a battle by the Athenian historian Thucydides:

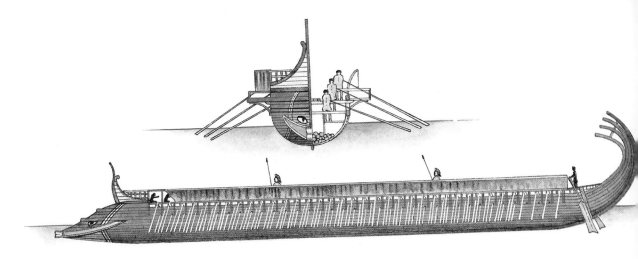

Fig. 9.41 A Greek trireme.

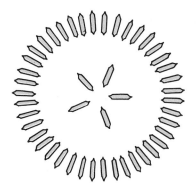

Fig. 9.42 Rings of triremes.

The two fleets together came to nearly 200 ships. They were jammed so tightly together in the narrow harbour that there was no opportunity for ramming or breaking back for a charge. There were frequent collisions, ship fouling ship as they attacked or fell back from one another. While two ships bore down on each other, the soldiers on deck showered their opponents with spears, stones and arrows. When they met, there was fierce hand-to-hand fighting as each crew tried to board the other ship.

Often, because of the cramped space, a ship had no sooner rammed its opponent than it was rammed itself. On several occasions two or more ships attacked the same enemy, and became entangled; steersmen frequently had to out-manoeuvre several enemy ships at once. The crashing and splintering of ship against ship caused great confusion, and made it impossible to hear the orders shouted by the officers.

a What does this description tell you about the technique of ramming?
b What were some of the other methods of fighting used in a naval battle?
   What did a 'steersman' do? What position would he occupy on a trireme? (See Fig. 9.41.)

10

Citizens of the empire: the Romans

The Etruscans

Fig. 10.1 Early Italy.

WHEN the ancient Greeks founded their colonies in southern Italy in about 700 BC they were not the only settlers in the long boot-shaped peninsula. A number of other groups of people were living in towns scattered throughout the countryside. Further north there were Etruscans living in Etruria and Latins living in Latium.

Etruria was bordered by the Arno River in the north, the Tiber River in the east and south and the Mediterranean Sea in the west. The Etruscans made good use of their land by draining the marshes, clearing the forests and building roads. Most people were farmers, but a large number lived in towns.

The townspeople produced well-made bronze weapons and ornaments, gold jewellery and terracotta statues. They built wooden temples and decorated them with terracotta sculpture. They lived in mud-brick and timber houses. They enjoyed horse racing, hunting, fishing and wrestling. How do we know all these things?

Most of our knowledge of the Etruscans comes from their cemeteries. At first, the dead were cremated or buried in a simple pit. Over a period of time the burials became more elaborate, until tombs were shaped and furnished like houses. You probably remember how in ancient Egypt people buried everything they thought the dead person would need in the next life. In Etruscan tombs, archaeologists have found a similar collection of everyday objects. However, no one really knows whether the Etruscan people believed in life after death in the same way as the Egyptians.

Some wall paintings in tombs tell us that the Etruscans used to sing and dance. You can see one of these paintings in Fig. 10.2. These paintings look like Greek paintings from about the same period of time. Because of this some historians think that the Etruscans must have had some contact with the Greeks in south Italy and in Greece itself. Much Greek pottery has been discovered in Etruscan tombs as well.

A number of terracotta coffins in the shape of dining couches have been found

Fig. 10.3 A terracotta funerary couch.

in Etruscan tombs. Usually a husband and wife are shown reclining together on the coffin-couch. These coffins and other evidence such as wall paintings suggest that women were much freer in Etruria than they were in Greece. You may remember that women in Athens were not allowed to attend dinner parties and so they were never depicted reclining on dining couches as they were in Etruria.

There were at least twelve Etruscan towns by about 700 BC. When their society was prosperous and well established the Etruscans began to take over territory to the north and south of Etruria. This included the town of Rome across the Tiber River in Latium.

Time to understand

The Roman culture that developed in Italy has things in common with both Etruria and Greece. Sometimes historians argue over whether the Greeks or the Etruscans had the greatest influence over the early Romans.

Fig. 10.2 A wall painting from an Etruscan tomb.

Fig. 10.4 An Etruscan soldier, cast in bronze.

Fig. 10.5 The interior of an Etruscan tomb.

1 Fig. 10.4 shows a statue of an Etruscan soldier, dating from about 500 BC. Compare this with the picture of the Greek hoplites shown in Fig. 9.12 on p. 159.

  a List the similarities in the appearance of the two kinds of soldiers.

  b Do you think that the Greek way of fighting may have influenced the Etruscans? Why?

2 Fig. 10.5 shows the inside of an Etruscan tomb. Some historians think it looks like the houses of the time. How would you describe this kind of house?

The early history of Rome

Our story now focuses on a group of people called the Latins of Latium. The territory of Latium was a coastal plain stretching from the Mediterranean to the Apennines, between the Tiber and Iris rivers.

In 800 BC about fifty small villages were scattered across the plain. Some of them were perched on hilltops. By about 500 BC, under the influence of the Etruscans, the villages had become larger, although there were now only about ten of them.

The most important of these villages in our story is Rome. The history of Rome tells how one small settlement became large and powerful enough to rule a vast empire. The empire at its peak stretched from Britain in the west to Asia Minor in the east.

Rome had the best position on the plain of Latium. It was later called 'the city of the seven hills' because of the seven hillocks included in the original settlement. It was close to the Tiber at one of the few places where the river could be crossed safely and therefore easily defended. Because of its closeness to the Tiber, Rome had access to the sea.

Most historians believe that Rome was originally ruled by kings and that the last two or three of these were Etruscans. This part of the story of Rome fits in well with what we know about Etruria.

Romulus and Remus

Most of the traditional story of early Rome is not accepted by modern historians. The story was developed by Roman historians such as Livy. They tried to link the fall of Troy in about 1200 BC (see p. 152) with the beginning of Rome.

191

The story goes like this. Aeneas, a Trojan prince, and his followers, sailed to Italy after the Trojan War. Aeneas married the daughter of the king of Latium. When his father-in-law died, Aeneas became king of Latium. He was succeeded by his son Ascanius who founded a town called Alba Longa.

Many years later Numitor became king of Alba Longa. He had twin grandsons, Romulus and Remus. Amulius, the brother of Numitor, took the throne from his brother and ordered that the twins be drowned in the Tiber. However, the boys survived. They were first nursed by a she-wolf and then by a shepherd and his wife.

When they grew up they killed Amulius and gave the throne back to their grandfather, Numitor. Romulus and Remus decided to found a new town called Rome on a hill (one of the seven!) called the Palatine in 753 BC. Romulus built walls around the town. Remus made fun of him by jumping over the walls. Romulus became angry and killed his brother. This left Romulus as the only ruler of the new town.

After Romulus there were six more kings of Rome. The last three of these had Etruscan names and ruled from 616 to 510 BC, according to the story. Historians agree that the Etruscans probably took over Rome, as well as other towns in Latium, in about 650–600 BC. So the story probably has some fact in it, even though it is largely based on legend and mythology.

Fig. 10.6 A sculpture showing the she-wolf nursing Romulus and Remus.

The growing city

The evidence available through archaeology and some written sources tells us that the Etruscan kings helped to turn Rome from a small town into a city. They built new temples to the gods and new, straight roads.

One of the most important steps was the planning of a city centre called the Forum,

Basilica: in the provinces town council meetings were held here. In Rome itself there were a number of basilicas used for business and law courts.

Colonnade: here shops and business offices were located. In Rome shops were found in a separate marketplace.

Statues and columns: generals and emperors often erected these at their own expense to make themselves and their victories widely known.

Rostrum: a public speaker stood on the rostrum to address the assembly of people gathered in the forum.

Curia: originally the curia was the meeting place of the Senate in Rome. In the provinces it was probably used for religious and other special occasions.

Triumphal arch: these were built in honour of an emperor or a military victory. They were often decorated with sculpted reliefs telling the story of the campaign or the emperor's glory.

Temples: the most important temples were usually included in the forum. In the temple of Vesta in Rome a flame was kept burning constantly.

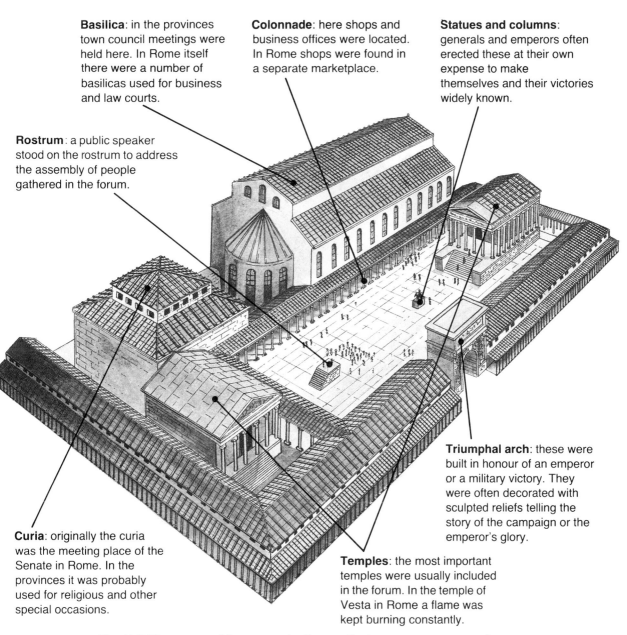

Fig. 10.7 The centre of Rome was the Forum. Business, government and important religious ceremonies were all conducted there. Almost all Roman towns in the provinces (see p. 212) were built around forums as well.

Fig. 10.8 The ruins of the Forum in Rome today.

or market place. The ground on which the Forum was built was low-lying and sometimes flooded by the Tiber. A huge drain was built to carry off excess water. Old houses were pulled down and a pebble floor was laid over the whole area.

Another project of the Etruscan kings was the laying out of the Circus Maximus. This was a large sportsground for races and games.

The last Etruscan king was Tarquinius Superbus who became very unpopular with the Romans. His rule was harsh. The people of Rome drove him from the city and established a new form of government called a *republic*. You will learn more about the Republic in the next section of this chapter.

Time to understand

When Livy wrote his history of Rome he included a story about a Roman hero called Horatius Cocles. Livy said that when Tarquinius Superbus was driven from Rome he returned with an army mustered in another Etruscan town. He wanted to become king of Rome once again. Now read on.

Note: The Janiculum, the Palatine and the Capitol are the names of three of the seven hills of Rome.

On the approach of the Etruscan army, the Romans abandoned their farmsteads and moved into the city. Garrisons were posted. In some sections the city walls seemed sufficient protection, in others the barrier of the Tiber. The most vulnerable point was the wooden bridge, and the Etruscans would have crossed it and forced an entrance into the city, had it not been for the courage of one man, Horatius Cocles — that great soldier whom the fortune of Rome gave to be her shield on that day of peril.

Horatius was on guard at the bridge when the Janiculum was captured by a sudden attack. The enemy forces came pouring down the hill, while the Roman troops, throwing away their weapons, were behaving more like an undisciplined rabble than a fighting force.

Horatius acted promptly: as his routed comrades approached the bridge, he stopped as many as he could catch and compelled them to listen to him. 'By God,' he cried, 'can't you see that if you desert your post escape is hopeless? If you leave the bridge open in your rear, there will soon be more of them in the Palatine and the Capitol than on the Janiculum.'

Urging them with all the power at his command to destroy the bridge by fire or steel or any means they could muster, he offered to hold up the Etruscan advance, so far as was possible, alone. Proudly he took his stand at the outer end of the bridge; conspicuous amongst the rout of fugitives, sword and shield ready for action, he prepared himself for close combat, one man against an army. The advancing enemy paused in sheer astonishment at such reckless courage.

Two other men, Spurius Lartius and Titus Herminius, both aristocrats with a fine military record, were ashamed to leave Horatius alone, and with their support he won through the first few minutes of desperate danger. Soon, however, he forced them to save themselves and leave him; for little was now left of the bridge, and the demolition squads were calling them back before it was too late.

Once more Horatius stood alone; with defiance in his eyes he confronted the Etruscan cavalry, challenging one after another to single combat, and mocking them all as tyrants' slaves who, careless of their own liberty, were coming to destroy the liberty of others. For a while they hung back, each waiting for his neighbour to make the first move, until shame at the unequal battle drove them to action, and with a fierce cry they hurled their spears at the solitary figure which barred their way. Horatius caught the missiles on his shield and, resolute as ever, straddled the bridge and held his ground.

The Etruscans moved forward, and would have thrust him aside by the sheer weight of numbers, but their advance was suddenly checked by the crash of the falling bridge and the simultaneous shout of triumph from the Roman soldiers who had done their work in time.

The Etruscans could only stare in bewilderment as Horatius, with a prayer to Father Tiber to bless him and his sword, plunged fully armed into the water and swam, through the missiles which fell thick about him, safely to the other side where his friends were waiting to receive him. It was a noble piece of work — legendary, maybe, but destined to be celebrated in story through the years to come.

1   Why did Horatius decide to defend the bridge?
2   What instructions did he give to the other Roman soldiers?
3   How could they destroy the bridge by fire? By steel?
4   Why did two men help Horatius?
5   Describe how Horatius and the others held back the Etruscans.
6   What do you think Livy meant when he wrote 'with a prayer to Father Tiber'?

Can you think of any other society which offered prayers to a river?
7   Do you remember the Greek hero Achilles? Make a list of the qualities of the two heroes.
8   Why do you think Livy described this event in such detail? Does Horatius suit the modern meaning of the word 'hero'? Why?

From republic to empire

Governing Rome

The new form of government in Rome was a republic. This meant that the rulers were chosen by the people of Rome themselves in an assembly. Each year the people met to elect their rulers or *magistrates*.

The duties of the king were divided between two magistrates called consuls. The office of consul was the highest achievement of any man who had a political career. Each magistrate was elected for one year only. This system was designed to prevent one man from becoming too powerful.

Some magistrates looked after festivals and games, some after the law courts and some after the finances of Rome. One of the duties of a consul was to lead an army in battle if necessary.

The consuls were advised by a council of men called the Senate. Only ex-magistrates could become members of the Senate. The Senate gradually became more powerful than the magistrates and, in fact, governed Rome.

Originally there were two main social classes. The upper class, called *patricians*, were probably the descendants of the early inhabitants of Rome. They owned the most land and were wealthy. They were usually well educated.

The lower class, called *plebeians*, were usually peasant farmers and craftsmen. They were often very poor. Later, the merchants and traders who were also wealthy formed a class in between these two. They were known as the *equites*.

At first, only patricians were allowed to be magistrates. Patricians also had more votes in the elections of the magistrates. However, between about 490 and 360 BC things changed in Rome. The plebeians outnumbered the patricians and threatened to revolt if they were not given more say in the government. In 367 BC a plebeian was elected as consul. This showed how much things had changed.

Spreading out

For many years the Romans concentrated on building up the strength of their own city and the territory of Latium. Eventually the other inhabitants of Italy fought with the Romans over territory. Rome developed an effective army which defeated the Etruscans in the north and the Samnites in the south and east by 290 BC.

The most serious threat to Rome around that time was a tribe called the Gauls. The Gauls lived in part of what is now France. They invaded northern Italy and in 390 BC entered Rome. They burned and ransacked much of the city, destroying many historical records. The Romans saved themselves by paying the Gauls a huge sum of gold. The Gauls then settled in the north of Italy in territory called Cisalpine Gaul.

The Romans had defeated the Greek colonies in south Italy by 275 BC. This meant that all Italy below Cisalpine Gaul was under the control of Rome. The Romans treated the other Italians fairly as allies or friends rather than as conquered

Fig. 10.9 A Greek temple built at the colony of Paestum, in southern Italy.

enemies. They had to pay tax to Rome and supply men for the army but otherwise were allowed to live freely. Gradually the Roman language (called Latin), Roman law and Roman religion spread throughout Italy.

Roman merchants traded both to the east and to the west across the Mediterranean. However, they found that the Carthaginians of North Africa resented other merchants trading in the Mediterranean. Eventually war broke out between Rome and Carthage when the two states became involved in a quarrel over Sicily in 264 BC. The Carthaginians were defeated. Sicily was overrun by the Romans and became the first province of the Roman empire in 241 BC. This meant that it was forced to pay tax to Rome and was governed by a Roman magistrate.

Within a few years the islands of Sardinia and Corsica became Roman provinces as well. The Romans soon realised that provinces brought extra wealth and extra land to Rome. Soldiers were often given land in the provinces after they returned from war.

Over the next 150 years Rome successfully conquered most of the countries around the Mediterranean and

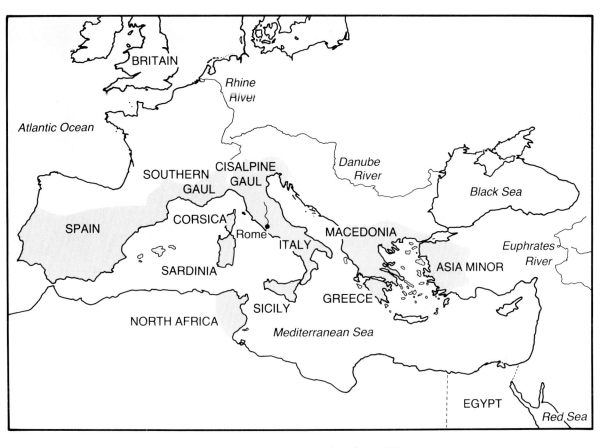

Fig. 10.10 The Roman empire about 120 BC.

east to Greece and Asia Minor. By about 120 BC Rome controlled Spain, North Africa, Sicily, Sardinia, Corsica, Greece, Macedonia, Asia Minor, Cisalpine Gaul and southern Gaul, an area which is now part of France. You can see the extent of the empire in Fig. 10.10.

One of the effects of the conquest of Greece was the adoption of Greek culture by the Romans. Educated Romans even learned Greek as a second language.

Julius Caesar

Over the next 100 years, Rome's empire expanded but the government of Rome began to break down. Ambitious consuls and strong army leaders competed against each other for control of the government and Rome.

One of the most famous of these is Julius Caesar. He became consul several times. He also led an army which conquered northern Gaul. This gave Rome a new province.

Eventually a war broke out in Italy over who should control Rome. Julius Caesar and his army were victorious. He was called *imperator*, which meant 'commander-in-chief'. The word 'emperor' comes from the word *imperator*.

In 45 BC Caesar became the ruler of Rome. He introduced a number of changes which greatly helped the poor. Unfortunately, most of the patricians

Fig. 10.11 Julius Casesar, depicted as a general.

Fig. 10.12 The Emperor Augustus wearing a toga.

disliked him. Many felt that they had no say in the government. They also thought that he was going to become king of Rome. Romans hated the idea of a king. On 15 March 44 BC, Caesar was stabbed to death by a group of patricians.

Antony and Cleopatra

After Caesar's murder there was another period of war in Italy. Two men emerged as winners and they divided the empire between them. Their names were Mark Antony and Octavian, the adopted son of Julius Caesar. Octavian ruled the west; Mark Antony ruled the east.

Antony fell in love with Cleopatra, the queen of Egypt. He began to neglect his duties as co-ruler of the Roman empire. In 31 BC Octavian declared war on Antony and Cleopatra, and the next year he invaded Egypt. Antony and Cleopatra committed suicide rather than be captured.

Egypt was conquered by Octavian. It became a Roman province. Octavian was the sole ruler of the Roman empire. He ruled wisely and made people believe that the old form of government was restored. He was called *Augustus* which meant 'His Majesty'.

198

Augustus and afterwards

Augustus introduced many reforms to Rome and the empire during his reign of 44 years. New roads were built between Rome and the provinces. Trade prospered. A police force and a fire brigade were set up.

Over the next 200 years there was peace in the empire. This period is sometimes called the *Pax Romana* (Roman Peace). However, things were not always easy and peaceful in the provinces.

The first four emperors after Augustus were related to him. After Nero, the last of the four, the emperor was usually a successful or popular general.

Time to understand

The Romans usually built aqueducts to bring water from a natural supply such as a river or spring to towns. The water travelled down the slope of an aqueduct. If the slope was too great the water pressure built up and sometimes burst pipes. The regular slope was 0.5 centimetres over 30 metres. Sometimes the aqueduct passed underground or through solid rock.

Fig. 10.13 shows how water reached the town and what happened to it there.

1 Three main supplies of water led off the castellum or water tower. If there was a shortage of water which supply was cut first?

Do you think this was planned? Why?

2 Why do you think that public fountains and public baths had an equal level of supply?

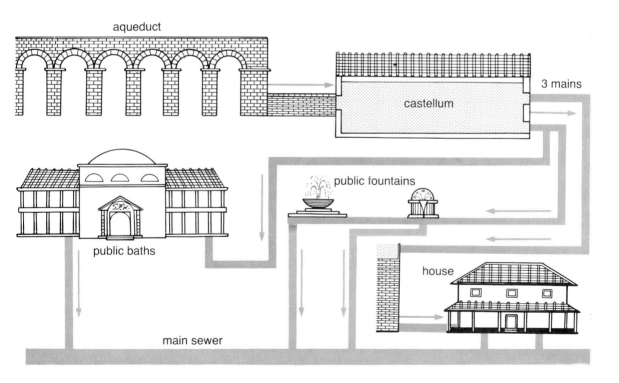

Fig. 10.13 Roman water supply system.

Fig. 10.14 A Roman aqueduct in France.

Fig. 10.15 The interior of a Roman house.

3 Why was it important to have a good drainage and sewage system? How else could water be disposed of?

4 Aqueducts were covered even if above ground level. Why was this important?

5 When an engineer was designing an aqueduct how would he decide whether it should be built above the ground or below ground level?

The Roman family

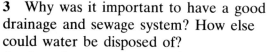

Family life in Rome was very important. A Roman family was much larger than most families today. It included not only the husband and wife and their children but also slaves.

The father, as head of a household, had the power to punish any member of his family, even with death. He was also in charge of religious ceremonies in the home.

Usually each house had a small shrine where household gods were worshipped. The *Lar Familiaris* was the protective spirit of the household. He was often depicted as a young boy. Vesta, goddess of fire and the hearth (or fireplace), was also worshipped. This was because fire was essential for living, for warmth and light and cooking. Prayers and sacrifices were made at dinner before the last course or dessert.

The mother of the family worked hard. She organised the work of the slaves, looked after the early education of the children and spun wool. Many famous Romans praised their mothers for bringing them up well.

Marriages were often arranged, sometimes by professional brokers and sometimes by the father. When a woman married she became a member of her husband's family or household. If the husband had not yet set up his own household the newly married couple lived in his father's home.

When a child was born Romans believed that a *genius* or guardian spirit was born with it. Birthdays were celebrated in much the same way as today with gifts and good wishes, except that offerings of wine, flowers, incense and cakes were made to the *genius* as well.

Nine days after a child was born special ceremonies were performed. A *bulla* or locket was hung around the baby's neck.

Fig. 10.16 A Roman woman (left) performing a religious ceremony, perhaps for the goddess on the right.

Taberna: Rooms at the front of townhouses were often used for business. In this example one of the front rooms was a tavern. People could buy wine and food such as grapes and dates. Where do people go for casual refreshments today? Are food and drink shops still part of people's houses?

Peristylium: Most Roman houses had a well-organised garden at the back. It often contained fountains, statues and even pools of water, as well as shrubs, trees and flowers. Part of the garden was surrounded by a row of columns which was usually covered. Do modern houses have an equivalent to the peristylium? How is this used?

Triclinium: If the weather was good, the family ate in the peristylium. Otherwise the triclinium or dining room was used. Why would the architect have placed the triclinium in this position?

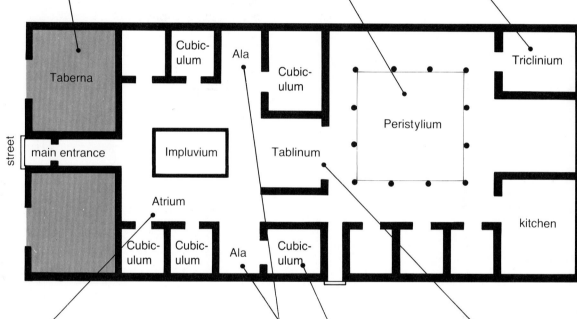

Atrium: This was the central room around which other rooms were placed. It was open to the sky. In the centre was a depression in the floor called the *impluvium*. This was used for catching rainwater. What would life have been like in a Roman house without the *atrium*? Why do modern houses not have an *atrium*?

Alae: These were small alcoves off the atrium. Usually these contained wax busts of the family's ancestors. What kinds of records do we have of our ancestors today? Why were these not used by the Romans?

Cubicula: These were the sleeping quarters. Do you know the meaning of the English words cubicle or cubby? Do you think they were derived from the Latin word for bedroom?

Tablinum: This was the father's study or office. It could be closed off with doors or curtains. Why do you think the tablinum was placed in the centre of the house?

Fig. 10.17 Plan of a typical Roman house based on those at Pompeii. The rooms all had special purposes, as they usually do in houses today. Roman houses faced inwards. This means that there were very few windows or doors opening on to the street. Light and air came through the doorways opening on to the atrium and the peristylium which were both unroofed.

He or she wore this right throughout childhood. This was meant to protect the child from 'evil forces'.

Clothes showed a person's position in society. Boys wore a knee-length tunic called a *toga praetexta*. If they came from wealthy families it had a purple band around the edge. When a Roman boy reached manhood he wore a *toga virilis* over his tunic. It was very important to drape a toga correctly. Sometimes very wealthy men had slaves just to look after their togas.

Women and girls wore a *palla*, which was the female equivalent of a toga. Most cloth was made of wool. It was dyed different colours and woven in different textures for variation. When it was cold cloaks were worn as well.

Poorer people wore a simple tunic tied at the waist. If it was hot labourers wore a loincloth. Most people wore leather sandals on their feet.

Only the rich could afford 'extras' such as jewellery and make-up. Good teeth were valued and were cleaned with water and ground pumice stone. Hairstyles for women were elaborate and sometimes wigs were worn. For most of the long period of Roman history, men wore their hair short and were clean shaven.

The whole family ate together, unless there was a formal dinner party. Breakfast was bread and honey, or bread dipped in wine. Sometimes dates, olives or cheese were added. Lunch consisted of eggs, bread and cheese. Dinner was the main meal and was eaten after the day's work, early in the evening. The array of food included fish, meat, salads, poultry, herbs, fruit and cakes.

Romans followed the Greek custom of eating on dining couches. These couches were quite wide and held up to three people.

The menus described above were for the wealthy. The poor often ate a kind of gruel, which was wheat boiled with bits of vegetable, meat or fish, as well as bread, cheese and fruit.

Time to understand

In many ways Roman children were educated like Greek children. As well, a young man from a patrician family always

Fig. 10.18 The life of a Roman boy.

completed his education with training in oratory or public speaking. This was very important if he was going to try to become a government official or magistrate later in his life.

1 Fig. 10.18 shows the education of a young boy from infancy to about the age of ten. What does each scene depict about his life?

2 The poet Horace had a different view of his early schooling:

> I don't dislike the works of Livius,
> Or want them all destroyed. When I was
>   young
> Orbilius (or Flogger, as we called him)
> Taught us them all by heart. Now, I'm
>   surprised
> To find them hailed as masterpieces — high
> Unblemished works of near perfection —
>   when
> In fact, if one good line or phrase stands
>   out,
> It keeps the rest (unjustly) still alive.

    a Why would pupils have called Orbilius 'Flogger'?

    b How were boys expected to learn the works of Roman and Greek authors?

    c Are either of these methods of learning common today? Why or why not?

3 Juvenal, another Roman writer, gives us the schoolmaster's view. We can also learn something about the conditions in a schoolroom.

> Even the most brilliant schoolmaster never gets the salary he deserves. And even this amount (less than any professor gets) is whittled away by the pupil's attendant slave, the greedy swine — and the school secretary takes his cut too. You come in the same class as some door-to-door salesman peddling winter clothes, so there's no point in fighting the system, as long as you get something for sitting there from early dawn,

in conditions which no blacksmith or wool-workers' overseer would tolerate for a moment; as long as you get something for living with the stink of the lanterns, one per boy, that cover every Horace and Virgil with soot from cover to cover.

    a Boys in Rome, like those in Athens, were taken to and from school by a slave. What were these slaves called in Athens? Why were they present in Roman schools? Why do you think the schoolmaster gave him a 'cut' of the money he earned?

    b At what time of day did school begin in Rome? How can you tell?

Working in Rome

In ancient Rome, the kind of work a man did each day depended on his class. Patricians or men of the upper class were very restricted in the work they could do. They were not supposed to do any physical labour or take part in business such as trade or craftwork. This was seen as the work of the lower classes.

Patricians

Patricians often became lawyers. They were not allowed to charge fees but people often gave them gifts. Lawyers gave advice and worked in the law courts. They were well educated and interested in politics and government. Many patricians were elected as magistrates and became politicians.

Only men from wealthy families could become lawyers and politicians. This was because men were not paid wages while serving as a magistrate or in the Senate. Occasionally, a lawyer came from a lower class family. Brilliant army commanders sometimes managed to enter politics as well.

Patricians made money by owning large farms worked by slaves. Often, they had inherited land and wealth from their fathers and grandfathers. The most common crops grown on these farms were cereals such as wheat and barley, olives and grapes. Large flocks of sheep were kept, as good profits were made by selling their fleece. Wool was used for almost all clothes.

Equites and plebeians

The class below the patricians were the knights or *equites*. These were the businessmen, bankers and merchants of Rome. They organised the building of public works such as temples and aqueducts. The Romans are famous for their engineering achievements such as providing a running water supply to towns and building bridges.

The lowest class or free plebeians did most of the manual labour. Their occupations ranged from bakers, butchers, barbers and shopkeepers to painters and sculptors. If necessary a plebeian woman helped her husband in his shop or bakery.

Slaves

Many slaves worked in these jobs for their masters as well. Some slaves were 'state slaves'. They were bought in slave markets with public funds collected by taxation. They worked on things like public buildings and road making. Some slaves worked as fullers. They cleaned and mended togas and stolas. Instead of soap they used carbonate of soda, potash or fuller's earth. Then they bleached the clothes by spreading them over wickerwork frames with sulphur burning underneath.

Male slaves could also be employed as minor officials or scribes in the government. They were paid wages out of public funds. Sometimes they were slaves who had been well-educated in their home country.

A day at work

Work began at dawn after a light breakfast. Shopkeepers opened the shutters of their shopfront so that it was completely open on street level. The shopkeeper sat behind a long counter while shoppers surveyed his wares. Other craftsmen and labourers were busily at work by early morning.

Patricians and lawyers worked at home in the early hours. At about 9 am they made their way to the Forum which was originally the market place of Rome. By the time of the Republic it had become the centre of city life like the agora in Athens. The law courts, the Senate house and the biggest temples were all found in the Forum. Successful generals and emperors each added new temples or huge columns.

All roads radiated out from the Forum. They were well surfaced and broad. As the roads led away from Rome they joined other roads on which people could travel to distant parts of the empire. The saying 'All roads lead to Rome', was originally true. Good straight roads made communication between the provinces and Rome faster. They also made the transportation of goods easier.

By about eleven o'clock in the morning most business in the Forum had finished. After lunch everyone in Rome had a midday rest; many then went to the public baths. Shops opened again in the afternoon but only very busy lawyers worked after lunch. If there was important business to discuss the Senate also met in the afternoon.

Fig. 10.19 The construction of a Roman road.

In the morning the Forum was full of men bustling with public business and law cases. In the afternoon the atmosphere in the Forum was more relaxed as people strolled among the magnificent buildings, enjoying an afternoon walk.

Most women stayed at home looking after the house. However, they were much freer than Athenian women. They were allowed to go out more in public and attend dinner parties. The wives and daughters of patricians and equites did not go to work. Some plebeian women worked as midwives, nurses and hairdressers; others helped their husbands in their work.

Time to understand

Here is a list of the prices of some goods in Rome about 300 AD. Below is a list of some people's wages. By comparing the prices of goods we can understand a little more about life in Rome even if we do not know the value of the goods today.

Note: All prices are in denarii, the Roman currency.

Wheat	11 d. per litre
Barley and rye	6½ d. per litre
Lentils	11 d. per litre
Rice (cleaned)	22 d. per litre
Salt	11 d. per litre
Wine (various types)	16–60 d. for just over one litre
Beer (various strengths)	4–8 d. for just over one litre
Oil (various types)	24–80 d. for just over one litre
Honey (various types)	16–80 d. for just over one litre
Pork and lamb	36 d. per kilo
Beef, mutton and goat	24 d. per kilo
Ham	60 d. per kilo
Lucanian sausage	30–48 d. per kilo
Sea fish	48–72 d. per kilo
River fish	24–35 d. per kilo
Cheese	24 d. per kilo
Pheasant	125 or 250 d. each
Goose	100 or 200 d. each
Chickens	60 d. a pair
Eggs	1 d. each
Cabbage and lettuce	0.4 or 0.8 d. each
Peaches	0.2 or 0.4 d. each
Patrician shoes	150 d. a pair
Soldier's boots (no nails)	100 d. a pair
Military saddle	500 d. each
African cloak	500 d. each
Dalmatian tunic (unmarked)	2000 d. each
Hooded cloak, Laodicean	4500 d. each
Four-wheeled wagon with yoke (excluding ironwork)	1500 d. each
Transport of wagon load (550 kilos)	32 d. per kilometre
Transport of donkey load	6 d. per kilometre

Wages

Farm labourer	25 d. with keep per day
Stonemason and carpenter	50 d. with keep per day
Barber	2 d. per customer
Primary teacher	50 d. per month per boy
Rhetoric teacher	250 d. per month per boy
Fuller	175 d. for cleaning one new hooded cloak of Laodicea wool

1 Wheat, barley and rye can all be ground and made into bread. Which kind of cereal would be used by most people? Why do you think wheat was more expensive?

2 Was salt an expensive item? How can you tell?

3 Which do you think was the most common drink served in taverns? Why?

4 Which kinds of meat and fish would be considered delicacies? Why would this be so?

5 Why would pheasant be more expensive than chickens?

6 Find out where Dalmatia and Laodicea were located. Then explain why both these items of clothing were more expensive than a wagon.

7 Was a farm labourer poorly paid compared to a primary teacher? Why?

8 How many people would a barber have to shave per day to earn as much as a farm labourer? If he spent an average of twenty minutes on each customer how many hours would he have to work each day to earn as much as a carpenter?

9 How long do you think it took a fuller to clean a new cloak? His daily income was probably about the same as a stonemason.

Leisure hours

Morning was the time for work in Rome. In the afternoon Romans relaxed by exercising at sportsgrounds, playing ball games or going to the public baths. They could also be spectators at the amphitheatre or circus. Wherever Romans established a province these forms of entertainment became common. In places such as Britain, North Africa and Jordan, archaeologists have excavated the ruins of amphitheatres and bathhouses.

The bathhouse

Some people had private bathrooms in their homes. Most, however, preferred to go to the large public bathhouses. These were built by the government and a small fee was charged for admission. Sometimes a wealthy Roman citizen who wanted to be consul paid for everyone's admission to the baths for a short period of time. He did this to become popular with the people who were going to elect the consuls.

At the baths men could wear a kind of swimming costume but most bathed naked. Women who went to the public bathhouses had separate baths and wore a loose fitting garment.

After taking off their togas and leaving them on shelves in a changing room, men went to the *tepidarium* or warm room. Once they had adjusted to the warmth they moved on to the *caldarium*. In this room there was a large sunken hot bath. Some men soaked in the hot bath, others sat on the benches around the walls, perspiring in the steamy atmosphere.

The next step was a quick swim in the cold pool in the *frigidarium* or cold room. Some bathhouses had outdoor swimming pools as well. Finally men went to the *unctorium* where they would oil themselves completely and scrape it off with a strigil. Towels, oil flasks and strigils were all carried to the bathhouses by personal slaves.

The bathhouse was very much like a Greek gymnasium. Men went to the baths to relax and perhaps discuss business with other men they met there.

Bathhouses were heated by a furnace. The heat circulated underneath the floor. The rooms which needed the most heat were closest to the furnace. The frigidarium, which did not need heating, was not connected to the furnace at all.

Fig. 10.20 The Roman baths at the city of Bath in England.

Chariot races

The Romans did not have weekends but had many festivals and holy days. On these days games and contests were held.

The word 'circus' simply means a circle or ring. In Rome, a circus was a racetrack. It was really more rectangular in shape with a semi-circle at one end. Rows of seats lined both sides of the circus, continuing around the semi-circle. In the middle of the racecourse was a wall called a *spina*, with posts at either end. Once around the spina was a lap. The largest circus in Rome was the Circus Maximus. It could hold up to 250 000 spectators.

Each race started at the barriers at the opposite end to the semi-circle. Two or four horses drew each chariot. Normally eight chariots were entered in a race.

The charioteer wore a short tunic and a helmet. He held a whip and a knife. He used the knife to cut the reins, tied to his wrist, if the chariot crashed and he was dragged along the ground. Most crashes occured at either end of the spina. Slaves were on duty to drag chariots, horses and men off the track if there were collisions.

Betting on races was common. There were four main clubs — white, red, green and blue. People usually supported one of these chariot clubs just as people support football clubs today. By the end of a race the whole crowd of up to 250 000 people was on its feet screaming. The winner of each race left the stadium through a triumphal gateway in the semi-circular end.

Gladiators

The Colosseum was a huge amphitheatre in Rome. This was the setting for gladiatorial contests. Originally gladiators were criminals or slaves. Later, during the time of the empire, they were prisoners of war. All were specially trained to fight. If they did not fight properly in the amphitheatre they were whipped or threatened with red-hot irons.

Gladiators fought in pairs or in very large groups. Each fight ended in the death of one of each pair.

Basically, there were two kinds of gladiators. One wore only shin guards and a loincloth. He was armed with a dagger, a trident (a three-pronged spear) and a net. His opponent was much more heavily armed and protected with a helmet and a shield. The netman aimed to entangle the other gladiator in his net.

Gladiators were also trained to fight wild animals. Sometimes criminals were left in

Fig. 10.21 The ruins of the Colosseum in Rome today.

Fig. 10.22 The remains of a Roman amphitheatre at Nimes in France.

Fig. 10.23 Mosaic at the Capitol Museum, Rome showing theatrical masks.

the arena to be torn to pieces by lions or bears. Christians also suffered in this way because they refused to worship the gods of Rome.

Today the stories of the shows at amphitheatres recorded by the Romans themselves horrify us. These forms of entertainment ended as the Roman empire became Christian after about 300 AD.

The theatre

The theatre was another form of entertainment. Like the shows offered in amphitheatres and circuses, plays were staged during daylight, usually in the afternoon. Roman theatres were similar to Greek theatres, although there were some differences. In Roman theatres there was no orchestra and the stage itself was very long and narrow. The standard background was the outside of two houses, perhaps with a lane in between.

Plays were based on Greek comedies and tragedies. Some Roman drama has survived. However, it was not as popular in its time as the gladiatorial shows and chariot racing.

Time to understand

In a letter to a friend, Seneca, a Roman philosopher, described what it was like living in an apartment near a public bathhouse.

> I have lodgings right over a public bathhouse. Now imagine to yourself every kind of sound that can make one weary of one's years. When the strenuous types are doing their exercises, swinging weight-laden hands about, I hear the grunting as they toil away — or go through the motions of toiling away — at them, and the hissings and strident gasps every time they expel their pent-up breath.

When my attention turns to a less active fellow who is contenting himself with an ordinary inexpensive massage, I hear the smack of a hand pummelling his shoulders, the sound varying according as it comes down flat or cupped. But if on top of this some ball player comes along and starts shouting out the score, that's the end! Then add someone starting up a brawl, and someone else caught thieving, and the man who likes the sound of his voice in the bath, and the people who leap into the pool with a tremendous splash.

Apart from those whose voices are, if nothing else, natural, think of the hair remover, continually giving vent to his shrill and penetrating cry in order to advertise his presence, never silent unless it be while he is plucking someone's armpits and making the client yell for him! Then think of the various cries of the man selling drinks, and the one selling sausages and the other selling pastries, and all the ones hawking for the catering shops, each publicising his wares with a distinctive cry of his own.

1 What could people do at the bathhouse, other than bathe?
2 What sorts of things often happened at a bathhouse? Do you think the same sorts of things happen at public swimming pools today?
3 What kinds of food could people buy at the bathhouse?
4 In your own words, describe the bathhouse scene.

Life in a Roman Province: Britain

Conquering Britain

Britain was first attacked by the Romans in 55 BC. The commander of the expedition was Julius Caesar. He made another attempt a year later in 54 BC. Both of these were unsuccessful because many of the ships that had transported the armies across the English Channel were wrecked by storms.

The Britons were related to the Gauls whom Caesar had conquered a few years earlier. Both the Britons and the Gauls were descended from the Celtic race described in Chapter Seven.

The Romans did not attempt a further attack on Britain until ninety years later, in 43 AD. There were a number of reasons for this. They were preoccupied with their own troubles back in Rome. Then, after Augustus restored peace and order, he decided not to extend the empire any further.

The emperor Claudius sent an expedition to Britain under Aulus Plautius. The Britons did not give up their land easily and fought the invaders fiercely. It took three years to conquer most of south-east Britain.

As the Romans moved across Britain they built roads, bridges and forts. This slowed their progress a little but made it easier to transport goods and march armies across land they had conquered.

Fig. 10.24 A section of Hadrian's Wall today.

Some tribes in the north of Britain resisted the Romans for twenty or thirty years. One of these tribes was called the Silures. They were led by Caratacus who had escaped from the Roman conquest of south-east Britain. The Silures fought bravely but even Caratacus was captured in 51 AD.

When Caratacus was taken to Rome, Claudius was impressed with his dignity and courage. Caratacus was pardoned and allowed to live as a free man in Rome itself.

Fig. 10.25 Some of the outlines of ancient Silchester, a Roman town, can be seen in this aerial photograph.

Hadrian's Wall

By about 84 AD the Romans had conquered Britain as far north as central Scotland, but this did not last. By the time of emperor Hadrian (117–138 AD), the Scottish tribes had attacked the Roman forts in Scotland and forced the Romans back into England.

Hadrian decided to build a huge wall separating Scotland from Wales and England. The wall was over 6 metres high and wide enough for sentry patrol on top. Along the wall there were sixteen forts through which roads passed. Each of these forts contained barracks for about 600 soldiers, stables for horses, workshops, a hospital and storage rooms.

Between the forts were milecastles which housed one hundred soldiers each. Between each milecastle were two watchtowers that housed sentries. The sentries were supposed to take turns in keeping a 24-hour watch. Altogether 1400 soldiers were needed to man Hadrian's wall at any one time.

Roman Britain

Most of the settlements in Celtic Britain before the Romans came were really only villages. The Romans built towns based on the model of their own city, Rome. These towns became the centre of trade and government in each area.

The Roman governor of Britain, like the governors of other Roman provinces, was an ex-magistrate. His appointment as a provincial governor lasted one year. He was responsible for directing the troops in his province, keeping law and order, and collecting tax.

Each town had a forum with a basilica or town hall, as well as shops, temples, public baths, houses and, in some cases, theatres. Each town also had a water supply. It would not have been possible for a large number of people to live in a town without a drainage system and a water supply.

At first, the towns were unwalled but by about 200 AD most were surrounded by stone walls. The towns were small by today's standards and probably had a maximum of 5000 inhabitants. Most of the people were still Britons even though there were a large number of Roman soldiers, engineers and officials. Each town was governed by local men, using the Roman idea of magistrates and a town council.

Sometimes a colony of retired Roman soldiers was established. These colonies grew to be towns in their own right.

All these things helped to 'Romanise' Britain. At first, only important Britons were given Roman citizenship. This meant they were equal to free-born Roman citizens. They could, in theory, elect magistrates in Rome. They usually wore Roman togas very proudly. In 213 AD ever free-born subject in the Empire was granted Roman citizenship. This helped to spread Roman customs, such as wearing togas and speaking Latin.

Most of the population during Roman rule lived in the country. Farmhouses of wealthy Britons looked like Roman country villas. Some even had private baths. These farms were worked by peasants. Farmers paid tax to the Roman governor. It was probably collected as farm produce which, in turn, fed the army protecting Britain from attack.

What did Rome gain by defending Britain from foreign attack? The answer is metals. Only one Roman gold mine has been discovered in Wales. However, numerous other mines from the Roman period show that coal, lead, tin, iron and copper were produced. These mines were worked by slaves and criminals.

Roman rule in Britain ended in 410 AD when the Roman garrisons stationed in Britain were recalled. They were needed to defend other parts of the empire and Rome itself.

Time to understand

Fig. 10.26 (over) shows a Roman legionary (ordinary soldier) as he would have looked in about 100 BC. Equipment used for setting up camps was carried by each soldier. He wore chain-mail and carried a leather-covered shield. His weapons were spears, a sword and a dagger.

Fig. 10.27 (over) shows a Roman legionary dating from about 100 AD. His weapons are still the same but his protective armour has changed.

1   List the differences between the equipment of the two soldiers.
2   In what kind of action would the legionary of 100 BC have been engaged? Why?
3   What kind of work did the soldier of 100 AD probably do? Why? What kinds of places was he likely to have been posted?
4   Can you think of any reasons why the armour would have changed? Do you think it had something to do with the places they fought or defended?

Pompeii and Herculaneum

On 24 August 79 AD, Pliny, the Admiral of the Roman fleet, looked out from his villa and saw a huge black cloud in the distance. He lived at Misenum on the Bay of Naples. It did not take long to work out what was happening on the far side of the bay. About 6 kilometres from the water line, Mount Vesuvius was erupting for the first time in recorded history. The nearby towns of Herculaneum and Pompeii were threatened with catastrophe.

Pliny sent a fleet across the bay to Stabiae to help evacuate people fleeing the volcano. He sailed across as well but never returned.

As the day wore on, ash and volcanic rock poured down on Pompeii, which was a prosperous centre of wine production and trade. The terrified inhabitants tried in vain to escape the suffocating, poisonous fumes.

Fig. 10.26 A Roman legionary, 100 BC.

Fig. 10.27 A Roman legionary, 100 AD.

Fig. 10.28 At the entrance to a house at Pompeii a mosaic which says: 'Beware of the dog'!

Fig. 10.31 The plaster casts of people overcome by the fumes of the eruption of Mount Vesuvius.

Fig. 10.29 Ovens and mills in Pompeii.

Fig. 10.32 The remains of many Roman houses have been found at Pompeii. This one, which was quite large and elaborate, obviously belonged to a wealthy family.

Fig. 10.30 A street in Pompeii.

Nearby, Herculaneum was buried in an oozing wave of scorching mud and lava. When the wave finally subsided Herculaneum lay buried to a depth of up to 15 metres.

At Stabiae many of the inhabitants were also suffocated by the fumes and smoke, including the admiral Pliny. His nephew, also called Pliny, recorded this in two letters to Tacitus, his friend in Rome. A dark cloud spread across the whole of the Bay of Naples.

Two days later, even Rome was covered with a thin layer of white ash, driven north by the winds from Mount Vesuvius. The Roman emperor, Titus, sent out a team to investigate the disaster. However, attempts to dig to recover property or to find out what had happened were hopeless. Sometimes excavators died inhaling the poisonous fumes still caught in pockets beneath the surface.

Even though Pliny recorded the event, people gradually forgot about the disaster. After centuries, the location of Pompeii and Herculaneum was lost and their existence became a legend. It was not until 1592 that the first signs of Pompeii were accidently discovered when a canal was dug across the city. During the nineteenth century serious excavations began.

The volcanic eruption that overwhelmed Pompeii and Herculaneum has given us a superb picture of Roman life. Many of the houses were preserved intact except for the roofs. Many perishable objects were *carbonised* (turned to charcoal) by the heat and burning lava. This meant that they did not rot away. In some cases, food was left on the table as families fled for their lives.

At Pompeii excavators were at first puzzled by large holes in the layers of ash and rock. They then realised that these holes had been formed by the bodies of people and animals which had been buried and later decayed. By pouring liquid plaster into these holes archaeologists were able to take plaster casts of their shapes. The shapes show the agony of those who died in the eruption of Mount Vesuvius.

Religion in Rome

At first the Romans believed in invisible gods and goddesses associated with nature. Later, through contact with the Greeks, they adopted the Greek gods and goddesses. The only difference was that the Romans changed their names. For example Aphrodite, goddess of love and beauty, was called Venus by the Romans.

You probably remember that the Greeks built temples for the statues of their gods and goddesses. They worshipped them with sacrifices. The Romans adopted all these practices.

As the empire grew the Romans had contact with many other forms of religion. Some cults were brought back to Rome and became very popular. The Egyptian goddess Isis and the Persian god Mithras are two of the best-known cults.

From the time of Augustus the emperor was also worshipped as a god. Each emperor expected people to bow down to his statue to show their respect and awe. As long as people worshipped the emperor and the old Roman gods and goddesses (such as Jupiter, Juno, Mars and Vesta), they were allowed to worship other gods as well.

After the death of Jesus Christ, the Christian religion began to spread throughout the Roman empire. It attracted a large following because Christians believed that God was kind and loving. They also believed (and still believe) that

Fig. 10.33 The temple of the goddess Vesta in Rome.

their sins would be forgiven if they believed that Christ was the son of God. The Christian religion promised that after death people would go to heaven if they had lived good lives and believed in Christ.

The early Christians refused to worship the emperor and the old Roman gods. For this reason they were persecuted by the Roman emperors. Many Christians were executed or thrown to the lions and other wild animals in the amphitheatre.

However, the Christian religion continued to grow in popularity, and by about 300 AD it was the major religion of the Roman empire. The emperor Constantine, who began to rule in 305, decreed that everyone was allowed freedom of worship and religion. This meant that no one would be persecuted for his or her religious beliefs. Constantine himself became a Christian just before he died in 337. In 392 the emperor Theodosius made Christianity the official religion of the Roman empire.

Time to understand

The extract below is taken from the book of Luke in the New Testament of the Bible. It tells the story of the birth of Jesus Christ. Read the extract before answering the questions.

> In those days a decree was issued by the Emperor Augustus for a registration to be made throughout the Roman world. This was the first registration of its kind; it took place when Quirinius was governor of Syria. For this purpose everyone made his way to his own town; and so Joseph went up to Judaea from the town of Nazareth in Galilee, to register at the city of David, called Bethlehem, because he was of the house of David by descent; and with him went Mary who was betrothed to him. She was expecting a child, and while they were there the time came for her baby to be born, and she gave birth to a son, her first-born. She wrapped him in his swaddling clothes, and laid him in a manger, because there was no room for them to lodge in the house.

1 When was Augustus the Roman emperor?
2 What did the writer mean when he wrote the 'Roman world'? Which countries did it include during the reign of Augustus?
3 Today we call this kind of 'registration' a *census*. Look up the meaning of the word 'census' in the dictionary. See if you can find out the original Latin word.
4 Why, do you think, Augustus took the first census of the Roman world? How could he use this census?
5 Use a dictionary to find out the meaning of the words 'swaddling' and 'manger'. Now describe the scene of the birth of Jesus Christ in your own words.
6 Why is the birth of Jesus Christ so important in the study of history?

The end of *Pax Romana*

After the reign of Augustus the empire continued to grow. You read, earlier in this chapter, that Roman soldiers and governors helped to keep the borders of frontiers of the empire safe from attack. By about 200 AD the empire had reached its maximum extent.

However, attacks on the frontiers became more frequent. Tribes such as the Goths needed the land inside the frontiers. The Romans called those who lived outside the empire barbarians. This was because compared to the Romans themselves, the tribespeople looked uncivilised.

As time went on more and more soldiers were needed to defend the empire. Sometimes the Romans trained one group of tribesmen to fight against another foreign group. It became difficult to organise the defence of the furthest frontiers.

Within Rome itself ambitious men were fighting for power. It was not uncommon for an emperor to be murdered by a rival who would then become emperor himself. During these times the governing of the empire was forgotten.

Roman governors collected tax in the provinces to pay for the defence of each province. Heavy taxes forced many small farmers to abandon their farms. With less farm produce, trade declined. Famine and diseases such as the Plague spread through parts of the empire as well.

Finally, the emperor Diocletian was strong enough to introduce reforms which improved farming and trade. In 295 AD he decided to divide the empire in two. He ruled the eastern half while a general called Maximian ruled the west. Things ran more smoothly until his death, when rivalry and disorder erupted once again.

In 330 AD the emperor Constantine reunited the empire. He ruled from Byzantium, which he renamed Constantinople. However, the western half had its own governor. By about 395 the empire had again been split in half.

Attacks on the western empire became more and more frequent. The eastern empire remained secure. In 410 AD garrisons in Britain were recalled to defend Rome itself, which was being attacked by a German tribe called the Visigoths.

By about the middle of the fifth century AD the western Roman empire had virtually ceased to exist. Poorly defended and poorly governed, it was overrun by barbarian tribes.

11

The first Americans

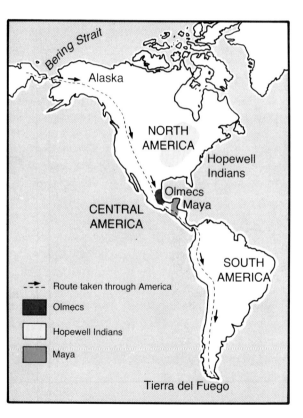

Fig. 11.1 The Americas. This map shows how the first Americans moved from north to south and where the three groups of people studied in this chapter lived.

W HEN Christopher Columbus first saw America in 1492 he called it the 'New World'. He was very wrong. The land he discovered was not new at all; in fact, people had been living there for many thousands of years. Columbus called it the New World because it was one of the last areas to be discovered by Europeans. It was a new world to Europeans; an old world to the people who lived there.

There are two large continents in the Americas, as you can see from the map in Fig. 11.1. They are North America and South America. The continents are linked by a narrow strip of land called Central America. North America and South America share a 'backbone'. This is a mountain range which starts in Alaska in the north and runs right down to the tip of South America. In the north this mountain range is called the Rocky Mountains; in the south it is called the Andes.

Time to understand

Look at a map of the Americas in an atlas and try to answer the questions below.

1 The two continents are surrounded by water. Can you name the seas and oceans that surround the two continents?

2 There are two mighty rivers in the Americas: the Mississippi and the Amazon. Can you find them in your atlas? Where does each one flow? Which is the longer river? Do you think these rivers would have been important to the early people who lived in the Americas? Why?

3 Can you find the equator in your atlas? Which parts of the Americas are close to the equator? What kind of climate do you think they have?

4 Tierra del Fuego is the southernmost place in the Americas. It is also the southernmost place in the world where human beings live permanently. What sort of climate do you think it would have?

The first Americans

Look again at your atlas. Can you find Siberia and the Bering Strait? The first people in the Americas probably got there by crossing the Bering Strait from Siberia in Asia to Alaska. Today the Bering Strait is quite shallow and less than ninety kilometres wide. Even today, the Eskimos of Alaska cross the Bering Strait to Siberia in small boats made from animal skin. Many thousands of years ago, the Bering Strait was much wider. During the Ice Age, when the earth's climate became much colder, most of the water of the strait froze. The sea level dropped because so much water had turned to ice. When this

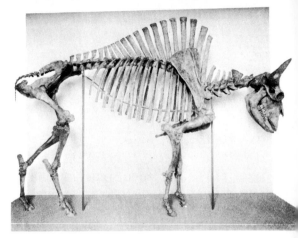

Fig. 11.2 The skeleton of an extinct bison, found in New Mexico.

happened, Asia was joined to America by a land bridge, or perhaps by a series of rocky 'stepping stones'.

Ancient animals wandered across the strait — small animals like rats, and bigger ones such as mammoths and oxen, bison and moose, elks and bears. Groups of hunters followed them across the land bridge. It did not matter to them whether they were in Asia or America. Later, when the ice melted and the sea level rose again, the Bering Strait was once more covered with water. Both the hunters and the animals were cut off from their old homes.

We do not really know when these early hunters went to the Americas, nor do we know how many of them there were. They may have started moving east about 40 000 years ago, at about the same time as the Aboriginal people came to Australia. They probably crossed the strait in family groups or small bands. We do know that these people gradually worked their way from Alaska right down to the tip of South America. You can see the route they took in the map in Fig. 11.1.

You might wonder how we know this — or think we know it! When several pieces of evidence are put together, they build up a picture that helps us understand the past. Here are some of the clues that help to make the picture:

— Geologists have studied the Bering Strait and found a large area of rock just 100 metres under the present sea level. They believe that this rock was above the sea level many thousands of years ago.

— In the south-western part of the USA archaeologists have found some ancient fire pits. Near them they discovered ancient spear heads. They were used by early hunters to spear animals for food. Scientists have used Carbon 14 tests (which you read about in Chapter One of this book) to find out that these spears are over 37 000 years old.

— Ancient rock and cave paintings found in America show the animals the earliest people hunted.

Time to understand

1 Do you know how the Aboriginal people came to Australia? Where did they come from? (Books about the Aboriginal people in your library will help you to answer these questions.) Was the way the Aboriginal people came to Australia at all like the way the first people went to America?

2 In Chapter One you read about some Australian prehistoric animals. Use reference books about prehistoric animals to find the names of some of the ancient animals that once roamed through the Americas. Draw and label a few of these extinct animals in your book. Are they at all like the animals you read about in Chapter One? Can you find out *why* they became extinct?

A new home

By 10 000 BC there were people in all parts of America, from the Bering Strait to Tierra del Fuego. The way they lived and the food they ate depended on where they lived. They speared animals, caught fish and collected wild plants. After about 7000 BC some groups of Americans began to grow food as well as hunt and gather it Like people in other parts of the world at

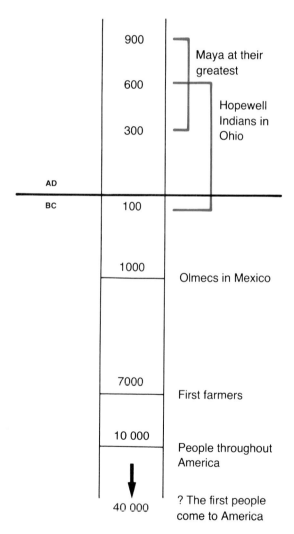

Fig. 11.3 A time-line of early American history.

221

Fig. 11.4 Like other Indians, the Eskimos are descended from the first people who crossed to America. Because of their harsh lands, the Eskimos have never become farmers.

this time, they settled in small villages near their crops. But many of these first Americans never became farmers. Some, like the Eskimos or those who settled on the dry plains, lived in places where farming was difficult or impossible. Others found plenty of food by hunting, fishing and gathering, and had no reason to become farmers.

One of the first plants to be tamed by Americans was the avocado, around 7000 BC. Later, the people learned to grow squash, chilli pepper, maize (the American word for corn), beans and sweet potatoes. These early farmers used what has been called the 'slash and burn' method of farming. First they cleared a small patch of land. This must have been a long and tedious job, particularly in the thick jungle areas of Central America where farming began. The people had either to cut down the tall jungle trees with their stone axes or ringbark them and wait for them to die. They piled up the dead timber, set it on fire, and planted their crops among the charred tree stumps. After several sowings the land was exhausted and the people had

to move on to another place and start all over again.

As the villages became more permanent, the farmers built better houses. What they were made of depended upon what was available: stone, ice, whalebone, wattle and daub, cane and mud bricks were all used in various parts of America. Most people seem to have lived in small huts, each one big enough for one family. Groups of families lived together as a clan or tribe. Each person had a special part to play in the clan's life. The young men were farmers, warriors or hunters; the old men were the lawmakers; the women gathered and cooked food and cared for the children.

Time to understand

1 The Eskimos settled in the very north of America, one of the harshest places that human beings have ever lived in. They were hunters and their lives depended on their knowledge and understanding of the weather and how it affected the animals they needed for food. The Eskimos divided the year into six seasons. These seasons are described below. Draw a suitable picture to go with each season to make up an illustrated calendar of the Eskimo year.

— *March–April* (*early spring*): Snow falls heavily but there is a little sun. The Eskimos hunt seals and sometimes shoot a stray caribou.

— *May–July* (*late spring*): The snow begins to melt and people move into their summer tent homes. They catch seals on the edge of the melting ice.

— *August–September* (*summer*): The Eskimos move around to catch birds and fish and to gather berries. They hunt whales and seals also.

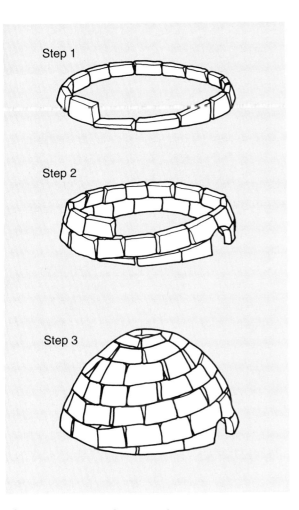

Step 1

Step 2

Step 3

Fig. 11.5 How an igloo is made.

— *October–mid November* (*autumn*): Snow falls heavily and the lakes freeze up. The days become shorter.
— *Late November–December* (*early winter*): The people have built their snow or stone houses, for the ground is now covered with thick snow and ice. They hunt seals and walruses at the edge of the ice.
— *January–February* (*late winter*): It is dark and cold. Seals can be caught through breathing holes in the ice, and Arctic hares and foxes are sometimes trapped.

2 The diagrams in Fig. 11.5 show three stages in building an Eskimo snow house or igloo. Use these pictures to write instructions called: 'How to build an igloo: notes for beginners'

Do you know, or can you find out, why:
- a the igloo was covered with a thick layer of snow?
- b the entrance tunnel was often under the floor level?

The Olmecs

The giant stone head in Fig. 11.6 (over) was found in the jungle of Mexico's Gulf Coast. It is more than three metres high and was carved from a single block of rock. It was made between 1200 and 900 BC by people called the Olmecs. Other similar heads and statues have also been discovered. They may be the faces of the Olmec rulers.

These giant heads and statues tell us something about the people who made them. They show that the Olmecs must have had an organised society. It would have been impossible to drag the rock and have it carved without a powerful ruler and people who were prepared to do what their leaders told them. There must have been Olmec sculptors and stonemasons to do the work, as well as overseers and people to grow food for the craftsmen. The Olmecs were among the first people in the Americas to develop this kind of organised society.

The Olmecs did not build cities but they did build impressive places where they held ceremonies. One had platforms and courtyards, artificial lagoons and drains, all laid out on an artificial plateau over 6 metres high. Another ceremonial centre, at

Fig. 11.6 A giant stone Olmec head from La Venta on the Mexican Gulf Coast.

Fig. 11.7 The 'crying baby', an Olmec stone carving.

La Venta, on the Gulf Coast in Mexico, was built on a small island surrounded by swamps. At one end was a pyramid made of clay, over 30 metres high. There were courtyards and tombs and some unusual buried pavements. The people had dug out huge pits, lined them with stone blocks and then filled them in again! One pit was 8 metres deep and filled with 1000 tonnes of slabs. There were also three identical mosaic pavements made of flat green slabs decorated to look like jaguars. Like the pits, it seems that they were covered up as soon as they were made. They may have been offerings to the gods.

Time to understand

1 The Olmec statues are made from volcanic rock which was probably brought from a quarry 100 kilometres from where the statues were set up. Imagine you were in charge of this project. You have to find the right kind of rock for the statues, dig and hack it out, get it back to the settlement, have the statues carved and set them in place. How would you go about it? What sort of people would you have to employ? How would you organise them? How would you feed them? What problems might you have to solve? How would you try to solve them?

2 The stone figures in Fig. 11.9 (on p. 226) are 18 centimetres high and stand beside upright pieces of jade. They were discovered, in the position they are standing in the picture, at the Olmec ceremonial site of La Venta. Historians do not know what they were doing. What do *you* think? Can you suggest why they were buried *under* the ceremonial pavement at La Venta?

3 In Chapter Three of this book you read about the building of the pyramids in

Egypt. What similarities can you find between the building of the pyramids and the building of an Olmec ceremonial centre? Have you read of other building projects in this book that were similar to these two?

The mound builders

Further north, other early Americans built very different monuments. These people lived along the Ohio and Mississippi rivers and built thousands of earth mounds over the graves of their dead tribespeople. Some are shaped like cones; others like pyramids. Sometimes the people heaped up earth to make huge geometric or animal shapes. These monuments were built between 100 BC and 550 AD.

These people have been called the Hopewell Indians, after the man on whose land some of their remains were discovered. A better name would be 'great earthwork builders'. Their mounds were often clustered together, and sometimes enclosed by earth walls to make square,

Fig. 11.8 The serpent mound' in the present-day state of Ohio in the USA, built by the Hopewell Indians.

225

Fig. 11.9 Olmec figures, carved from stone, standing beside jade blades (see p. 224).

circular or rectangular patterns. Many of the mounds are between 6 and 9 metres high and up to 50 metres long, although some are up to 140 metres long.

Perhaps the Hopewell Indians saved bodies until there were enough for a mass burial. They may have kept them high in the trees. Arranging a funeral must have been a long process. First they built a wooden frame in which the dead bodies could be placed. If there were many bodies to bury, the frame could be up to 60 metres long. The individual graves were made inside this frame. When the bodies had

been prepared and placed inside, along with all the dead people's possessions that were to be buried as well, the wooden frame was set alight. As it burnt the people danced and chanted, until the priest stepped forward to tell them to prepare the monument. Then, in long rows, they moved backwards and forwards collecting earth and stones in baskets and carrying them to the charred remains, gradually building up the mound.

Burial mounds were not all that the Hopewell Indians built. They must have conducted elaborate religious ceremonies at the serpent mound. This model of a giant serpent — you can see a drawing of it in Fig. 11.8 — is over 400 metres long — longer than the world's tallest building today. A fire burned in an altar inside the head-shaped part of the model. The Hopewell Indians built ramparts, too, to defend themselves from their enemies. The largest of these, Fort Ancient, rises 82 metres above the ground. The walls, which stretch for more than 6 kilometres, are surrounded by a ditch.

The Hopewell Indians were traders. They brought in the hard, black stone called obsidian for their spear points; claws and teeth from bears in the Rocky Mountains for their necklaces and buttons; copper, shark teeth, shells and alligator bones for decoration. They collected freshwater pearls from the rivers around them. Many of these things were used in their ceremonies, and some were saved for the graves of priests and other important people.

Unfortunately, little has remained of the villages of the Hopewell Indians. This is because, unlike the mounds, they were built near the riverbanks. As the years went by, they were washed away and covered with silt. From the foundations that have been discovered, we know that the houses of the mound builders were circular, and between 6 and 20 metres in diameter. The walls were made on a framework of poles. Spaces between the poles were filled with twigs and then the whole frame was plastered over with clay and chopped twigs. The roof was probably made of bark overlapping in strips, with a small hole to let smoke out of the house. Early Australian settlers built their homes in a similar way.

No furnishings have survived, but the mound builders probably slept on beds of animal skins and grass. Many of their

Fig. 11.10 A Hopewell Indian house.

skeletons have deformed leg bones and from this we can guess that they often squatted on their heels.

These early Americans grew maize, beans and squash but depended for most of their food on the deer, rabbit and turkey they hunted and the fish, turtle and shellfish they collected. There seems to have been plenty of food for the Hopewell Indians because some people in the group were able to spend their time making works of art instead of growing or finding food. Their carvings show many living things, particularly the duck hawk. There were many abstract patterns too.

Like so many other people we have studied in this book, the Hopewell Indians seem to have disappeared just as their society was at its height. Around 600 AD their culture ended. There may have been floods, droughts or hurricanes. Perhaps they were attacked by other groups of people. The great ramparts show that they were afraid of attack. Many of the people must have migrated, and merged with other groups.

Time to understand

1 Do you remember any other people you have read about in this book who built great earthworks — mounds and ramparts? Who were they? When and where did they live? Were their earthworks built for the same reason as those of the Hopewell Indians?

2 Look again at the picture of the Hopewell Indian house in Fig. 11.10. Does it resemble any of the other houses pictured in this book? Which ones are they? Why do you think this style of building was used by ancient people?

3 When Christopher Columbus reached America in 1492 he believed that he had come to the East Indies (now Indonesia). He called the native people he found there — the first Americans — 'Indians', and they have kept that name ever since. There were (and still are) many different groups of American Indians, descendants of those people who first crossed the Bering Strait into America. What can you find out about the following Indian groups?

    a Woodland Indians,
    b Plains Indians,
    c Pueblo Indians.

Write a paragraph or so about each group, explaining what made each one unique.

The Maya

It is odd that some groups of early Americans chose to live in the low-lying rainforests of Central America. Much of the land there is marshy and swampy, with trees growing high to reach the sunlight. The climate is hot and humid and it is very difficult to travel far or fast through the thick jungle. It was here in the jungle that the Maya people lived. Their civilisation was at its height between 300 and 900 AD. Here they built great ceremonial centres –– without metal tools, wheels or beasts of burden. Around these centres the Maya cleared enough land to grow crops and build homes. Near the temples they raised tall stone monuments, intricately carved with hieroglyphics and strange figures.

The Maya were descended from those first people who came down from Alaska into Central America. At first, like other early Americans, they were hunters; only gradually did they become farmers. Between about 1500 BC and 300 AD the Maya learnt to grow food, spin cloth and make pottery. Maize, their main crop, was thought to be a gift from the gods. The people came to think of the grain itself as a god.

What we know about the Maya comes from two different sources. First are the remains of Maya buildings that have been discovered and explored in the jungles where they were built so long ago. From these we have been able to learn about Mayan art and architecture. Carvings and sculptures on the buildings have taught us a lot about the people's appearance and clothes.

All the Maya wore similar clothes: loincloths for the men and loose sack-like dresses for the women. But the clothes of the priests and nobles were made of finer material and richly decorated with beads and shells. For ceremonies they wore elaborate head-dresses.

To our eyes, the Maya had strange ideas of beauty. They often made notches in their teeth and filled them with bits of jade. They pierced their ears and wore huge jade earrings. Sometimes they put

Fig. 11.11 A Mayan dignitary.

Fig. 11.12 A Mayan priest.

Fig. 11.13 One of the pyramids at the Mayan centre of Tikal. It is more than sixty metres high. Only the priests were allowed to enter the temple or shrine near the top of the pyramid.

Fig. 11.14 Another of the pyramids at Tikal.

229

Fig. 11.15 A statue of the maize god, carved from basalt and found in the ruins of the Mayan centre called Copan. Husks of maize are growing from his head.

small bits of pitch into their children's hair, hoping that its constant swaying in front of their eyes would make them cross-eyed. They liked flat foreheads and 'squashed' faces. To achieve this they bound their babies' skulls between two pieces of board for several days.

Gods, priests and pyramids

Our second source of information about the Maya are three Mayan *codices*, or books. Each book is made from a strip of bark cloth, folded like an accordion to make the pages. In the codices are pictures of Mayan gods and hieroglyphic writing. Scholars have not yet deciphered all the hieroglyphic

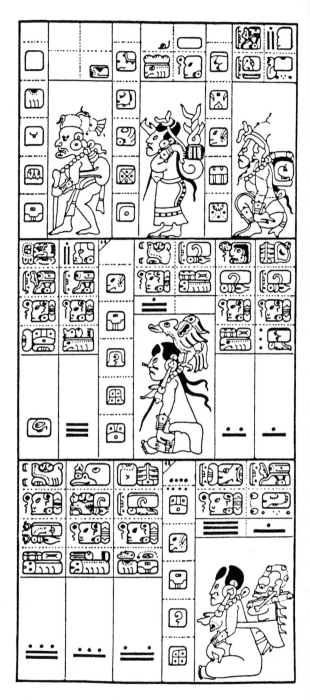

Fig. 11.16 Mayan hieroglyphics, from one of the codices now in Dresden, Germany.

writing but they understand enough of it to think the codices are religious books. They seem to have been made so that priests could work out the good and bad aspects of the gods. They used this information to help them predict the future.

Ordinary farm workers did not understand the complicated Mayan religion. They had to accept what their priests told them. The priests said that temples had to be built where sacrifices could be made to the gods. For more than a thousand years, generations of Mayan people toiled in the jungle to support their gods. They cut down trees, quarried stone, dragged it to the temple site and built mighty pyramids. At the top was a shrine that only the priests could enter.

The pyramids and the area around them were centres of religion and ceremony. The priests and skilled craftspeople may have lived near them but most people — the farmers — lived in villages some distance away from these impressive religious centres. They came to them only to watch a pageant or ceremony. They probably gathered in the courtyards while masked men and musicians paraded and danced in front of them. The priests, wearing high, feathered head-dresses, chanted and swayed as they sacrificed an animal — or sometimes a human being — in the shrine on top of the pyramid.

The Maya also built ball courts. These were ceremonial enclosures in which Maya youths played a sacred ball game. We do not know the rules of this game, but we do know that the players used a rubber ball and that they could hit it only with their elbows, hips and thighs, not with their hands or feet.

Time to understand

1   The illustrations in Fig. 11.17 were drawn from Mayan sculpture. At first they look just like patterns, but if you study them more closely you should be able to find pictures of Mayan gods in each one. Here is what the drawings represent.

   a   The head of the maize god comes out of a maize plant.

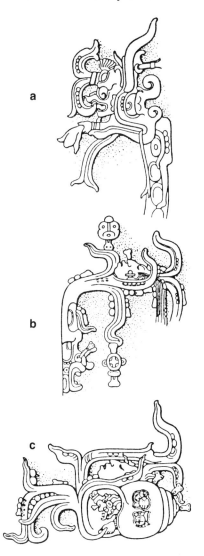

Fig. 11.17 Mayan gods: which is which?

b A small god comes out of a shell. He holds a maize plant inside which is the head of the maize god.

c A long-nosed god comes out of a serpent's jaws.

Can you work out which picture fits each description?

2 Fig. 11.18 shows a Mayan priest dealing with captives.

    a Can you see the priest's mask? Why do you think he wore it on this occasion?

    b Describe the priest's clothing and the clothing of the captives.

    c Are there any similarities between the priest and the captives?

    d What do you think is happening in this picture? Why?

Fig. 11.18 A priest and his captives.

Past, present and future

The Maya seem to have been obsessed with time. They worked out many ways of measuring it. They believed that things went in circles and that in order to understand what would happen in the future, they had to measure what had happened in the past as well as what was happening in the present. They thought that the gods controlled time. Priests had to be expert mathematicians as well as religious leaders. Often they became the rulers of the people as well.

The Maya believed that each day was a god that carried the weight of time on his back, just as a porter carries a heavy load. Time was a never-ending passage of day gods, night gods, week gods, month gods and year gods, moving from the past into the future. The priests' job was to work out how all the gods were linked at a particular time. This helped them to find out what influences would be important on a given day — past, present or future. To work this out they used complicated calculations that stretched many, many years into the past and future.

To measure the passage of time, Mayan priests studied the movements of the sun and moon and the planet Venus. There was a lot they did not understand — they believed the earth was flat, for example — but they watched the skies so closely that they were able to make very accurate measurements. Their records were so accurate that the Maya were able to predict eclipses of the sun. They made up

Fig. 11.19 Mayan symbols for measuring time.

Baktun	Katun	Tun	Uinal	Kin
400 Tun	20 Tun	360 days	20 days	day

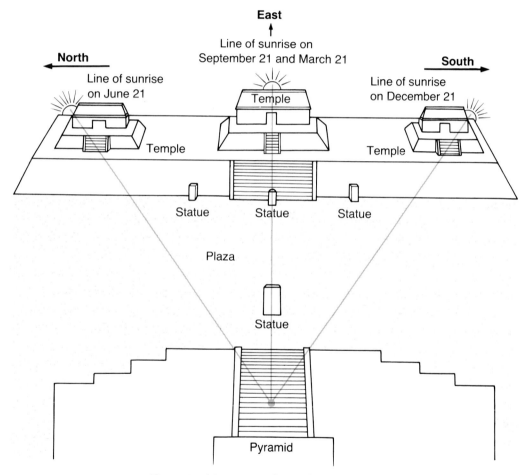

Fig. 11.20 Mayan temples and astronomy.

a calendar which had eighteen months of twenty days each, making 360 days in all. To make the year 365 days, they added five 'unlucky' days.

Time to understand

1 Fig. 11.20 shows a plan of the Mayan temples at Uaxactun in the modern country of Guatemala.
  a What can you learn about the Maya from this diagram?
  b Why was the sun important to Mayan priests?
  c Earlier in this book you read of another structure that may have been built to study the sun. What was it? Did it look at all like a Mayan temple?

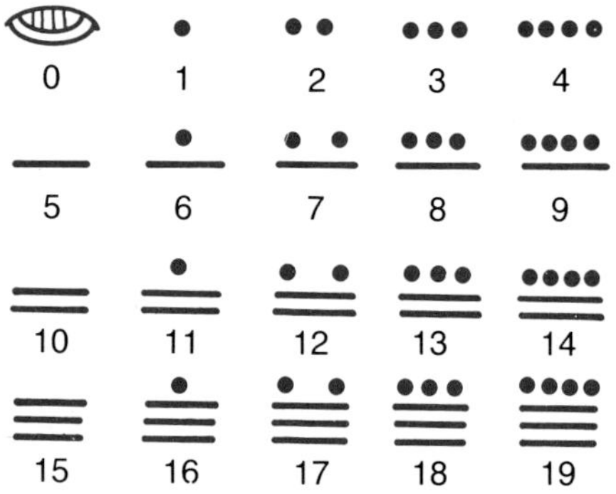

Fig. 11.21 Mayan numbers. The Maya also had symbols for numbers over twenty.

2 The symbols in Fig. 11.21 are the Mayan numbers up to nineteen.
  a Can you find these numbers in any other illustration in this chapter?
  b How would you do the following sums using Mayan numbers?
     i   6 + 7
     ii 9 × 2
     iii 18 − 10
     iv 16 ÷ 4
Would these numbers have been easier or harder to use than the numbers we use today?

A Mayan burial

One of the most important discoveries about the Maya was made in 1952. An archaeologist was working in the Temple of the Inscriptions at Palenque, one of the Mayan pyramid centres. He found one stone slab with finger holes in it. It seemed to have been made to lift up. When he lifted the stone he found a staircase that went underneath the pyramid. Slowly he and his team worked their way down, clearing away hundreds of years of rubble as they went. About 18 metres under the floor of the temple they came to a wall that blocked their way. Outside the wall were shells and pottery and pearls. Further on they came to six skeletons. They knew now that they were approaching the grave of a powerful person, somebody important enough to have people sacrificed in his honour.

When the last slab was removed the archaeologists found a burial chamber, about 10 metres long. The figures of nine richly dressed people had been carved on its walls and in the centre was a great stone slab, carved with the figure of a young man. Inside the stone grave was the skeleton of a priest-ruler, surrounded by jewellery. The Maya had made this elaborate tomb for him in the same way as the people of Egypt built huge pyramids for their dead rulers.

Time to understand

You have read about several elaborate burials in this book. Do you remember where they were? In what ways were they similar to the burial described above?

Fig. 11.22 The Temple of the Inscriptions at Palenque. It was under this pyramid that the hidden burial was found.

Fig. 11.23 The tomb under the pyramid at Palenque. A skeleton was found in the grave, its face covered by a jade death mask.

The end of the Maya

This rich burial took place in about 700 AD. About a hundred years later the Mayan culture began to collapse. During the 800s the pyramid centres were abandoned. Unfinished buildings were left just as they were. Could there have been a war? The Maya were usually peaceful people. Their pyramid centres rarely had walls to keep raiders out. Were there too many people to feed and support? Had the soil been farmed for too long so that it became poor? Did the people rebel against the priests who had been telling them what to do for so long? Were they tired of working so hard to keep the priests and gods happy? Perhaps they had just been doing the same things for too long — perhaps their society was simply worn out.

What happened to the Maya? It seems that at least some of them moved north. After about 1000 AD Mayan people settled in Yucatan where they built a new religious centre called Chichen Itza on the site of a much earlier Mayan settlement. Their descendants lived there until the

1200s; they still live in various parts of Central America.

Time to understand

1   The Maya have been called 'the Egyptians of the New World'. Can you explain why?

2   Alfred Maudslay was one of the first archaeologists to work among the Mayan ruins. This is how he described his working conditions:

> Excavations became filled with water as soon as they were made, and no moulding could be done until a watertight roof had been made over the monument which was to be moulded. At one time the flood-water covered all but a few feet of ground on which our palm-leaf shanty had been built; everything in camp had turned green with mould and mildew, snakes and scorpions became very troublesome, and mosquitoes were a continual torment.

   a   What do you think Maudslay meant by 'moulding'? Why was he 'moulding' the monuments he had discovered?

   b   What problems did Maudslay have to face while he was working on this site? Why do you think he stayed there?

3   Using the illustrations in this chapter, design your own pattern in the style of the Maya. You can include hieroglyphics, gods and the patterns found on Mayan sculpture and buildings. How would you describe the Mayan style of art?

4   The Aztecs and the Incas were two other groups of early Americans. The Aztecs lived in Central America, north of the Mayan homelands. The Incas lived further south in what is now Peru. Their cultures were at their greatest later than the culture of the Maya. What can you find out about the Aztecs and the Incas? Can you find any similarities between them and the Maya? What happened to destroy the Aztec and Inca societies?

Acknowledgements

We wish to express our appreciation for help in obtaining photographs, to the Australian Institute of Archaeology, Melbourne, Mexican Consulate-General, Sydney and Dr. David Rich, Sydney.

For permission to reproduce photographs and illustrations we should like to thank the following: Aerofilms Limited, London, Figs. 7.5, 7.19; Archivi Alinari, Florence, Italy, Figs. 10.6, 10.11, 10.12; Ashmolean Museum, Griffith Institute, Oxford, U.K., Figs. 3.33, 3.34, 3.35, 3.37, 3.39; Australian Government Information Service, Canberra, Fig. 1.7; Australian Institute of Archaeology, Figs. 2.17, 3.5, 3.18, 3.29, 3.31, 3.32, 3.38, 4.4, 4.12, 4.15, 4.17, 4.18, 4.19, 11.6, 11.13, 11.14, 11.22; Banpo Museum, Shaanxi Province, People's Republic of China, Fig. 6.5; BBC Hulton Picture Library, Figs. 3.4, 9.2, 9.28; Trustees of the British Museum, London, Figs. 2.6, 2.8 (and cover detail), 2.13, 2.18, 3.13, 3.22, 3.23, 4.8, 5.14, 6.7, 7.13 (and cover detail), 7.20, 7.21, 9.15, 9.16, 9.35 (top), 11.15; British School of Archaeology in Jerusalem, London, Fig. 4.13, China Welfare Institute (*China Reconstructs*), Peking, Figs. 6.11, 6.13; Denver Museum of Natural History, Colorado, U.S.A., Fig. 11.2; Egyptian Museum, Cairo, Figs. 3.6 (both), 3.8, 3.9, 3.16, 3.27, 4.10, 4.11; Embassy of Pakistan, Canberra, Figs. 5.2, 5.3, 5.5, 5.7; Alan Foley Pty Ltd, cover background; Photographie Giraudon, Paris, Fig. 3.11, Robert Harding Picture Library, London, Fig. 2.2, Govt. of India Tourist Office, Fig. 5.12 (and cover detail); Q. Jones, University of NSW, Fig. 1.11; Makor Library and Resource Centre of Victoria, Fig. 4.6; Mansell Collection Limited, London, Figs. 9.10, 10.18; S. Mellor, Figs. 3.2, 3.3, 3.10, 3.21, 3.25; Metropolitan Museum of Art, New York, Figs. 9.24, 9.37, 9.39; Consulate-General of Mexico, Sydney, Figs. 11.9, 11.23; Mrs S.G. Milston, Sandringham, Vic. Fig. 6.10; Musées Nationaux Paris (Louvre), Figs. 2.12, 9.30; Museo Nazionale Etrusco di Villa Giuila, Rome, Figs. 9.13, 9.18; Museum of Fine Arts, Boston, Figs. 9.17, 9.35 (bottom); Qantas Airways, Fig. 5.13; Richcolour, Sydney, Fig. 6.15, Roger Wood Library, London, Fig. 3.26; Royal Commission on Historical Monuments, Figs. 1.6 (and Mr W.A. Baker), 7.8, 7.17, 7.18 (and The Society of Antiquaries), 10.25; Scala Istituto Fotografico Editoriale, Florence, Italy, Fig. 10.16 (and cover detail); Peter Schouten, Sydney, Fig. 1.9; Silkeborg Museum, Denmark, Fig. 1.17 (and cover detail); W. Skilbeck, Fig. 3.24; State Organization of Antiquities and Heritage, Ministry of Culture and Information, Baghdad, Fig. 2.19; David Syme & Co Ltd, Fig. 3.40; Dr Alan Thorne, Canberra, Fig. 1.8; Uni-Dia-Verlag, Munich, Fig. 3.31; U.S. Information and

Communications Agency, Fig. 11.4;
Vatican Museum, Rome, Fig. 9.14; Victoria
and Albert Museum, London, Fig. 5.15;
Werner Forman Archive, London,
Figs. 11.7 (and cover detail), 11.11, 11.12.

While every effort has been made to
trace and acknowledge copyright of
photographs, in some cases copyright
proved untraceable. Should any
infringement have occurred, the publishers
tender their apologies.

Index

240